Formative Spirituality

Volume Seven

TRANSCENDENCE THERAPY

Formative Spirituality

Volume Seven

TRANSCENDENCE THERAPY

• ADRIAN VAN KAAM •

CROSSROAD • NEW YORK

1995

The Crossroad Publishing Company
370 Lexington Avenue, New York, NY 10017

Printed in the United States of America

Library of Congress Cataloging-in-Publication Data

Van Kaam, Adrian L., 1920–
    Transcendence therapy / Adrian Van Kaam.
        p.   cm. — (Formative spirituality ; v. 7)
    Includes bibliographical references and index.
    ISBN 0-8245-1512-9
    1. Man (Christian theology).   2. Philosophical anthropology.
3. Pastoral counseling.   4. Psychotherapy.   5. Spiritual formation—
Catholic Church.   6. Catholic Church—Doctrines.   7. Van Kaam,
Adrian L., 1920 –   .   I. Title.   II. Series: Van Kaam, Adrian L.,
1920–   Formative spirituality ; v. 7.
BT745.V26   1995
253.5—dc20   95-22228
                                                                          CIP

Contents

Introduction

At the end of World War II during the Hunger Winter in Holland, I lived with people I helped to hide from deportation. The long, dark winter nights in the countryside gave us ample time for discussions. We talked about the characters of collaborators with the enemy, of profit mongers, and of the uncommitted and indifferent who did not help us. We came to the consensus that what was needed in the future was a concerted effort to understand and foster what I would come to call "transcendence therapy."

Out of this concern grew a whole theory of character formation in relation to the new science of formation and spiritual counseling I initiated in Holland and later continued in graduate programs at Duquesne University and postgraduate programs at the Epiphany Center in Pittsburgh and elsewhere. At the center of this formation theory of personality I put what I designated as the character, heart, or core form. I have to admit a major part of my life's work has been to develop the discipline of character formation and the practice of "transtherapy" in recognition of the human spirit we all share.

Initially, my efforts raised the same question all "threshold thinking" does: Would they work? Then, a number of psychologists, educators, pastoral counselors, and social workers began to show kindred interest. Early books of mine like *Religion and Personality* (New York: Prentice-Hall, 1964; rev. ed., Pittsburgh, PA: Epiphany Association, 1991) and *The Art of Existential Counseling* (Wilkes Barre, PA: Dimension Books, 1966) became, in their own right, bestsellers. In 1982, I received the distinguished William C. Bier award from Division 36 of the American Psychological Association—psychologists interested in religious issues and spiritual values. I recognized then, and even more now, that colleagues in the field were beginning to see that a transcendent view of life could have a positive effect on healing. I was not alone in my concern for character formation and religious (e.g., Christian) counseling. Fortunately, this praxis-oriented interest of mine coincided with my initiation of a new human science I called "formation science."

One of the main models of the scientific mind, perhaps the one most familiar to us, is the informational paradigm. Guided by mostly quantitative methods of research, it informs us about the measurable aspects of human life and its development. The expression "character formation" brings to our mind the need for a special way of focusing our attention on human unfolding. I call this focus of attention "formational" to distinguish it from "informational." My subsequent formation paradigm complements and at times corrects the indispensable contributions, models, and techniques of quantifying information.

My formation paradigm pursues through research, study, and practice the way in which we can formationally implement in education, spiritual direction, formation counseling, and, above all, in transcendence therapy, the wealth of information presently available to us. My interest resides in how and why it can serve our own and others' experiential character formation.

Any paradigm in the social, psychological, therapeutic, and education disciplines challenges one to approach the object under study from a specific angle of cognitive and experiential interest. Such a paradigmatic disposition determines the way in which we focus our powers of attention and observation on specifically selected phenomena.

Looking at life through the window of always-ongoing formation influences our thinking, our theorizing, and our therapy. The fact that we are always giving form to life and receiving form from life affects the choice and development of our research and our methods of practice. It also directs our attention empirically to the experiences, needs, demands, and dynamics presently afoot in our society.

A paradigm shift is usually linked with some change in the overall perception of a growing majority of people in a society. It signals a change that is taking place in their worldview or mind-set. In the case of Western culture, this shift is from a functionally oriented and predominantly informational society to one that is concerned increasingly with transcendent-functional and transformational issues and values.

Needless to say, the responsible addition of a new paradigm, such as my formation science proposes, demands intensive thought. In this book I intend to probe the new assumptions arising from the changing worldview we are witnessing as well as the significant paradigmatic shifts it entails. Meanwhile, the demands of post-therapeutic practice remain one of my concerns. In spite of this practical concern, it will be impossible to restrict myself to only a consideration of the practical implications of character formation. To clarify the new paradigm underlying this new transtherapeutic approach, I need to give some personal and theoretical background. Let me begin with the former.

As a professor of psychology and as the initiator of formation science and formation theology, I felt that it was my calling not only to take into account the formationally relevant findings of the human and social sciences but also to uncover and appraise the hidden shallowness of psychologism and transpersonalism, two giant waves in the fascinating sea of contemporary thought. Buffered by them, the ship of transcendent-immanent character and personality formation may take on water and eventually sink! I have spent many years in the effort to prove that the human spirit as distinctively human is inseparable from the formation of one's transcendent-immanent character and personality. My research revealed the following:

Human Spirit as Guiding Character
and Personality Formation

Today, an increasing number of scientists are trying to understand mind-body, psyche-soma, interaction. This was not the case fifty years ago when I initiated the new science of formation. I made my primary concern an understanding of the interaction between the human spirit and the formation, reformation, and transformation of human character and personality. Researching this interaction required that I study the interformation that occurs between the transcendent dimension and the functional, vital, and sociohistorical underpinnings of any character and personality formation as a whole. Central in this matrix of meaning are formation traditions that have a profoundly formative or deformative effect on a person's life and growth.

The focus of formation science and its underlying transcendent anthropology is not simply character formation as such but how this formation is rooted in an entanglement of formation traditions. This aim explains why my approach to a transcendent theory of personality differs essentially from the aim of transpersonal psychologies. They do not pay explicit and detailed attention to faith and formation traditions as powerful sources of personality unfolding but focus instead on the self in relative isolation from its entire field of traditional unfolding.

The human spirit as distinctively human lifts our powers of formation beyond sheer functional categories. Functional intelligence, not enlightened by the human spirit, can be observed in animal behavior, and some aspects of it can be duplicated in artificially programmed robots and computers. Therefore, the study of the transcendent human spirit takes a prominent place in the anthropology that guides and integrates research and practice in formation science.

To keep properly focused, I had to find and pursue research methods appropriate to an understanding of the human spirit—the human spirit not as isolated but as interforming continuously with mind and body. Moreover, the human spirit as inserted in sociohistorical (form-traditional) and cosmic situations. Such situations impact continuously upon our embodied and embodying personality formation. At every step of the way, I would have to take into account the influence of sociohistorical formation traditions (see volume 5, *Traditional Formation,* in this formative spirituality series).

I am not alone in my search. People representing a variety of distinctively human formation traditions, cultures, periods, ideologies, and religions have experienced, described, and analyzed different aspects of the human spirit. They examined its conditions and dynamics, its interaction with the functional mind, the vital body, and the historical socialization of persons—all within their field of perception and action. The oral-traditional, artistic, symbolic, lingual, and written communications of this mostly prescientific search span more than six thousand years. This explains why remnants and resources of this oldest search of humanity abound in all cultures known to us.

A review of such varied sources taught me that the quantifying methods of the positive sciences, while helpful, are not sufficient to clarify all possible aspects of our distinctively human experiences, dynamics, and practices in regard to their impact on transcendent-immanent character and personality formation. The deepest constituents of spiritual formation cannot be completely quantified. Neither can one fully explain their meaning by experimental research alone. Needed, I believe, is the qualitative empirical-experiential research that characterizes formation science. Without it a full anthropological account of transcendent-immanent human formation is not possible to attain. Let me turn now to some more theoretical and methodological considerations. What I will communicate in chapter 1 is essential for an in-depth understanding of my original work in transcendence therapy and its successful use by a growing number of practitioners.

CHAPTER 1

Transtherapy and the Human Spirit

Transtherapy and the Human Spirit

I initiated my transtherapy in the light of human experiences of the life of the spirit. Many disciplines use only quantifying methods. My approach is different. It is qualitative and experiential; it looks into experiences that are distinctively human or spiritual. It adds something new to the knowledge that comes to us from laboratory experiments and tests that can be quantified. I believe that in spiritual matters quantitative knowledge should be complemented by probing qualitatively what cannot be measured. This will help transtherapists and counselors to understand and appreciate the spiritual journey of their counselees.

My use of the word "appreciation" is important here. We should appreciate any sign of spiritual meaning in the stories of our counselees. Spiritual appreciation should mark any healing (making whole) approach of transtherapists. They should appraise and appreciate the spiritual call hidden in communications of counselees. They should do so no matter how disconcerting the character, life situation, or problem may seem. (See Adrian van Kaam and Susan Muto, *The Power of Appreciation: A New Approach to Personal and Relational Healing* [New York: Crossroad, 1994].) This is true not only for transtherapy but for all human relationships.

For example, friends of South African President Nelson Mandela have told how his character showed a disposition of appreciation of anything good in his enemies and even in his estranged wife. His colleagues were surprised. They kept comparing his changed character with the easily enraged, impatient dispositions he displayed before his imprisonment when he was a young revolutionary. His years of solitude may have worked as a spontaneous transtherapy.

To understand the spiritual character story of our counselees we may take into account any information we may gain from tests and laboratory data. But we should also go beyond such findings to discover what may be spiritually effective, especially in transtherapy. For instance, in the treatment of anxiety and depression in postoperative cancer or cardiac patients the art and discipline of transcendent appreciation can lead to marked improvement. The blending of both a positive-scientific and a transcendent-appreciative outlook is more effective in the vital healing process than either one of them would be without the other. The link between these two approaches is at the forefront of some contemporary research. I would call attention here to the work of medical doctors like Dean Ornish and Bernie Siegel. Applications of this insight in such fields as sports, business, education, art, and music are quite popular. It proves how interested people are in such integration. It confirms my anthropology of personality unfolding. Hence, its development has been one of my lifelong goals, especially in its transtherapeutic implications.

Qualitative Research

I believe, thus, that research of our distinctively human dimension of life has to be in great measure, if not exclusively, qualitative. My addition of a qualitative-experiential approach to the empirical-experiential ones raised a key question for me. What qualities are basic to distinctively human character unfolding? Let me reply by presenting my definition of the human spirit. I will use this working definition as the basis for my approach to transcendence therapy.

I see our spirit as the basic power and source of our distinctively human life. Our spirit enables us to be open to all of reality as well as to its sources and horizons. It is a pluridimensional openness. This power of spiritual openness can be actualized by any aspect of reality that becomes available to our consciousness.

Our spirit also makes it possible for us to bring together within a unifying formation anthropology all that we discover in such openness. Our spirit can relate this anthropology to our mind, character, body and to all of reality we touch upon. Such an anthropology and its corresponding transtherapy uses common, traditional, and uniquely personal principles of life formation.

Spirit is also the power of mind to continually form, reform, and transform our character and personality, often by means of some form of transtherapy. Our spirit transforms us in the light of its openness to disclosures of reality and its deepest source.

Our formation anthropology unfolds in the light of the classical consonant wisdom traditions of humanity. Transtherapy helps the counselee to personalize uniquely this formation anthropology and its roots in these traditions.

Let me reflect now on the salient terms of this admittedly lengthy descriptive definition.

Openness to All of Reality

What sets human life apart from other known forms of being on this planet? It is not our functional intelligence alone. Other life forms manifest some facets of the same type of intelligence. Moreover, humankind is increasingly able to duplicate aspects of our functional intelligence in its programming of robots and computers.

What makes us unique as a human race, is, among other factors, a dynamic potency to open up, at least in principle, to all of reality and its mysterious source. I say "in principle," for the necessary condition to actualize this potency is twofold: the availability of manifestations of reality to our consciousness and our willingness to be attentive to such disclosures.

Our human spirit is marked by restlessness. It is our spirit that drives us relentlessly to go beyond, to advance, to transcend. The spirit's gift of openness to all that is keeps lifting us beyond what we already know, feel, try, do, accomplish, suffer, or enjoy. This dynamism of our spirit is a powerful source of ongoing character and personality formation, reformation, and transformation. The spirit also stimulates us to engage ourselves in new enterprises, such as innovative research projects, daring adventures, surprising paradigms, explorations of new frontiers, useful inventions, alternative methods of healing, and so on.

Formation science and its anthropology of transcendent character and personality unfolding is rooted in this dynamic openness. It promotes, animates, and energizes original research and related formational endeavors and character dispositions, as I shall show in later chapters. Transtherapy helps its counselees to release this gift of openness when it has been paralyzed by loss of contact with the great wisdom traditions of humanity-in-formation.

Pluridimensional Openness

My transcendent theory of personality holds that human life unfolds in response to various dimensions of openness. Each gives access to a different aspect of reality. Many traditions try to summarize all such aspects under the simple canopy of a spirit-mind-body paradigm. Observation and reflection in transtherapy compelled me to divide these main dimensions further into the following categories:

1. the sociohistorical (our bodily presence to and involvement in the world puts transcendent-immanent character and personality formation and the corresponding transtherapy necessarily into a sociohistorical context);
2. the vital impact on character and personality formation (the psychophysio-

logical, sensual, temperamental, and neuroformational facets of our body-mind-spirit unity);

3. the functional influence in character formation (the pretranscendent functional mind facet of the body);

4. the functional-transcendent coformant of character and personality (the mainly pretranscendent reaching out of the still basically functional mind toward the realm of one's transcendent-immanent spirit dimension);

5. the transcendent-immanent spirit as the primary coformant of transcendent-immanent character (our spirit dimension as such);

6. the transcendent-functional as the main agent of ongoing transcendent-immanent character and personality formation. The spirit dimension in its full unfolding inspires, forms, reforms, and transforms our functional character and personality. The spirit does so in and through the functional dimension and its underlying vital body dimension. The human spirit takes the sociohistorical and cosmic context of these functional and vital dimensions into account. It enables us to disclose and implement their transcendent pointers. The transcendent-functional dimension, as well as the paths to its awakening, guides most of the transtherapy that takes place in group or private sessions.

Insofar as all of these dimensions open us to aspects of reality, they participate in the all-pervading power of the human spirit as such. Therefore, the knowledge of even higher animal life is not the same as human knowledge. For example, their sense knowledge lacks the depth that the human spirit imparts to all other kinds of human knowledge, also that of sense experience.

We may not be in touch with our spirit. Nevertheless, its power can seep through all of our life. It affects, directly or indirectly, our character and personality unfolding. Transtherapy is concerned with any relation of our life to our human spirit.

Sources and Horizons

Human experience always points beyond itself to horizons inviting further examination. For example, the inquisitive spirit of theoretical quantum physicists opens them to ever-expanding horizons of meaning as soon as previous quests for energy sources yield their secret. The same is true for all areas of human experience and knowledge. Our restless spirit, driven by the transcendence dynamic, presses ultimately toward a horizon of horizons. Is there such? Humankind has tried to answer this question many times over. Classical seekers as well as contemporary theorists seem to agree that this horizon of horizons is shrouded in a mystery that can be pointed to in symbols but never fully grasped. Many people experience this mystery in awe as the source of the reality to which the spirit of humanity opens up continuously.

I do not wish to question here the correctness or incorrectness of such advances nor their interpretation. I will leave that query to philosophers and informational theologians. My concern is with the personal and communal form people may give to such experiences in their unfolding character and personality and how this affects the process of transtherapy. My question is How does each specific character and personality form affect and how is it affected by such experiences?

Many people turn their disposition of awe for an ultimate source and horizon of life into the basis of the content with which they fill the spirit dimension of their mind. They give personal and communal form to that basic conviction. This form influences and is influenced by their always limited and limiting surroundings. Accordingly, formation science fosters research that sheds light on the interformation constantly taking place between all the spheres and dimensions of human life as such. Transtherapy is, for a great part, concerned with the consonance or dissonance of this interformation between the spheres and dimensions of the counselee's character and personality.

Actualization of Our Spirit Power

This part of my definition points to the fact that our transcendence dynamic is not all at once awakened. It slumbers in the infant, awakens in the child and adolescent, and expands during the many phases of adult formation. Full, continuous unfolding depends on the corresponding character dispositions. This dynamic potency of spirit can be actualized by any aspect of reality that becomes available to any region of our consciousness. The awakening of our spirit goes through crises of purifying initial formation, illuminating reformation, and unifying transformation of our distinctively human character. The power of our transcendence dynamic may be refused, denied, or rationalized. Our functional reason may close in upon itself. We may value only or mainly measurable success, power, and possession. On the other hand, excessive fear of any expression of vital passion may halt our prudent progress into untried transcendent territory. All kinds of dissonant traditions may distort the course of our transcendence dynamic. All these movements will affect our functional mind and vital body. In the long run some of them may be reflected in our character and personality dispositions. Therefore, students of transtherapy should be attentive to such interformations and the way they function in their present or future counselees.

Consonant Frame of Reference

My definition of spirit refers also to its power of synthesizing. Our spirit is not satisfied with the disclosures of fragments of reality. Spirit is openness to reality as a whole. The purpose of its disclosure is not merely to assess each fragment for its practical, functional, or academic use. The spirit wonders how each fragment tells us something of the whole of our existence. How is each aspect of life linked with all others? How does each experience point to the meaning and mystery of our life as a whole and to the unfolding of our character at its center?

Such questions can be asked by philosophers or informational theologians. Their expertise is not the same as that of my formation science and the formation theology it spawns and sustains. For the same questions can be asked empirically-experientially-formationally. We do not focus then in detail on the questions that arouse the interest of more informationally focused theologians or philosophers. How do people give form to their transcendent-immanent experiences of reality? Are there common ways to be found in the classical wisdom traditions of humanity? How do people use or abuse such traditions empirically-experientially in their character and personality unfolding? How does this use affect, and how is it affected by, present vital-functional experiences within people's sociohistorical, situational, and cosmic surroundings? What does this mean for transtherapy?

Common, Traditional, and Unique Principles
of Consonant Formation

My definition points to our spirit as the forming principle of distinctively human character and personality formation. I mention some basic principles of experiential integration. The spirit strives to bring life experiences together in a coherent frame of reference. How people implement this striving in their character and personality depends on the principles of experiential integration they use, often prefocally.

Many people live by principles of experiential integration that they share implicitly. For example, they look for relationships between experiences that are commonly felt to be connected. Take the beauty of sea and sky one beholds while sailing away from shore. This experience can be associated with similar aesthetic experiences and with the experience of awe for the mystery of beauty in and behind all of them.

Others take their principles of transcendent integration from a faith and formation tradition to which they adhere. Followers of Islam, for instance, may integrate their life experiences into awe-filled wonder in the face of the powerful will of Allah. Adherents to the orthodox Freudian faith and formation tradition may integrate thoughts and feelings into a libidinal, deterministic frame of reference, leading to a kind of downward transcendence. Others, again, live very much in the light of their unique-communal life call. They insist on relating transcendent experiences to this call. At the same time, they try to benefit from common and traditional principles of experiential integration. A Jewish artist I met in Israel relates any transcendent experience she has to her vocation to express herself in sculpture. She feels that her work must give form to her innermost emotions. That is the unique aspect of her unique-communal call. As to its communal side, these experiences reflect also the story of the chosen people, in which she participates according to her tradition. She brings to life, moreover, common transcendent symbols of humanity, translating them into both a personal and a traditional style of expression.

Here again, what is of first concern to qualitative researchers in formation science and to transtherapists is not only the underlying faith traditions. Their preferred focus of attention is on the unique-communal embodiments of such faith traditions in formation traditions that evoke and unfold one's latent character and personality. They ask, How does a form tradition, as concretely experienced, interform with socially situated vital and functional experiences? How wholesome, healing, and effective is this interformation for our personal-communal unfolding? Or how disturbing, weakening, and inhibiting is it for the consonant character unfolding of the person as a whole? What do the answers to these questions mean for the practice of transtherapy?

Formation, Reformation, Transformation

My definition of spirit takes into account its personality-evoking potency. The human spirit is an all pervading power of openness. It is blessed with a receptive capacity second to none. The spirit, however, reveals also a creative, dynamic, form-evoking power that as transcendent-immanent has to be distinguished from the capacity for merely pretranscendent personality development.

The fact that we can actualize our unique-communal personality potencies and develop our world is inherent in our vital, functional, and functional-transcendent makeup. Our ability, however, to form, reform, and transform mere pretranscendent development into something "more than" resides in the all-pervading mystery of spiritual formation. It is only the human spirit that can open our heart or character, our personality as a whole, to this mystery. Transcendent character and personality unfolding is, thus, the fruit of the confluence of the powers of pretranscendent development and of transcendent formation by our human spirit as enlightened by the mystery of formation and the consonant classical wisdom traditions of humanity touched by this mystery.

Forms of life other than the human, like animal life, also go through a process of development. Their founding form is a gift of the forming mystery, too. The difference is that they are programmed, and we are not. What makes the human life form distinctive is that the mystery enables us to elevate our development to the level of spirit. We are called by the mystery of life to participate in the purifying formation, illuminating reformation, and unifying transformation of our stages of development. How we do so affects and is affected by both our developmental and our formational patterns of mind and body. These unfold in continual interplay with our character in its dialogical interaction with life situation, tradition, perception, and action.

Faith Tradition and Formation Tradition

Having explained the main terms of my definition, I would like now to touch on some related issues. As I pointed out earlier, the oldest wisdom of humanity centers around a transcendent-immanent unfolding of character and personality. This wisdom has been sedimented in two kinds of traditions.

To express my original observation of these two traditions, I initiated the terms faith tradition and formation tradition. Both are intimately interrelated. For example, the religious faith tradition of Hinduism is expressed in a variety of Hindu formation traditions. Similarly, the ideological faith tradition of humanism gave rise to diverse formation traditions. Obviously, formation science, as empirical-experiential-formational, has to leave the research and appraisal of religious and ideological faith traditions as such to their faith-informational theologians and philosophers. Otherwise formation science would lose its identity by leaving its identifying preferential focus of attention.

The matter of formation traditions, which are one of the preferred focuses of transtherapy, is more complex. My war experience with people of various persuasions and personality structures whom I helped to hide in The Netherlands confirmed the need to distinguish between faith and formation traditions. Each one's formation tradition is carried by a corresponding faith tradition. As a formation scientist and transtherapist, I cannot tamper with the tenets of each one's faith tradition. There is, however, much in formation traditions that falls under the preferred focus of formation science, its transcendent-immanent anthropology, and its transtherapy.

My research of formation traditions made it clear to me that people adopt them to make their faith tradition effective in their empirical-experiential life with others with whom they share their public or personal life situation. This general striving of humanity makes it probable that a formation tradition may disclose some empirical-experiential conditions and dynamics, which adherents may have in common with all of humanity. This aspect of formation traditions can be legitimately researched and evaluated by formation science and transtherapy. Research like this deepens understanding of my interformational paradigm. It can also disclose more fully the meaning of the formation traditions under investigation. Examining the results of this kind of research can affect, in turn, the patterns of living that are expressed in the traditions in question. Wise appraisal of the results attained can enable people to become more effective and healthy in their character and personality unfolding without compromising their own underlying faith traditions.

Subject-Object and Subjectivism

The task and responsibility of formation science, its guiding anthropology, and its transtherapy direct its research in the realm of the human spirit to how one's character and personality concretely unfold. This research seems to me most timely in this period of heightened interest in the topic of spirit and spirituality and of character and personality formation in our families and educational institutions. The absolutizing of the quantitative empirical-experimental methods of research led to the mistaken notion that everything that cannot be researched in this way is merely a product of one's subjectivistic imagination. This belief in absolutized subjectivism can yield unexpected side effects. One of them is the emergence of all kinds of subjectivistic "spiritualities," not verifiable by any strict method of objective, qualitative empirical-experiential research.

We can look at spiritualistic subjectivity as an uncontrollable proliferation of arbitrary "spiritual" feelings, images, and wishes without much objective ground or order behind them. By contrast, we can also look at the subject of the spiritual life as a "subject-object" intertwining. In this "subject-object" we can disclose and describe certain universal qualities of objective order, certain observable patterns, and dynamics. We can demonstrate that these can be found in a significant number of people when and if they are exposed to similar inner and outer conditions of subjective and objective spiritual formation. One can establish how such patterns of a "transcendent subject-object" interform with the vital, functional, and sociohistorical dimensions of human character and personality. I initiated and developed such methods, beginning in 1944, and later published them in volume 4 of my Formative Spirituality Series, *Scientific Formation.*

This subject-object criterion could help formation scientists and personality theorists to separate subjectivistic research projects from those that are about the subject-object in its objectifiable (not reifiable) patterns. Such patterns are distinct from either subjectivistic or reified patterns of spiritual living and their concomitant character and personality deformation.

As I have said earlier, our human spirit can inspire us to develop a theoretical formation anthropology. Transtherapists, formed in this anthropology, assist their counselees in the awakening of their corresponding spirit power. This power can help them to disclose and unfold their own unique-communal character.

By its very nature a theoretical formation anthropology is always provisional, but it ought not to be arbitrary. I will show in the upcoming chapters how empirical-experiential research, quantitatively or qualitatively done, can correct and expand a transcendent-immanent formation anthropology. Before proceeding, I would like to add that research in the spheres, dimensions, regions, and ranges of my interformation field paradigm is an essential part of this unfolding formation anthropology and of its implicit pointers to transcendence therapy.

CHAPTER 2

Transtherapy as Scientific and Trans-scientific

Transcendent formation and transcendence therapy include trans-scientific facets that are not fully observable. The richness of a formative event cannot be captured in scientific formulations alone. Still, such trans-scientific facets are crucial for our growth in transcendence.

In my early work in "transtherapy," I knew I had to take into account, yet go beyond, an empirical-experiential approach to transcendent transformation. It demanded also a systematic examination of the basic pre- and postscientific facets of transtherapy and its underpinning formation science. Such pre- and postscientific aspects guide a great part of our journey from pretranscendent to transcendent living. But let me not get ahead of my story.

Basic Structure of Human Sciences

I developed my formation science as a human science in service of distinctively human formation and transtherapy. I knew from the start in Holland over fifty years ago that I could not exempt it from the basic structure of all human sciences. This structure is pre- and postscientific as well as scientific. First of all, the selection, direction, and formulation of empirical research in each human science are also always based on prescientific anthropological assumptions. Second, the same human science applies and articulates its findings in post- or trans-scientific applications and articulations.

For example, clinical psychology is sustained by empirical-experiential research. That research goes on in the light of certain prescientific anthropological assumptions about human life. Its findings are then postscientifically applied to groups and individuals in tentative ways. The results of these postscientific therapy and counseling experiences may then be articulated systematically and in a scholarly way in papers and discussions. Such articulation stays in tune with the science as a whole by using, besides its own *clinical* metalanguage and theory, the *basic* language and theory used by the same underlying science.

Transcendent Transformation as a Scholarly Discipline

Insofar as one uses pre- and trans-scientific approaches, the experiential science of transcendent formation becomes more than an empirical human science. It gains as well the dignity of being a scholarly discipline. Over and beyond their empirical research and its results, representatives of experiential human sciences may engage in prescientific anthropological considerations. They may ask themselves at least implicitly, What is the nature of the human life and the society that we are studying empirically? How can we make some of our prescientific assumptions explicit? How can we report and clarify in a systematic way post- or trans-scientific articulations and applications of our sciences to persons and communities?

Such tentative applications may be political, economical, social, or clinical, depending on the human science in question. Many tentative articulations are "coformed" by the unique situatedness of these communities and individuals under consideration. Hence, they do not always lend themselves to the universal scientific formulations that rigid empirical research strives to attain. Yet there must be a way to clarify systematically some facets of experience. Otherwise, experiential sciences cannot be effective. They would not be able to deal as such with the concrete personal and communal predicaments of people. Practitioners of the human sciences, including transtherapists, face these upsets and interruptions of their merely empirical theories in everyday life, especially in their counseling experiences.

Unity of Formation Science,
Formation Anthropology, and Transtherapy

In a similar vein, I raise the following questions: How do we safeguard the unity of transcendent formation? How can it be the object both of a human science and of a scholarly discipline? Will such a difference in approach rip the fabric apart of a structure as subtle and complex as, for instance, the study of their corresponding transcendence therapy? The unity of formation science, formation anthropology, and transtherapy can be maintained to the degree that they are directed to the same focus of research and praxis. The special focus of any discipline provides it with its unifying identity. Relentless fidelity to this focus is the only way to maintain the unity and identity of the discipline in question.

In the case of my discipline, the identity of its preferred focus of study, namely, distinctively human or transcendent formation of character and personality and of the corresponding transtherapy, guarantees its unity. The scope of the unifying focus makes it possible for me to develop more than a merely scientific theory. It enables me to take into account the immeasurable empirical-experiential facets of transtherapy. At the same time, it allows me to go beyond these aspects. Thus, I am able to formulate a theory relevant to transcendent formation, reformation, transformation, and transtherapy as a whole. This overall theory integrates the results of prescientific, scientific, and transscientific studies within my overall discipline of formative spirituality and makes it serviceable to transtherapy.

Formative Spirituality and Transtherapy as Dialectical Disciplines

The above three approaches and their findings modulate each other. They remain in a continuous dialogue. This results in formulations and directives that increasingly sustain and explain each other. This integration is fostered by the use of the same basic metalanguage, theoretical concepts, and constructs developed within formation science. The metalanguage and theory of this discipline as a whole expand and deepen through the dynamics of what I call "dialectical modulation." This means that all three approaches are mutually complementary and corrective. They become increasingly consonant by modifying each other continuously in this dialogue. Transtherapy assists its counselees in developing a similar dialectical modulation for their personal life. I discovered its effectiveness in my initial transtherapy with the war victims in Holland.

Prescientific Underpinning of the Disciplines of Transcendent Formation and Transtherapy

As in other disciplines, so, too, in the disciplines of transcendent formation and transtherapy there are implied prescientific assumptions. The preferred focus of both formation science and transtherapy is the empirical-experiential aspect of transcendent human life in formation. Accordingly, their assumptions have to be based on an explicit formation anthropology (see volume 6 of my Formative Spirituality Series, *Transcendent Formation*). My formation anthropology selects its assumptions in the light of their relevance for theoretical and experiential integration of the findings of my formation science and transtherapy. I should caution here that my assumptions of the foundational transcendence of all human formation are not in all respects identical with those of particular religious or ideological faith and formation traditions. The assumptions of the disciplines of formation science and transtherapy should be basic enough to be compatible with a significant number of both kinds of tradition. Each tradition can complement and correct this minimum of shared formation knowledge in the light of its own more specialized, formational theological or ideological anthropology. The transtherapist should take the latter respectfully into account when he or she has to deal with adherents of different faith traditions.

As in other disciplines and sciences, so, too, in my formation anthropology, one may discover later that some of my assumptions reveal an affinity to—though not an identity with—certain philosophical statements in a wide variety of different philosophies. This is not surprising. Both formation anthropology and other philosophies touch at times on similar characteristics of human formation. Statements that may appear interchangeable, but are not fully identical, may emerge. However, my formation anthropology did not start out from an existing philosophy, even if it points in passing to some analogical similarities it may discover later in a variety of philosophical assumptions. Neither does my formation anthropology aim at the development of a full-fledged philosophical system. This may be the goal of professional philosophers. The same could be said of numerous theological or ideological anthropologies initiated in the theologies or ideologies developed by many religions or philosophical schools of thought.

The elaboration of full-fledged philosophical or theological anthropologies lies beyond the competence and interest of experts in formation science, formation anthropology, and transtherapy. This is not to deny that many ideological philosophies and theologies can offer formation anthropologists fruitful suggestions. Conversely, my formation anthropology can do the same for ideological philosophies and theologies, especially if they touch on the realm of transcendent empirical character formation and transtherapy. Many philosophical and theological anthropologies still seem weak in this area of study. They may thus benefit from the work done by my formation scientists, scholars, and practitioners, especially in the area of transcendence therapy.

Relevant Assumptions

The task of my formation anthropology is limited by the preferential focus of my formation science and transtherapy: distinctively human or transcendent formation and therapy of character and personality. This focus delineates rigorously the selection and elaboration mainly of those anthropological assumptions that are formationally and/or transtherapeutically relevant.

Some sciences may prefer that their assumptions remain implicit, but this would be undesirable for the disciplines of transcendent formation and transtherapy. I have observed that the implicit assumptions of people about their formation have an impact on the direction they give to their life. I found especially influential the hidden assumptions they absorb from formation traditions and social, clinical, and educational disciplines insofar as these are popularized. As long as such assumptions are left implicit, people have little control over borrowed orientations that direct their life implicitly. Hence, it was necessary for me to make explicit the anthropological assumptions behind my formation anthropology and transtherapy. I want them to be available to scholarly and scientific as well as to form-traditional and popular scrutiny. My aim was not to develop a full-fledged philosophical anthropology but a coherent and self-consistent anthropology of formation and transtherapy. My purpose was to bring together logically and systematically the insights and findings of the three branches of my formative spirituality—the prescientific, scientific, and trans-scientific.

Scientific Approach to Transcendent Formation and Transtherapy

The study of pre- and trans-scientific facets of my formation spirituality and transtherapy is enlightening because both these facets play a basic role in our spiritual growth. Therefore, it is not surprising that many spiritual masters and edifying writers over the centuries in various cultures have limited themselves to one or the other of these two facets. Writers who wrote before the rise of the empirical sciences were not confronted with the forming and deforming influence on their readers or listeners of popularized human sciences, pretranscendent therapies, and the many diverse formation traditions that are impinging upon us today.

Today it is irresponsible to restrict ourselves to only a pre- and/or trans-scientific approach to transcendent formation and transtherapy. We are obliged as students, thinkers, and practitioners to examine any facet of formation that lends itself in whole or in part to empirical-experiential investigation. Spirituality-as-formative, as well as its transtherapy, is concerned with the concrete unfolding of human character and personality as distinctly human. It addresses the way transcendent transformation happens within a variety of empirical life situations. Some of these situations are already explained in part by certain historical and by some presently emerging form traditions along with the findings of other human sciences. I established in Europe as a principle of my formation science and anthropology that a full and balanced approach to concrete spiritual formation must take into account all formationally relevant facts and findings, not denying or bypassing any of them. All should be appraised in the light of the pre- and trans-scientific foundations of my transcendent formation theory and transtherapy. An effective appraisal of my formative spirituality and transtherapy implies, therefore, a concrete grasp of its empirical-experiential "hooking in" points.

Necessary Emergence of Formation Science

The effective transcendent formation of human life demands that people learn to cope spiritually with the empirical reality of their field of daily presence and action. They must meet events as they appear concretely in the spheres, dimensions, ranges, and regions of their formation field. Empirical clarification facilitates the transcendent effectiveness of people when it comes to contending with such happenings. Certain empirical appraisals are already absorbed by them uncritically through the popularization of form traditions and of the human sciences. These popularizations coform implicitly the mentality of modern men and women, children, and adults.

From the viewpoint of my formation science and especially my transtherapy, such implicit popular coformation is often a deformation, more a hindrance than a help, on the journey of wise and reasonable transcendent-immanent unfolding. Such deformation necessitated, among other things, my development of formation science, formational anthropology, and transtherapy. I had to find a way to clarify empirically and experientially the nature, functions, dynamics, and conditions of the empirical life from the viewpoint of transcendent formation and transtherapy. One can know these from classic formation traditions, while taking into account human observation and the achievements of theoretical-experiential reason. People have to embody their distinctively human life in observable fields of presence and participation. Would it not be foolish to overlook the wisdom of classical empirical formation traditions? I argued in Europe that these fruits of the laboratories of millennia of formation history should be critically appreciated. The same applies to the embodiment of one's own particular form-traditional spirituality in a concrete pluritraditional formation field. Without this clarification, concepts and constructs incompatible with one's form-traditional formation may slip unnoticed into one's traditional life directives, deforming them in the process. To assist people in healing this specific deformation is one of the purposes of my transtherapy.

Three Approaches Implicit in Formation Traditions

Spiritual masters, edifying writers, and numerous formation traditions take into account, at least implicitly, the three approaches I systematize in my discipline of transcendent formation—the prescientific, the scientific, and the trans-scientific. The masters, writers, and traditions of which I speak do pay attention to the empirical-experiential components of spiritual formation. We should examine them in a methodical, empirical-experiential way that takes into account the formationally relevant findings and methods of the empirical-experiential human sciences.

For example, in the works of John of the Cross, there are references to dynamics of attachment and detachment that can now be examined empirically by the science of formation and its auxiliary sciences. Teresa of Avila speaks about coping with symptoms of low-grade depression, some aspects of which can be observed and analyzed empirically in terms of their concrete impact on transcendent formation and transtherapy. Ignatius of Loyola deals with the workings of the inner and outer senses in meditation. These, too, can be traced empirically. The noted French spiritual master Francis Libermann discusses the experiential and physiological impact of tropical climate on the spiritual life of European missionaries in his description of the prayer of practical union. Masters of the Eastern formation traditions examine at length contemplative prayer practices involving breathing exercises that are amenable to disciplined empirical-experiential investigation.

The attention of spiritual masters, writers, and traditions to the empirical-formational facets of spirituality cannot be denied. To be sure, their sayings were usually premethodical, often implicit and unsystematic. In their time, they had to go by personal observation and the prescientific information available to them. They did not yet have at their disposal, like I do, systematic, valid, and reliable approaches that can yield general insights into the empirical-experiential spiritual life of all people. Neither did they have a systematic, foundational formation theology that can profit from the concepts and constructs of a systematic, pretheological formation science, as does the Judeo-Christian formation theology I have been developing since 1944.

Emergence of My Formation Science

The emergence of empirical-experiential sciences in the past two hundred years pressed me to develop more systematically the empirical-experiential facet of transcendent character and personality formation. I used for my work the evolving history of formation traditions. I adopted and complemented some findings of the empirical sciences if they were obviously relevant to any specific topic I was researching in this field.

The emergence of the empirical sciences challenged thinkers like myself. It inspired me to create and develop my own methodology and theory both in general and within specific formation traditions.

One function of my discipline of transcendent formation and therapy is to keep its servant science of formation in dialogue with the more fundamental pre- and trans-scientific approaches of the same discipline. One purpose of this dialogue is to prevent my discipline from contamination by assumptions that are implicit in concepts or constructs borrowed from other sciences, arts, disciplines, and traditions. The dialogue of formation science and transtherapy with formation anthropology enables me to appraise the compatibility of such assumptions with the distinctly transcendent nature of human life formation and/or transtherapy.

I witnessed the vast popularization of pretranscendent directives for human development and the consequent neglect of transcendent directives. This one-sided leaning gnawed away at my consciousness. As far as I was concerned, it made the emergence of a discipline of transcendent formation and transtherapy

an absolute necessity. Without it, a number of people freely and fully committed to their own spiritual formation traditions could unwittingly assimilate less
congenial or incompatible tenets of other traditions. Such assimilations could
conflict with the formation traditions to which they themselves had pledged to
adhere wholeheartedly. For them, their own tradition is the basic frame of reference for consonant character and personality unfolding. The result of such
confusion can be a split in their personality between pretranscendent development and true spiritual formation.

Conflicts like these can be fostered unwittingly by the media and by education. They can be facilitated by insufficiently critical pastoral counseling or by
religion courses that borrow concepts too naïvely from the clinical, educational, and social disciplines. Such a split, if not disclosed and transcended,
could undermine, after one or more generations, the adherence of persons and
groups to essential facets of their own faith and formation traditions. When this
happens, people may need to consult with "transtherapists."

CHAPTER 3

Formation and Transformation in Relation to Transtherapy and the Formation-Field Paradigm

The qualifying term "formation" is by no means a new addition to the spiritual life. All life is formative, also the spiritual life. All classical spiritual formation traditions include the formational aspect of the spiritual life, implicitly or explicitly. Formative spirituality makes this aspect the focus of its research and practice. Formative spirituality also considers all formation from the viewpoint of transformation. Every time it uses the term "formation" instead of human development, it intends to convey a relationship of our pretranscendent development and education to the transcendent horizon of our distinctively human life and character.

Unlike other approaches to the transcendent life, my formative spirituality makes this aspect of transcendent character and personality formation the primary focus of its research, theory, and praxis. In the process, it draws critically and creatively on relevant information from, first of all, classical and classics-compatible formation traditions. Second, it consults arts, sciences, and empirical disciplines. Some of their findings too could be relevant to formation science and transtherapy. Formative spirituality develops its own research methodology, theory, metalanguage, and methods of application. I distinguish this approach from other human sciences and from other pretranscendent therapies as well as from philosophical, theological, and historical disciplines.

Formative spirituality examines thus the formational facets of the transcendent life. Both as a prescientific formation anthropology and as an empirical human science, it asks the question, Is there some common ground to which all consonant, transcendent formation traditions and their formational practices may point?

The discipline of transcendent formation may choose to articulate a specific formation tradition. Each specific foundational tradition tends to develop a number of subtraditions. Each subtradition offers its own particular elaboration of the shared foundationals of the wider tradition to which it belongs. An example are the special spiritualities of religious communities that may emerge in certain traditions. For example, the specific formation tradition of the Buddhist *soto* form tradition has various *soto* subtraditions in different locations. So does the specific Catholic Franciscan tradition; it has many subtraditions in many independent Franciscan communities. Here again, the discipline of transcendent formation, because of its foundational focus, poses the questions: What foundations do the subtraditions within a specific faith and formation tradition have in common as subforms of that tradition? Why is it important for transtherapists and counselors to take into account how counselees who belong to such a subtradition assimilate and live that formation tradition in their own unique-communal way?

Healing of Inner Dissonance
Owing to Contaminating Assumptions

Many concepts and constructs of the human and social sciences are popularized today. With this comes an indirect popularization of their prescientific assumptions. Such assumptions may be incompatible with the transcendent-immanent nature of human formation. They may also be at odds with the formation directives of the specific tradition to which one adheres. This incompatibility may take many forms. The contaminating assumptions may be reductionistic, rationalistic, gnostic, vitalistic, materialistic, functionalistic, deterministic, pantheistic, autotheistic, or merely profane, to name only a few possibilities. People may try unwittingly to live their lives in the light of popular concepts and constructs pulsating through society. They themselves, and perhaps even some of their "pastoral" or "catechetical" instructors, directors, and counselors, may not realize that such popular ideas as absolutized self-actualization, human development, nondirectiveness, self-centeredness, self-esteem, collective unconscious and archetypes, *can* be contaminated by assumptions incompatible with their own faith and formation traditions. The result can be a dissonance between the profane and the faith-traditional direction of a person's life formation. This dissonance can affect an individual or a whole segment of the population. It can even become epidemic. For this reason, too, I saw the need for a critical science and discipline of transcendent formation and its application in transcendence therapy.

Once this discipline exists, it is the responsibility of its theorists, researchers, and practitioners to point out such dissonances. They must disclose how people unwittingly teach or live by popular concepts, constructs, or directives of formation that are incompatible with their own tradition. One must show how these have been borrowed uncritically from sciences, disciplines, or formation traditions other than their own through the popular use of certain words and ideas that have become common parlance in their society, in its schools, and in the media. Critical appraisal is necessary by experts in spiritual formation and transtherapy who have been trained to assess the unacceptable, albeit implicit, anthropological assumptions that may have contaminated the popular formulation of these concepts and constructs.

Discipline-Related But Not Interdisciplinary

Formation science is about distinctively human or transcendent-immanent formation wherever and however it manifests itself inside or outside any organized religion or ideology. The pursuit of knowledge of this focus of study includes the examination of relevant formation facts and findings. These may be found in ideological and religious formation traditions as well as in other arts and sciences. Like other autonomous sciences and disciplines, so, too, formation science refers to sources of information not in an interdisciplinary but in a discipline-related fashion. What is the difference?

Discipline-related arts and sciences are essentially different from interdisciplinary fields of study. The latter are proximately constituted by their own focus of practical concern such as, for instance, pastoral counseling. Their remote academic ground is a collection of theoretical insights drawn selectively from various academic disciplines or schools of thought because of their relevance to a proximate practical concern. Interdisciplinary fields do not aim at the full critical development of a unique systematic discipline as such. Beyond their own practical, applicative research, they may explore how certain of the theories, concepts, and constructs developed in various academic disciplines can justify, illumine, and serve their practical purposes.

Something essentially different happens in formation science and in other autonomous human sciences. They develop their own academic ground and theory. They cannot be identified as such with interdisciplinary fields of inquiry. Similarly, scholarly disciplines, such as theologies and philosophies, cannot be reduced to merely interdisciplinary enterprises on the basis of the fact that they refer in their research reports to relevant information gained from other disciplines, such as archaeology, linguistics, or theoretical physics.

Presently, not only formation science but almost all the arts, sciences, and scholarly disciplines refer to findings of sources other than their own. They do so if such findings can contribute significantly to a topic of research in which their students are involved. At the same time, they maintain their own autonomy, identity, focus, integrity, methodology, theory, and metalanguage. For example, the discipline of informational theology utilizes the insights and findings of archaeology, linguistics, hermeneutics, and ontology. It does not thereby relinquish its own identity nor its theological metalanguage.

By contrast, the concern of interdisciplinary approaches is not one art or science as such. They focus on a common field of practical purposes. This practicality is best served by a flexible amalgamation of relevant findings from a variety of arts and disciplines. Only those findings and insights are chosen that bear directly on the praxis under examination. Examples of such interdisciplinary fields are pastoral counseling, international diplomacy, labor relations, marriage preparation, public health, social justice, holistic health care, and so on. In contrast, transcendence therapy and counseling are not rooted in an amalgamation of findings from a variety of therapeutic schools and theories. They are firmly based on formation science and formation anthropology. These, in turn, may have critically assimilated and reformulated some formationally relevant insights of another school of therapy and counseling.

Autonomy of Formation Science
and Its Transcendence Therapy

When we compare the discipline relatedness of a science or discipline such as transtherapy with interdisciplinary endeavors, the essential difference between the two becomes evident. The scientists or scholars of an autonomous science or discipline refer to other sciences and disciplines only insofar as some of their insights or findings may be relevant to a topic of their own research. This consultation is not merely or mainly done in service of a common, practical cause. Rather, it is meant to foster the growth of the autonomous consulting science or discipline itself.

The term *autonomous* comes from the Greek *autos,* referring to self or self-identity, and *nomos,* "rule." On strictly academic grounds, an autonomous science, discipline, or school of therapy establishes its own rules of expansion by its own research. These rules include rigorous methods of adaptation and subsequent adoption of relevant outside information. Any adoption is done in the light of strict adherence to its own focus of research and practice. Autonomous sciences can only survive in their unique identity by exclusion of any interdisciplinary amalgamation. The latter approach must be replaced by critical, discipline-related, adaptive integration in service of the focus of research of the autonomous science. The same applies to transtherapy in relation to other therapies. It is not inter-therapeutic, but it can be related to other types of therapy insofar as some of their findings can be adapted to transtherapy.

As I said earlier, the praxis of transcendent transformation goes beyond the empirical-scientific mode. It implies a faith experience that may be monistic, theistic, or theistic-epiphanic. A more refined treatment of such praxis must either restrict itself to one of these three visions of the transforming mystery or treat each of them at length separately. I usually restrict myself by exemplifying this in one specific formation tradition, the Christian, with which I am most familiar. This shows the possibility of articulation of formation science and its transtherapy within a specific faith and formation tradition.

In other words, I believe in the absolute necessity for adherents of a specific faith tradition to complement formation science as empirical-experiential with the wisdom of their own classical transcendent formation traditions. To compare this with another field of study, pretheological philosophies of the life of the spirit stressed the necessity of complementing their philosophies of transcendence with the wisdom of one's own faith tradition.

One last point has to be made. The general formation anthropology and its subsequent general transtherapy, which I am addressing here, have to be distinguished from specific traditional formation anthropologies. General formation anthropology and general transtherapy strive for at least a minimum of formation knowledge that most people may agree upon. They aim at the disclosure of certain general tenets of transcendent formation and transtherapy that may be compatible, at least analogously, with those of a significant number of classical transcendent formation traditions. The crucial term is *analogously.* Analogously in this context means partly the same in some general basic way and partly different when it is further articulated in one's particular form tradition.

Utmost care should always be taken not to identify the pretheological formulation of formation anthropology itself with any of the different articulations any specific tradition may give to it. I can see the danger of such deceptive identification, for instance, in some adherents of movements, cults, New Age spiritualities, transpersonal psychologies, and in a variety of counseling and therapeutic centers. To clarify this point further, let me explore the difference between the articulation of the analogical concepts in certain (by no means all) humanistic transcendence movements and a Christian articulation.

Christians cannot accept certain humanistic assumptions that tend to permeate education, the media, and society at large, especially if, for example, something like Jungian gnosticism has been elevated to an ideological faith and formation tradition by some of its followers. My pretheological formation science and anthropology aim in part to assist Christians in their resistance to the distorting influence these movements might have on their own faith and formation tradition. Such distortions could foster a progressive silent alienation from their Christian churches.

This concern inspired my counterconcept of the formation field. I located at its center not the so-called higher and cosmic self but what I named the "radical formation mystery." Purposely, I designed the field as a "formation field." It represents my well-thought-out response to the humanistic term "field of consciousness." In my early formation theology and anthropology, I did not deny that consciousness plays a crucial part in one's formation field. On the contrary, I developed a theory of regions of consciousness and their interformation that some consider more sophisticated than any other they know. What I resisted is the reduction of the whole field to only a field of consciousness. This can lead to a mind-centered humanism, which would hold that the cosmic and human mind covers all of reality. This view, in turn, can give rise to an excessive, one-sided subjectivism.

The Term "Formation"
in the Phrase "Formation Field"

By the term "formation" in the phrase "formation field," I emphasize the form-giving power rooted in the intelligence and free formation will of the human person. My notion counteracts the assumption of some humanists that the field of life totally determines our human formation acts. The assumption of a relatively free formation field is also meant to avoid the presupposition of some humanists that this field is merely a "field of life" or a biological field determined by an idolized, impersonal "life force."

I locate the radical mystery of formation at the center of the field to resist the tendency to make a cosmic-human "higher self" the exclusive center of the human field of formation. This tendency gives rise to a humanism of a cosmically enclosed human self, realizing itself by autonomous self-actualization as ultimate. This notion is incompatible with monotheistic faith and formation traditions and specifically with the Judeo-Christian tradition, to which I adhere. The analogous term, formation mystery, leaves an opening for different interpretations by different traditions, if they can also agree—as a number of contemporary quantum physicists do—on the basic mysteriousness of life as we know it.

Spheres and Dimensions of the Formation Field

I replaced the common assumption of successive levels of human life with the notion of spiraling spheres and dimensions. My main contention was that these spheres and dimensions are equally and simultaneously present in any human life form from the beginning, potentially or actually. This innovation resisted the idea that all higher development in human life was some kind of sublimated unfolding of all-determining biological needs on the lower level of the hierarchy of human needs. This false notion could undermine faith in the reality of the free-forming human person. It could also lead to a denial of the absolute freedom of the radical formation mystery.

In my conception of the field, this mystery at its center is free to activate at any time the always already-preformed higher potencies. It can do so even if the lower potencies in the hierarchy of needs are not yet fully activated.

In my original field design, the spheres and dimensions, potential or activated, radiate or spiral out from the radical mystery at the center of the field. They are called to represent the existential formational embodiment of the essence of life as preformed in the radical mystery of formation. This challenges the humanistic assumptions of an atheistic existentialism. Existentialism replaces the existential radiation of the preforming mystery and of its numinous, spiraling reflections in countless essences. Among them the human essence gives rise to the foundational human life form or dynamic unique-communal life call. Existentialism has no faith in the moorings of any existence in essence nor ultimately in the preforming ground of all essences and existences, namely, the radical mystery of formation.

Social-Personal Interformation Sphere

The social-personal interformation sphere is only one of the basic spheres of the human formation field. Like all other spheres, this one, too, flows or spirals in and out of the mysterious center of the field. Its effectiveness, communally and personally, depends on the measure of its consonance with the mystery and with all the spheres and dimensions of the field. This assumption of my empirical-experiential formation field anthropology is the opposite of a humanistic idolizing of a social history, social movement, or social action as isolated from the radical mystery and from the other spheres and dimensions of the field. Such views do not take sufficiently into account needs, aspirations, and inspirations that complement and deepen the social emphasis they see. This approach sets the stage for a merely social humanism. The subsequent neglect of the intrasphere and the center sphere of the formation field can lead to a partly paralyzed inner life that often looks for healing in transtherapy sessions.

Sociohistorical Faith and Formation Tradition

Another function of the personal-social interformation sphere in my field paradigm is its pointing to the reality of the sociohistorical or vertical interformation with humanity's historical past. Crucial for human formation is its interformation with the sociohistorical movements known as the classical and classics-compatible faith and formation traditions. They have influenced profoundly my invention of the pyramid of formation traditions that coforms our character formation, a model I explain in detail in my book *Traditional Formation* (volume 5 in this series). Experiential reflection on this internalized pyramid of formation traditions plays a significant role in transtherapy.

Denial of the Power of Tradition

Social, clinical, psychological, and educational disciplines tend to underestimate, ignore, or even deny the basic all-permeating and coforming power of tradition. They do not spend much time in the detailed analysis of formation traditions and their powerful dynamics. Without a detailed understanding of tradition in each specific case, no character formation or deformation, neither its problems nor their transtherapeutic solutions, can be fully grasped.

For example, Christians who receive pretranscendent or merely functional-transcendent counseling or psychotherapy may be infected by transpsychological, cosmic, or gnostic humanistic faith and formation traditions. This may weaken and obscure the formational power of their own Christian tradition. In many cases, this tradition happens to be the most substantial base of their character structure. Experts in this field must apprehend and appraise the influence of the interior pyramid of various form traditions. Otherwise, understanding in depth is bound to be severely handicapped and so is transtherapy.

The stress in my field paradigm on interformational traditions strengthens our spiritual immunity. It protects us against contaminations and the subtle schizoid consequences for character formation. Therefore, we cannot refuse to address the impact of traditions. That is why my approach to transtherapy aims at a formative integration and a well-appraised, consonant expansion of one's form tradition pyramid. It intends to heal the harm of form-traditional disintegration. This noxious side effect can accompany even a well-intentioned, partly successful, counseling or therapy process.

Differential Appraisal of Humanistic Approaches

I applied my formation field paradigm empirically to the Dutch Life Schools for Young Adults, about which I speak extensively in my book *Transcendent Formation* (volume 6 in my Formative Spirituality series). It proved to be remarkably effective. This revolutionary paradigm implies a critique of certain forms of humanism with two disclaimers: (1) it does not claim that there are no compatible forms of classical humanism available besides the less compatible ones that seem in some measure to dominate our present-day society;)2) neither does it imply that formation theology and its pretheological formation science cannot find some wise and helpful insights in these less compatible humanisms, in spite of some of their unacceptable assumptions.

No humanistic ideological faith and formation tradition can study human nature for a sufficient period of time without disclosing—already by the statistical laws of chance—certain elements of human nature we all have in common. On top of this, empirical-experiential anthropologies, unlike speculative philosophical anthropologies, deal with detailed observations and analyses. Their empirical findings, when released from some of their absolutized humanistic assumptions, can often be complemented, corrected, and reformulated in the light of formation theology and/or its pretheological formation science, anthropology, and transtherapy. Following this critical process, a wise integration in the formation theology of one's religion and/or its auxiliary disciplines becomes possible.

Crucial Problem with Absolutized Humanistic Approaches

One crucial problem with absolutized humanistic approaches will always remain; for example, Christians, Orthodox Jews, or Islamites may be college or graduate students. They may be, moreover, therapy and counseling clients, readers of self-help books and articles, and/or listeners to talk shows. It is improbable that each one of them can appraise what is really implied in such presentations. The religious base of their character formation may be hollowed out before they even suspect what is happening to them. They will be less able to come up with a wise and balanced integration of what may be compatible with their religious heritage. They are in dire need of a systematic formation theology, catechetical or otherwise, within their own faith and formation tradition. This theology in turn should be aided by a serious pretheological formation science and an empirical formation anthropology. These may enable them to criticize creatively already-developed approaches to character and personality formation. To name only a few, the psychoanalytic, nondirective, existentialistic, Jungian, behavioristic, cognitive, gestalt, and rational-emotive theories and therapies.

CHAPTER 4

Psychoanalytic Traditions
and Transtherapy

In volume 5, *Traditional Formation*, I critiqued the psychoanalytic tradition from the viewpoint of formation science because of its sociohistorical impact directly on pretranscendent and indirectly on transcendent traditions. I want now to focus on some aspects of psychoanalysis as relevant to transcendent formation anthropology and transcendence therapy.

The psychoanalytic tradition offers us a sophisticated theory of personality as well as a remarkable technique of psychotherapy. Psychoanalytical theory carries its own original anthropology. This anthropology made psychoanalysis one of the leading theories of human development. My disciplines of distinctively human formation and transtherapy takes this theory into account critically and creatively as it does all other theories of human development.

A significant aspect of the psychoanalytical developmental and therapeutic tradition is its theoretical model of character formation. In my own theory, I developed the concepts of core form, heart, and corresponding character of life. My concept of core or character form has a different position, meaning, and genesis than what psychoanalytic theories point to in their description of "character formation."

Pretranscendent, Individualistic Bent
of Psychoanalytic Tradition

The psychoanalytical model of core or character formation takes its clue from the pretranscendent life of Western populations. Unlike psychoanalysis, I reserve the term "formation"—as well as its subdivisions of initial formation, reformation, and transformation—for human development insofar as it touches the transcendence dynamic or is touched by it. Briefly, my science takes into account relevant developmental insights and findings of social, clinical, educational, and other disciplines but always from the viewpoint of its own focus, namely, the transcendent-immanent formation of humanity and world.

Many people in the West try to actualize themselves as absolutely autonomous individuals on a pretranscendent level of life. Psychoanalysis holds out a helping hand for those who suffer from conflicts and failures in pretranscendent integration. It makes them aware of disturbing dynamics in their infrastructure. In service of this aim, psychoanalysis seeks to help its clients to disclose and analyze certain potentially disruptive developmental dynamics in everyday life. Psychoanalysts make it possible for people to gain more insight into the past and present pretranscendent history of their life. It helps them to see how their relationships with others affected their developmental history. The analyst uses interpretations based on the theories from the psychoanalytic tradition that spell out the main concepts to be taken up in their interpretation of pretranscendent life and its conflicts.

Diminishment of Transcendent Traditions

In the process, certain analysts may be inclined to look a priori at the internalizations of transcendent traditions in clients as though they were necessarily compensations and symptoms of psychopathology. They have linked transcendent experiences with crises in infancy. For Freud, these crises flared up in the oedipal stage. Certain analysts reduce religious experiences merely to a search for a new form of the past infant–mother bond. Enjoyment of this bond evokes, in their terminology, an oceanic feeling, an incidence of *symbiosis*. This new term could in some minds render the infant–mother relationship just a symbiotic event, an experience of the past that explains in full so-called transcendent experiences and longings felt later in life. For me the term "symbiotic," while pointing to a real possibility of mutual togetherness, carries connotations linking it with plant and animal life. The term I use in my theory is "fusion" or "fusional interformation," in keeping with the presuppositions of my formation science and its transtherapy.

Helpfulness and Limitations
of Psychoanalytic Interpretations

Psychoanalytic interpretations offer many insights into the dynamics of human development, some of which can be integrated into formation theory. However, they have to be corrected and reformulated in terms of the transcendent focus of formation science and transcendence therapy. For instance, spiritual mentors can appraise certain religious bindings as, at least in part, repetitions of relationships in infancy, provided they distinguish between true transcendent experiences and their immature or pathological look-alikes. This does not mean that one can appraise all religious bindings and experiences as reenactments of infancy relationships. I myself, along with other clinical professionals, would not think of reducing every possible transcendent-immanent striving to only pretranscendent processes.

Individualistic Autonomy of the Core Form
in Psychoanalytic Tradition

Some psychoanalytic traditions pose as ideal in the concept of character formation the pursuit of an individualistic autonomy. Analytic theory sets its sights on what I call in my theory the "intraformational life." It views this inner life in highly defined structures. In my own formation theory, these structures are viewed as pretranscendent. Some psychoanalysts define inner structures by rigid boundaries that set the "ideal" self-ruling person apart from others, from the life situation, from nature, cosmos, and the environment. Formation science would say that they split the intrasphere off from the transcendent sphere and from the epiphanic meanings and traditions disclosed to us in the inter and outer spheres of our field of life.

In other words, some analytic theories may set apart the images or intraforms we hold about ourselves and the images we bring to bear on others. They put great stress on the "healthy" directives of pretranscendent self-reliance, self- assertion, self-esteem, and individual self-actualization. We can indeed make pretranscendent self-directives the highest rule of our life, but we have to accept the consequences of so doing. It sets us apart from others and from nature as well as from their mysterious source. It hinders the way of self-transcendence. This view does not help us to mellow the boundaries of our pretranscendent "I," but makes these unwittingly ever more rigid.

Life-Call Appreciation

The dispositions addressed by the analytical traditions have some usefulness, to be sure, provided we can make them compatible with our transcendent-immanent life call and that we can remain open to their completion by the wisdom of transcendent traditions. To put our unique-communal call into practice in everyday life, it must be embodied in our pretranscendent sphere and through it in the pluritraditional field of life we share with others. This embodiment of our call is only hindered if we make absolute a life of pretranscendent ideals and projects.

To play our role effectively in daily life, we have to bring to it a measure of practical self-reliance, self-assertion, self-esteem, and self-actualization. But these lower formational dispositions should be monitored and moderated by our higher call. Therefore, I invented and initiated "life-call appreciation" or "call appreciation" as a better term than self-esteem.

Transcendence therapy in this context aims to help people cultivate not only their transcendent but also their pretranscendent life. Otherwise, one cannot take part in the functional-vital tasks one has to perform with others in our pluritraditional society. Our functional "I" in its practical, executive capacity makes it possible for us to give form effectively to our call and thereby to serve the common good. This managing "I," as inspired by a deeper call, enables us to accommodate without compromise a wide variety of changing social norms and historical situations. Whether we like it or not, we have to work with people, events, and things as they appear in our ever-changing, pluritraditional fields of life. Therefore, transcendent formation traditions that are well balanced clear the way for our pretranscendent dispositions now under the direction of our transcendent call. One of the principles of formation science and its transtherapy is that our life can only form itself in a healthy polarity of transcendence and immanence. The formational ideal I posit in transtherapy is that of a consonant transcendent-immanent way of life.

Limitations of the Self-Actualization Traditions

Transcendent traditions look at many developmental directives as helpful and often necessary but as incomplete. They can turn into obstacles to transcendence that may delay or prevent the formation of the human person as a whole. We must complement and correct individualistic directives by highlighting the transcendent bond among people, nature, cosmos, earth, life situations, and their mysterious source. Transcendence of individualism lets us grow in close and committed relationships of affective interformation when the situation makes this desirable. At the same time, we should not fall into the opposite extreme of denying the necessity of functional and vital relationships at a fitting time and place.

Our sense of life should not be a matter of individualism and division. In the light of transcendent traditions, our unique call lifts us beyond the boundaries of pretranscendent individuality—without neglecting its subordinate development. This ascendance facilitates our appreciation of others.

In my personality theory and transtherapy, I do not put forth as ideal a totally independent and self-actualizing person, as do many developmental theories. The ideal I hold out is that of a unique-communal person centered in a transcendent life call. We should strive to abide in the faith that our call is firmly planted in a transcendent mystery of initial formation, reformation, and transformation. I use in formation science the general term "formation" to point to all forms of human development insofar as they are related by us as thinkers or doers to the formation of human life by the formation mystery through the empirical-experiential transcendence dynamic. I subdivide this formation (1) in initial formation of any facet of human life; (2) in reformation or ongoing formation of such initial forms; and (3) in transformation by an always, also offered, special transforming power that lifts up our forming and reforming attempts. We share in the mysterious formation of cosmos and humanity. Such centeredness and rootedness give us a touch of calm amid the stresses and pulls we experience in our frantic societies.

Transcendent traditions appraise the directives of pretranscendent traditions as helpful but insufficient. They are wanting insofar as they center mainly around lower levels of self-actualization. They stress only pretranscendent self-esteem. They make us strive after individualistic autonomy, self-reliance, and self-assertion. Exclusive fixation on these kinds of core or character dispositions closes us off from the transcendent phases of formation so deeply respected in a transtherapeutic approach.

Limitations of Cognitive Interpretations
and Transference Relationships

My transcendence therapy does not put all of its faith in the healing power of the cognitive process of interpretation. The same goes for the transference relationship. Interpretation and analysis of transference fit well into the realm of pretranscendent counseling and therapy. Such approaches can also be useful in transcendence therapy, counseling, direction, or teaching. We may use them if pretranscendent problems show up in transcendence crises. I believe we should also pay attention beyond transference relationships to the interforming relationships occurring here and now between therapists and clients, counselors and counselees, directors and directees, teachers and disciples. We should acknowledge the relationship that grows between us and those who come for our help. We ought to appreciate it in the light of the mystery calling both of us to transcendent wholeness and healing. Past relationships do not always and necessarily color later ones in every respect.

Transcendent traditions think of such interformation as part of the "communal" facet of our unique-communal call. Therefore, I put personal-social interformation in its own special place in my basic paradigm of the five coforming spheres of the formation field. In this way I highlight it as distinct from overall, always ongoing interformation. This universal interaction occurs between all spheres, dimensions, regions, ranks, and horizons of my formation-field paradigm, including cosmic formation. Therefore, I designate my paradigm often as interformational. As I shall later show, personal-social interformation plays a special role in transtherapy.

Self-Individuation and Conflict between Archaic
and Added Layers of the Core Form

Self-actualizing traditions that stay on the pretranscendent level support individualism. Individuals are encouraged to come up with values for their own life. They are to feel free to pick and choose such values, to clarify them in tune with their own bent. In this process of "values clarification," many may come to feel as if they should be almost totally independent of the commanding directives written into their human nature and conscience. They may also feel that their "clarification" should not take into account any value of their families of origin or of any traditional sets of values. Their families may have offered them transcendent faith and form traditions. In their drive for self-sufficiency, the young can disregard these. It is understandable and even desirable that they turn away from the unreasonable idiosyncratic changes that may have been added to these traditions by one's family.

Undesirable from the viewpoint of formation is to cut oneself off totally from these traditions, even in their basic principles. This sets up a conflicted core form. One splits basic traditional dispositions off from newly borrowed or discovered values. One can turn down or turn away from one's original traditional dispositions, but they do not go away. They keep hiding in the core form of our life as its archaic layer. Part of our life call is to mine this ground for its hidden wisdom. We should purify it from deformational accretions. Then we may take over in our tradition pyramid reformulated consonant elements of self-actualizing traditions.

Our first deformational accretions come from our family. People have to pull themselves out of ties with their family that are too tight. Many go through a period of formation in which they strike out at certain aspects of their family-bound traditions. The resentment that is at the bottom of this aggressiveness may not come into focal consciousness. Transtherapy helps persons to become aware of it. It makes them experience how core conflicts between internalized divergent traditions tear them apart. Individualistic views spread by some social, clinical, and educational disciplines keep these inner clashes alive. They bring about crises of formation conscience. One may be able to solve these by a transcendent appraisal of pretranscendent ideals and processes. Pretranscendent disciplines study these dynamics. We can derive many insights from them about the processes that also show up in transcendence therapy and formation counseling. As long as we do not resolve this split of our core form, we will be handicapped in our transcendent-immanent formation journey.

Oedipus Complex and Alma Mater Complex

Psychoanalytic theory holds that certain dispositions are central in the history of personal development, notably the Oedipus complex. What is the link between such complexes and the transcendent traditions by which counselees and their families may feel they should live their life.

The Oedipus myth talks about son–mother–father ties that set up a "complex." This shows up in the developmental history of people who cast their relationship to their parents in the image of Western pretranscendent patriarchal form traditions. But the same does not necessarily hold for people who adhere to other traditions. For example, a vital-affective tie of fusion with the mother influences some believers in certain transcendent form traditions. She images for them the nourishing ground of the all-forming mystery. For instance, my research in Japan taught me that the son–mother, or what I call the "Alma Mater" complex, may run the life of many men. The son can be filled with rage over feelings of loss of his vital-affective tie with the mother. Later, he may look more at what she went through for him. He lets shame and remorse touch his moods.

Transcendent traditions draw people to a life-style of trust in a higher power. Appreciative parents and other authorities called forth this trust. Psychoanalytic theory as well as other related personality theories did not always develop the language to address this transcendent-immanent kind of relationship, but transtherapy does.

Pretranscendent Dependency Relationships in Followers of Transcendent Traditions

Pretranscendent traditions touch the life of all people who grow up in pluritraditional societies. For example, a Muslim, Hindu, or Christian in America often takes on the pretranscendent dependency conflicts that are common among his or her American peers, family members, colleagues, and acquaintances. They become even more familiar with such conflicts through popular novels, movies, articles, and talk shows that touch on such psychological problems. All people go through a pretranscendent phase of development; transcendent maturity, perhaps aided by transcendence therapy, may liberate them from the lingering traces of one-sided fixation in this phase of life.

The orthodox, analytic version of life seems to be more immediately helpful to people whose traditions have come apart at the seams. They have to pull their crumbling life together without the backing of transcendent traditions and communities. I must immediately add that many believers in transcendent traditions take on the very Western patterns of individualism I have critiqued. They, too, look for absolute autonomy and arbitrary values clarification. They pick up the free-floating, ideological tradition of absolute equality in all matters. For them, the directive of equality then takes the place of what I call "coformational complementarity." We are called to coform our lives together, not to outdo but to complement each other.

The psychoanalytic approach and its offspring in the theories that underpin various social, clinical, educational, and other therapies hold out great hope to those trapped mainly in the pretranscendent period of formation. Ideally, after learning how to take care of conflicts on this level, one should complement such beneficial psychological or developmental treatment by transcendence therapy, direction, counseling, or teaching.

Interpretive and Meditative Approaches

Transcendence therapy takes into account the necessity of rationality and cognitive self-reflection. Psychoanalytical approaches place a great deal of trust in rational, interpretive explanations. This ties in with their focus on the pretranscendent life. Pretranscendent thought, imagination, and action draw on the vital-functional dispositions of the personality. These dispositions can be cut off from the transcendent dimension of life. In that case, they do not leave room for the inspirations and aspirations of the life call. Our core or character then takes on only pretranscendent dispositions.

The opposite works in transcendent traditions. Intuitive and meditative means like symbols and rituals complement and elevate our pretranscendent approaches. Reflection accompanies meditation. Appreciative abandonment to the mystery of formation sets up a serene background for self-presence. Lower reason keeps in touch with higher reason. It makes us more appreciative of what other traditions stand for. It enhances our capacity for addressing the root causes of transcendence crises in the Western world.

CHAPTER 5

Individual Achievement, Transcendence, and Transtherapy

As followers of transcendent traditions we face two issues. The first one concerns our stand toward pretranscendent traditions. In this regard we ask: To what extent do our traditional dispositions tie in with the prevalent dispositions of pretranscendent life around us? The second issue raises another question, namely, how can we benefit from the dispositions developed by pretranscendent traditions? In other words, how far can our own core form, insofar as it is tradition-bound, be wisely expanded? Can it accommodate the dispositions of individualization? A related question concerns our actual life form. How can it tune into a society that for the most part seems guided by pretranscendent traditions? How are individual initiatives lived out by transcendent people? How do the answers to these questions affect transtherapy?

Achievement Disposition

A pretranscendent achievement disposition fuels our drive for self-actualization and individuation. Many may feel that followers of Mediterranean, Eastern, African, and South American transcendent form traditions are insufficiently disposed to the pursuits of individuation and achievement. Some people conclude that there must be an insurmountable conflict between any individual development and transcendent formation.

It is true that some high powered self-actualizers may drive themselves on ruthlessly. In comparison with them, many followers of transcendent traditions may "look" less energetic. It is true that they are not bent on achievement at any price. But one should not draw from this the conclusion that individuality and self-transcendence stand in each other's way. Commitment to transcendent traditions is not necessarily connected with weaker dispositions for individuation and performance.

I take exception to the opposite view that is often held in the social sciences, especially since David McClelland's work (*The Achievement Motive* [New York: Appleton-Century Crofts, 1953) on achievement motivation, self-realization, and American-style independence. As a formation scientist who taught many Asiatic, African, and Hispanic students, I feel uneasy about the tendency of many social scientists and educators to generalize to all people what they observe in westernized populations. People in the West developed such traits under the sway of traditions that are individualistic and self-actualizing in a merely pretranscendent sense.

By the same token, followers of transcendent traditions also show remarkable achievements. The history of the founders or leaders of religions, of religious communities, of industrial and social enterprises, of first-rate schools, as well as the records of saints, heroes, and mystics, tell the story. Their lives reveal that a transcendent tradition—if it is lived in a balanced way—can bring about amazing achievements and miracles of perseverance.

Sources of Achievement Dispositions

Of concern to me is not the achievement disposition as such but its source, motivation, and direction. The source of a pretranscendent achievement disposition is often a drive for popular confirmation, fame, status, power, and possession. One may hunger for acceptance and approval by important people who look successful in society.

Inspirations and aspirations, nor merely ambitions, are the sources of a transcendent achievement disposition. Transcendent traditions make us walk in the light of our call to coform with the forming mystery our field of presence and action, in short, to create a better world in and around us. This inspiration draws forth aspirations to do as well as we can in service of our calling—not only or mainly in service of doubling our bank account or building our career.

Source of Individuation Dispositions

Commitment to the successive probable disclosures of our call makes us look for means to carry out what it appears to ask of us. It makes us see our individual skills, aptitudes, and talents in a new light. It shows us how we can draw on these gifts to put into practice what inspires us. Transcendent traditions that are consonant do not cut off the development of our individual "I" and its aptitudes. On the contrary, we stand in awe of the variety of the individual character traits and aptitudes to be found in the lives of saints, spiritual mentors and masters, of scholars and entrepreneurs, of poets and thinkers, who were inspired by transcendent traditions. This inspiration sets their individuality apart from one that pursues merely pretranscendent aims and goals. The sources of this latter kind of individuation often turn out to be fears, ambitions, and functional or gnostic ideals confined mainly to a pretranscendent life.

The true sources of our individuation should be the appeals of our life call. The execution of this call depends on our powers of planning and action. To put these appeals into practice, we have to come down to earth in the concrete give-and- take of daily life.

When we draw on our skills, we bring out our individual form potencies. Committed followers of transcendent-immanent traditions do not make this actualization in and by itself the ultimate aim of life. They look at it as a side benefit of fidelity to their life call. For them, the voice of the mystery calls out in the needs of people and in the challenges facing society today. A loving response draws out both their higher and lower dispositions.

For example, the practical social achievements of volunteers are always laudatory. Some people give up careers and success to lend a helping hand to the poor, to uphold the rights of the downtrodden, to fight against oppression. They bring to life in themselves a strong managing "I." For them, this firm executive "I" becomes a necessary means to achieve a better life for others. The same goes for inspired scientists, artists, scholars, authors, publishers, editors, and captains of industry. They maintain their commitments through the power of transcendent performance dispositions.

In many followers of transcendent-immanent traditions, such aspirations may be dormant. Their actualization becomes entangled with dispositions for individualistic fulfillment, for monetary and honorary rewards, and for praise by others. Elements of popular individualistic traditions may then veil the radiance of their original transcendent inspirations.

Hierarchical Transcendent Traditions and Individuation

Many transcendent traditions are hierarchical. Adherents of such traditions show esteem for each other's position, no matter how modest it may be. They look at each rank as assigned or allowed by the forming mystery. Formation traditions often fail to live up to this ideal. Such failures are to be expected, for the followers of form traditions are often faced with a bewildering variety of situations, institutions, communities, and personalities. No wonder their efforts to respect people sometimes fall short of what their faith tradition really stands for. The more they fail, the more their own transcendent ascendance and that of those whose lives they touch may be interrupted or delayed.

Authoritarian Formation Traditions

Some personalities happen to be authoritarian. They may have turned out that way on the basis of their temperament or character. In others, authoritarianism is more the outcome of their personal or shared history. Still others fall into the authoritarian mold because they allow elements of traditions that are fascist or fundamentalistic to pollute their tradition pyramid.

The authoritarian disposition strikes down the mutual esteem and humility that ought to mark a truly transcendent hierarchy. Formation traditions, turned awry, can give rise to authoritarian dispositions. For instance, some ruling mullahs of the Iranian Shi'ite formation tradition show fellow Muslims, who are not of their own persuasion, despicable disdain.

Twisted formation traditions try to convince people that the authoritarian abuse of authority is somehow acceptable. They posit absolute obedience to authority at any price. They accept blindly anything authorities say or do. Merely human authorities are constituted as idols. The tendency to idolatry can make religious or ideological authoritarianism harsher to live with than other forms of authority. A more deadly combination is the coming together of an authoritarianism of political and ideological or religious form traditions. This was the case in Nazi Germany, Communist Russia, Eastern Europe, Red China, and North Korea, as well as in Shi'ite Iranian and some African and South American dictatorships.

Embodiment in Form-Traditional Institutions

Hierarchical traditions of formation embody themselves in such institutions as, for example, law, education, and the army. Often this institutional embodiment takes into account elements of other traditions. These are, at first, adopted in the tradition sets of their founders and followers. For example, the Protestant monastic institution of Taizé took over, in its tradition, elements of an ecumenical tradition. Such changes and adaptations alter the form one gives to the institutions in which they are concretized. Taizé became justifiably famous for its institutionalized ecumenical prayer services.

Individualization marks many ambitions of Western form traditions and their institutions. In such populations, elements of concern for individualization touch unavoidably upon the tradition pyramid of followers of hierarchical traditions. What often follows is a rebellion against authoritarianism, not necessarily against authority. People are apt to push for more leeway for individual development. For example, the code of hairdo and behavior in the institution of the Dutch Army has been more individualized under the pressure of self-actualizing traditions.

Today we want to know more not only about the life call but also about the individual possibilities and limits that will be employed in the carrying out of this call. At present, some leading persons in hierarchical traditions show more awareness of this desire. It strikes them that it is better for persons to come to know their unique-communal call and to develop some idea of how to carry it out in daily life. This will happen faster if each person is given reasonable room for thought and action, also on the individual level of life.

We thus see more flexibility in giving form to individual dispositions and directives, especially as these impact upon the fulfillment of one's call in everyday life. This gives me more hope that the journey of unique-communal transcendence can become a possibility for more people now than in previous eras.

Subordinated Individualization

The more followers of a transcendent tradition draw on its spirit, the more their individualization will be in tune with their life call as rooted in the transcendent. Their individualization differs from that of followers of mere pre-transcendent traditions.

While individual autonomy and initiative are on the upswing in some quarters, they do not necessarily hollow out the dispositions of wonder and awe for the mystery. Neither do they necessarily weaken the disposition to turn for wisdom to the treasures of transcendent traditions and there to seek guidance for living. Nor does consonant individuation do away with our obedience to the life call. Finally, such subordinated individuation does not interfere with our openness to the unveilings of the call in the concrete people, events, things, and situations we meet in the inter and outer spheres of our formation field.

Formation to Consonant Individuation

A transcendent-immanent tradition, as lived by parents, can show children what subordinated individuation looks like. The mother plays a foremost role in this area, especially when her children are from one to two and a half years of age. She is apt to confirm the first signs of the individuation of the child. Individuality emerges early in life. From the beginning, the mother can make room for the future breakthrough of the still-dormant potency for transcendence. This potency can only be personally and focally actualized in later formation phases. The mother is called by the formation mystery to set up the channels of practices through which, at a later stage, the transcendent meanings of her tradition can flow freely. Once these inspirations make themselves known later in life, their flow is eased and sheltered by the riverbed of already-existing disciplines and facilitating conditions firmly formed in the child by loving parents. While the deeper meanings of such disciplinary customs are not understood by children, they still give form to their neuroformational dispositions. In due time, these dispositions make us ready to live up to the deeper directives of our transcendent traditions once they are disclosed to us. The well-ploughed soil of childhood will make it easier for us to put these directives into practice.

For example, children who have been formed early in life in the custom of staying still during devout prayer or during the reading of the Bible, Sutra, or

Qur'an as done by adults will later be more ready for the prayer rituals of their religion or denomination. An early formation in respect for the toys of siblings plants the seed of receptivity for the message and meaning of justice and respect as taught by religions or ideologies later in life.

This fostering of consonant individuation in the early years is further played out in adolescence. In westernized fields of formation, adolescents have to make numerous options among a variety of social-formation opportunities. They then have to honor, sometimes for a lifetime, their ensuing commitments. They have to increase their chances to make more right than wrong choices. They must appraise their unique life call and the wisdom of their traditions. They should also dispose themselves to assess continually their individual capacities to make this call effective in their life situations. The room they have given to their individual development shows up when they put into effect in society the probable disclosures of their call of life.

We should look at our individuation in the light of our tradition. For example, Orthodox Jewish adolescents may develop to the utmost their individual talents for sports, art, commerce, medicine, or scholarship. Yet, as long as they stay committed to their religious tradition, they will not allow this concern for individual performance to overrun their Sabbath duties.

Individuation in Contemporary Transcendent Traditions

Transcendent formation traditions are communicated first of all by the family. These traditions follow a hierarchy of sorts within the family and also in other institutions that influence the formation of character. This hierarchy symbolizes the dependency relationships between the followers of the tradition and its transcendent-immanent focus.

Families who live by transcendent traditions put adolescents in touch with many ways of individuation and of individual skill development. They want their children to be trained in the scientific, professional, athletic, and business skills they will need to meet the competition in society for a limited number of good jobs.

In line with its transcendent tradition, the family wants this individuation to maintain a subordinated place. They do not want it to break up the affective bonding and the reasonable interdependencies of hierarchical relationships in their families and in the institutions of formation to which they belong. Thus, they do not look favorably on absolutized autonomy or individualism. Yet, as I noted earlier, the style and the limits of these interdependencies are inevitably contested and eventually do change. Changes in the way traditions are or are not carried out within pluritraditional societies can spawn crises of conscience.

They can give rise to conflicts between generations and especially between adolescents and adults who share the same traditions.

The five-part British drama series *Shalom Salaam* offers a striking example. In this drama the generational conflicts in a Jewish and Islamic family are central. We watch the interactions between the Muslim girl, Mumtaz, the Jewish boy, Adam, and his Catholic girlfriend, Jackie, in the city of Leicester in England. They go to the same pluritraditional high school. The home scenes bring out the conflicts between old and new traditions.

Shalom Salaam draws our attention to the powerful role tradition plays in character formation through its theme: people of different traditions trying to remain together and to maintain good feelings for one another. These youngsters strive to stay in tune simultaneously with the pluritraditional British society and with their families. They do not want to give up the foundations of their own tradition. They do not want to kill off their transcendence dynamic. The play shows nobody as a victim. *Shalom Salaam* tells the story of people who sometimes make the right, sometimes the wrong choices and take responsibility for them.

Transcendent-immanent traditions, insofar as they remain open and consonant, help us to rise above separation. They soften the striving for autonomy. They protect us against one-sided assumptions of social, psychological, clinical, educational, and managerial theories that are tied to observations of mainly pretranscendent westernized populations. What such disciplines tell us about individualization is not true in all cases. Not all of their findings apply to what I call "consonant individuation." Many followers of transcendent-immanent traditions go through a phase of pretranscendent individuation. They bypass their belief systems because they imbibe elements of absolutized self-actualizing traditions. This move may lead ultimately either to a deeper adherence to their tradition or to a lasting contamination of it. The same openness to pretranscendent individuation may nurture fidelity to one's unique-communal life call and one's capacity to fulfill the directives of one's own transcendent tradition. Transtherapy can be of great assistance in such internal tradition conflicts and their reverberations in one's field of life.

Changes in Institutions

Earlier I showed how new insights can soften the harsh edges of authoritarianism. Of late many institutions are making changes in their authority structures. One sees a diminishment of the tendency to lay new burdens on people by those in charge. Hierarchy by means of power is changing into a hierarchy based on quality. Command from the top no longer smothers the possibility of an interformation based on respect for one another. More companies foster participative servant leadership and initiative. They cut out excess structures. They mitigate the dominance of Western managerial faith and formation traditions that have led in some cases to functional megaorganizations that depersonalize workers and diminish dedication.

Tradition Modulations and Conflicts

Changes in traditions bring conflicts to the fore. Many followers of hierarchical traditions do not seem to have been formed in taking initiative and making decisions. Changes in their traditional institutions are apt to expect too much from them too soon. Strain and anxiety prevail. Many people in the changing republics of what was the Soviet Union show signs of being shaken by the turnabout in their way of life. Many experience stress under the pressure to show initiative and enterprise in the new free-market tradition. Some become paralyzed in their functioning. Others are tempted to turn their newly found freedom over to self-proclaimed "saviors." The more talented and spellbinding such types are, the more they endanger one's inner freedom. Their hold on people can compel higher hierarchical state and institutional authority to limit freedom more and more, ostensibly to preserve law and order.

Consonant individualization should be gradual. Upcoming anxiety can be offset by formation in the deeper meanings and resources of changing traditions. This re-sourcing-in-depth lays the ground for growth in inner equanimity. Peace of mind calms the fear and tension conjured up by the appeal to more personal responsibility for one's life. To put it briefly, efforts toward inner reformation should reflect changes in inter and outer demands. Transcendence therapy that is done in the light of the classic disciplines of transformation treasured by our tradition can make one more ready for the work of inner reformation and new tradition-consonant expansion.

In the area of parent–child, teacher–pupil, mentor–disciple interformation, conflict can be sparked by a changing tradition. This happens when parents, educators, television personalities, or work supervisors send out opposing signals. On the one hand, they talk about greater freedom and individuation; on the other, they make their charges feel that they should be excessively submissive. Prefocally, they want them to look the same as they did when they were children and when drastic changes in socialist, capitalist, and educational or other form traditions had not yet occurred.

Some grandparents, other older family members, aging teachers, mentors, or leaders may resist innovations in direct or indirect ways. This conflict, too, is illustrated in the movie *Shalom Salaam*. The older uncle and the Imam (the representative of the Islamic clergy) talk to Mumtaz and her brothers about absolute conformity to Islamic formation customs. This counsel disturbs them deeply. It seems to be at odds with the limited individual freedom allowed by their parents. The Jewish boy, Adam, finds himself in much the same plight with his grandfather and the rabbi.

Conflict of Changes in Fusional Traditions

The transcendent tradition may be not only a hierarchical but also a strongly fusional "we-tradition." Matters then become more entangled. Whereas consonant individuation brings out aspirations for initiative, self-expression, and creativity, a traditional fusion disposition can set up a need for warm appreciation and confirmation by those in charge. People who have been formed in hierarchical-fusional traditions function best as individualized persons when they are confirmed by others. They feel right only if those above them and around them show them warm appreciation. They do not strive spontaneously to undo the affective connectedness the vital-fusional tradition has instilled in them. The followers of pretranscendent self-actualizing traditions are different in this regard. They seek to establish their "individualistic I" as ultimate. They feel as if they must rebel to achieve their separation from former generations. This is one of the causes of the intergenerational conflicts typical of westernized pretranscendent populations. As ought to be clear by now, both the overly vital-fusional and the excessive self-actualizing traditions interfere with the transcendence dynamic and its expression. Transtherapy can in this case offer a road to clarification and to peace.

CHAPTER 6

Female Individuation, Transcendence, and Transtherapy

Changes in our field of life, especially since the Age of Reason, caused an upswing in the individualistic traditions that may affect the way to transcendence and thereby enlighten the process of transtherapy. At present, these traditions impact upon many women. Their hope for a more individualized, autonomous life prompts them to give form to an individual "I" of their own. They want to bring society to an awareness of the importance of their fight for freedom. Men have fought and won their rights to individuality; women want equal consideration.

This individualizing trend also affects women who adhere to transcendent-immanent traditions. They feel the tension between individuation and their higher call. The deeper they anchor themselves in a consonant transcendent tradition, the better they can cope with this conflict. Many men discriminated against them. A number of them used their individualistic bent, their hunger for ruthless self-actualization, to put women down. Many women show a deeper sensitivity to their life call and the mystery behind it than men do. Yet, society gave women less opportunity to put this call into practice by encouraging them to develop their individual aptitudes. Many more men got the chance to develop their skills. A number of them abused these advantages to keep women in their place.

As I learned in the decisive first year of drafting formation science during World War II, crises of individuation struck gifted and capable women especially . Courageous women who saved our lives inspired me to come to grips with our society's refusal to create room for their personal talents and unique-communal callings. We men had withheld from women many opportunities given to us by society. Now the need of the hour pushed us to share with them powers of decision, an equal voice, and a part in our undertakings. Often during the war their daring, inventiveness, and effectiveness put us to shame.

Women and the Individuation Crisis

Transcendent institutions inspired women to give of themselves whole-heartedly in a variety of religious and social causes. Effective engagement called for the expansion of individual skills and talents already used by women to serve the needs of their families. This prepared them for many demands of the women's movement that emerged beside other movements of reformation, such as the abolitionist in the nineteenth century or during the Vietnam protest and the civil rights movement of the 1960s.

The women representing transcendent traditions came into contact with the women's movement. The latter evolved from self-actualizing traditions that stood for individuation. The transcendent woman seeks this individuation less for its own sake, or for only careerism or protest. She certainly wants her rights. She stands up for them in solidarity with her discriminated against sisters. But her deeper purpose is to widen the range of putting into practice the transcendent call hidden in the core of her life.

A healthy drive for individuation complements her aspiration for transcendence. She wants to be a unique-communal person. She is that already by virtue of her anchorage in her unique life call. She demands also to be recognized more as a person in her own right. She insists that society should enable her to express her unique-communal life call also in her pretranscendent individuality. Often, this only happens if and when she can sufficiently express herself in effective public performance as an individual.

This drive meets with the inability of some men to bear with an open assertiveness on the part of women. They look at her as power hungry. This attitude can disrupt a male–female friendship or a husband–wife relationship. This happens when men, for example, link with their girlfriend or wife the image of a "power-hungry mother." Such conflict can strengthen the deformative attitude I call the Alma Mater disposition or complex in certain men.

Deeper conflicts of the heart thus set the stage for individuation crises in transcendent women. These lead to conflicts between old and new pretranscendent traditions as well as old and new transcendent traditions. The working out of such conflicts in transcendence therapy can foster a richer world of meaning. A well-balanced feminine field of life holds together the transcendent spiritual life of women and their now more differentiating, expanding individual life. It enables women from all states of life to tread the steps of the ladder of transcendent formation in a more integrated way than was previously possible.

Women's Inner Transcendence and Social Reserve

Transcendent women maintain a subtle barrier of social reserve. As I argued earlier, the boundaries of the individual life tend to be more flexible and permeable to the degree that the boundaries of one's transcendent life are better defined and kept. A less sensitive outsider may not catch the inner depth and richness in a transcendent woman. The easy flow, openness, access, and flexibility of the individual facet of her life may conceal the dignified reserve of her inmost being. If she lets one go beyond the boundaries of her transcendent life, one may find opening up a wider range of affects, intuitions, and wisdom than appears in many transcendent men.

To be trusting enough to show us something of this deeper life, a woman must feel sure of respect, of receiving refined appreciation and true empathy. She easily withdraws at any sign of a male superiority feeling, of arrogance, misunderstanding, or manipulation. The transcendent woman stays in touch with the deeper dispositions, directives, feelings, and motives of self and others—with things we hardly talk about in everyday company.

Pretranscendent Therapy and Transcendent Sensitivity

A therapist, counselor, director, mentor, or teacher should be in tune with this transcendent sensitivity. In pretranscendent therapeutic situations, women may share their story of the conflicts associated with individual self-actualization, of the tensions they experienced with either macho or fusional traditions. Yet they keep to themselves their spiritual aspirations, practices, and experiences. Sensing that many pretranscendent therapists may not be in tune with transcendence, they reserve to themselves their experience of this decisive, ultimate dimension of their life. They may later seek to complement successful pretranscendent treatment with transcendence therapy to make up for what was missing. A person turns to transtherapy to pull together the healed individuation of their lower life with their higher aspirations.

Pretranscendent therapists, teachers, administrators, and supervisors often show ambivalent, if not depreciative, appraisals of transcendent traditions and practices. This closed attitude makes transcendent women hesitant. They fear to reveal their spiritual aspirations to anyone who might not be open to their preciousness and beauty. The striving to make something of the spiritual realm of their lives remains private.

I am referring here, of course, to transcendence in the fullest sense, not to partial social, vital, functional, or gnostic transcendence that women and men may show at the beginning of the later stretches of their spiritual journey. Then the affective, exotic, social, or charming side benefits of such partial transcendence may be a preferred topic of conversation.

I hope my view of the integration problems of transcendent women confirms that I do not hold some of the standard positions of pretranscendent therapies. Often the latter diminish the pursuit of the transcendent life as a kind of pathology or regression. Therapists of this persuasion may pick up that the same person struggles with pretranscendent conflicts. They tend, then, to look on transcendent experiences as symptoms of the same conflicts. They explain, for example, the life of love and prayer in a hysterical patient as a sign of hysteria. In my opinion, unless the possible coformant of transcendent appreciation is fully appraised, therapy or counseling cannot proceed optimally.

Transtherapy and Conflict

Commitment to transcendent traditions can be genuine, without ruling out conflict. Transtherapy enables people to disclose and resolve certain inner and outer clashes in an effective manner.

A person advanced on the transcendent path is not free of deformation. Transcendent and formational defects can show up in a person at one and the same time. Elements of transcendence and of disturbances in formation touch each other. Together they make for a highly complex relationship. Each element bears on the others in its own way in varying degrees. A person can be quite transcendent and still be pulled and pushed by deformations. Another person can be relatively free of pretranscendent deformation, show a well-integrated individual core form but not necessarily live in the light of a transcendent life call and tradition. It is thus unfair to make fun of transcendent women because they may still fail on the pretranscendent level of life.

Evasion and Indirect Communication
of Transcendent Experiences

Transcendent women tend to be indirect when sharing their transcendent experiences. They want to preserve the uniqueness of their transcendent-immanent life, the mysterious founding form of their personality. Wise evasion prevents intrusion. Indirect talk puts a brake on getting too close to the life call of others. This prevents the mix-up of one's own call with that of other people. Inner stillness turns us to the unfolding mystery of the call we most deeply are.

A woman will often not risk speaking too openly of experiences, aspirations, and appreciations that are most intimate and transcendent, except to a really trusted other. She senses that she may not be understood by the mass of men nor by many other women. Misunderstanding, if it happens frequently, can give rise to depreciative thoughts and feelings by others. These can lead to alienation and despondency and drive a transcendent woman into loneliness. Her sense of isolation can become pervasive.

To prevent this from happening, she must turn back in time to the treasure of being alone (or all-one) with the transcendent in the depth of her being. She may sense that a like-minded husband or friend, a refined, sensitive therapist or mentor, is in touch with her inner world. With them, she may be less evasive.

Therapists formed in the art and discipline of transtherapy help their counselees to talk out and work through their conflicts in the light of the Transcendent. They do so through their empathic appreciation and confirmation of each probable disclosure of the call. They create a climate of transcendent participation. An unspoken intimacy with the all-forming mystery itself transcends, pervades, and guides the interformation of the therapist and the counselee.

Pretranscendent "I"-Conscience of Women

Attending to the transcendent horizon of a woman's life does not shut out attention to her pretranscendent life. As I have said, proper development of the pretranscendent life serves the transcendent life. Our lower life is an instrument of social-vital-functional information as well as a tool and an expression of higher aspirations in our concrete material and social field of life.

Formation therapy, mentoring, or teaching concerns itself with the pretranscendent life insofar as it bears on deeper living. It either prepares us for and faithfully expresses the depth of our existence, or it interferes with and misrepresents our transcendent zone of being. In that case, it is split off from the transformation of our life as a whole.

For example, the pretranscendent conscience of certain women may be driven by the assumption that all eyes are critically on her. This disposition may be found more often in women who have to labor under the pressure of macho formation traditions. The unbalanced man–woman position in such a secular, industrial, or political order may be ingrained in her lower, conditioned conscience. In many instances, the overbearing position given to males by a particular secular form tradition is identified with the underlying ideological faith tradition.

For instance, the position of women may be confined to the rules established by some Islamic form traditions that happen to be fundamentalistic. Women in these settings may reveal a more repressive conscience than that of Christian or Muslim women who belong to more flexible, open form traditions. The same would apply, of course, to other fundamentalistic form traditions, for example, to some Jewish, Hindu, indigenous African, and Christian form traditions as distinguished from their basic faith traditions.

Such a repressive lower conscience fuels the fire of hidden anger and assertiveness. A woman may feel that she will lose appreciation, love, and confirmation if people become aware of how angry she can be or how demanding of her rights. Women in some oppressive types of form traditions tend to keep such feelings in check. They hold them down by means of willpower, or they transpose them in other directions. This transposition in turn can give rise to somatic symptoms.

Often, a woman is furious at men near to her for not showing kindness and consideration when she suffers. She feels disappointed and upset. Her lower conscience forbids her to talk about such feelings to a friend who is superior in social rank, to a lover, husband, boss, teacher, or mentor. Soon she may develop a strong hidden sense of entitlement. She feels that she is entitled to special consideration, support, and empathy. Yet, she does not dare to tell directly what ails or pains her affective life or evokes its sometimes either irrational or justified demands. The less intuitive or the less sensitive a male is, the more difficult it is for him to read vague symbols, hints, and innuendoes. These expressions are diluted by the taboo placed on the direct communication of anger by women. The misreading of the signs from a male perspective is often inevitable. This lack of understanding deepens her sense of entitlement, indignation, rage, and blame.

Repression, Impression, Expression, "Transpression"

Repression does not resolve inner turmoil. That is why transtherapy helps people to make nonfocal "re-pression" focal. The search for a solution to repression also led me to develop the concept of "im-pression." In transtherapy this term refers to the deformative act and disposition of impressing deeper and deeper feelings of rage and blame into our emotional life. This happens when we ruminate over these experiences in our excited churning mind to such degree that they leave a lasting imprint on us.

Many pretranscendent therapies advise as their solution "ex-pression." But this too has disadvantages. Direct expression to others, before a woman has returned to the center in her transcendent life, may come across as irrational and overly emotional. This evokes in others feelings of disrespect and distancing. It reinforces the all-wise, overbearing disposition of some males. Her pent-up rage looks, by virtue of its explosive nature and passionate expression, less than reasonable. It gives the domineering male an opportunity to point out to her "solemnly and reasonably" the irrational excess of her fury, blame, and accusation. This tactic aims to throw her back on an overpowering lower "I" shame and guilt conscience. She apologizes, perhaps asks forgiveness, tells him how right he is, and makes promises she cannot keep in the future.

All of these actions strengthen the male disposition of superiority as well as a woman's own feelings of inferiority. It may chain her to the brick wall of a false formation conscience. Repeated expression inwardly or to others may grant momentary relief, but such repetition can also impress her rage deeper into her life of memory and feeling.

On the basis of my work in formation science and trans-therapy, I cannot advise without qualification repression, impression, or expression. Without denying the temporal benefits of qualified expression, my main interest lies in what I call "trans-pression." I find it most beneficial to people when their excessive feelings are neither pressed "under" focal awareness, *repression;* nor impressed —without transformation—into one's focal or prefocal consciousness, *impression.* Also, pressing them outward, *expression,* I do not consider the final solution of the problem. I believe that pressing them upward, *transpression,* to the transcendent-immanent zone of one's life is the beginning of a gradual solution. It begins to diminish an excess of inner rage and indignation. It leads one to dare to communicate firmly, effectively, reasonably, what one knows to be one's rights and demands. The more the silent majority of oppressed women overcome their own internalization of traditional male repression, the more potent and reasonable will the firm communication of their rights and demands be.

Ways of Transpression

My concept of transpression holds that a woman ought not to deny her feelings once they are disclosed to her focal consciousness. Identifying them with the courage of candor, she lifts them into the light of her transcendent faith, hope, and love. She supports that elevation by recourse to the best spiritual resources of the religious or ideological faith and formation tradition to which she is freely committed. This transcendent elucidation will slowly and gradually relativize her feelings. She will affirm their core of truth and only allow the corresponding appropriate feeling-tone to prevail. This will diminish less reasonable emotional excesses in her expression of feelings.

The formation energy released by excessive feeling is now used for the work of transformation by transpression. Energy triggered by extreme irritation and annoyance is transformed into a power for growth in the transcendent life. A tremendous loss of precious formation energy by the rehashing, churning mind is prevented; it is channeled in the direction of reasonable, effective release.

Another result of transpression is that her now-calmed mind dares to be in touch with her own vehement wishes and feelings without the fear of being overwhelmed by them. Without such transformation, many women will do too little for themselves on the pretranscendent level of life. As a result, the individual coformant of their life will remain stunted. They will be tempted to live up to the repressive expectations of others.

What happens is that they may overform their transcendent life and underform its pretranscendent level. Not tuned in to the full range of their own pretranscendent individual feelings, they cannot be emphatically in touch with similar feelings in others. They would also find it more difficult to attain the consonant transcendent-immanent quality of life that marks the fullness of the journey to transcendence.

Complementarity of Femininity and Masculinity

Considering the individuation problems of women who are committed to transcendent traditions, one might ask: Does the same not apply to males? The answer is, yes and no. It all depends on how well the man lets his sensitivity, intuition, and openness to transcendence unfold and have a bearing on his life. How much discrimination and subsequent prefocal repression of such feelings has he endured in a functionalistic society? These conditions impose on a small number of sensitive men a somewhat similar predicament with which women have to cope.

To the degree that this is the case, some of the formation dynamics highlighted in this chapter apply to men, some of whom may be artists, poets, or mystics, others creative leaders or thinkers. They may be sympathetic family men, counselors, therapists, teachers, and mentors. They are still the exception in mainly functional populations. This number may expand as a side benefit of the women's movement. Women and men may begin to realize that they are not identical. They are not totally equalized forms of human life. They are first of all human beings. They are equal in human dignity while being complementarily gifted in some prevalence of feminine or masculine form potencies. Within the relative boundaries of their basic femininity and masculinity, they are still called to be unique in regard to their own life call and life-style.

A beneficial fallout of individualistic form traditions and their reflections in the social, clinical, managerial, educational, and human disciplines has been the awakening of women to their repressed individuality. For women in transcendent traditions, this means an acute conflict in the area of harmonizing their delayed rights to individuation with their transcendent-immanent traditions. Therefore, I felt that this special chapter on women's problems of formative integration was necessary to point the way to a removal of serious obstacles for some women in the adventure of transcendent immanence and immanent transcendence. Let me now turn more specifically to the meaning and place of transcendent traditions in our life, an understanding of which is essential for the practice of transcendence therapy.

CHAPTER 7

Transcendent Traditions
and Transtherapy

Transcendent-immanent traditions presuppose that the mystery of formation calls us to a life filled with spiritual meaning. Their aim is to awaken
us to this call. In my view these traditions do not just emerge and disappear by
chance. I see them as evoked by the mystery that guides the formation history
of humanity. Classical and classics-compatible traditions remind us of our personal calling. This call lifts our profane existence up to new heights; it stays
with us even if we sometimes lose ourselves in the wake of vital passions or
functional drudgery.

Transcendent Faith and Formation Traditions
Transcendent-immanent traditions give rise to spiritual disciplines that
bring us peace and keep us present to the mystery of life. The faith tradition
that underpins our formation traditions lights the way to that mystery. Let me
say again that we should not confuse faith assumptions with the many form traditions that put them into practice. Faith traditions stand at the center of attention in the field of information theology. By contrast, form traditions are the
focus of formation science. Experts explore the articulation of this science in
their own or others' transcendent formation tradition and its completion in formation theology.

The basics of a faith tradition become sedimented in the hearts and minds of
people brought up with them. Believers carry their faith tradition into their
everyday world by means of one or the other formation tradition. Its wisdom
for living helps them to link their faith to their daily circumstances. They know
that too many trade-offs with the world will harm fidelity to their faith.

The transcendent dimension of life brings together, in the light of the forming mystery, our life call and our traditions insofar as both are disclosed to us
here and now. It integrates them with all that happens in our field of presence
and action. An authentic transcendent tradition is thus open to all dimensions
of life. The ways in which we integrate our lives vary in individuals and whole

populations. Asian and African populations, for example, did not look at life initially in an individualistic way. They showed less individualization than Western people do. They were open to wider horizons.

Transcendent *faith* traditions of a Judeo-Christian origin kept a foothold in Western Europe, North America, and Canada. Some of their *formation* traditions lost touch with the deepest wisdom of their faith traditions. Certain artistic and philosophical groups as well as contemplation-oriented religious institutions tended to keep the deeper wisdom of a tradition alive. Examples of the latter would be the Carthusians, the Camoldolese, the Benedictines, the Trappists, and the Carmelites in Catholicism; the Quakers, the Shakers, and Taizé in Protestantism; the Kabbalists and Hasidim in Judaism. All draw on the spiritual depths of their own traditions.

Today, we see a rebirth of interest in transcendent formation traditions. We find such concern not only in those called to a contemplative, religious apostolic, or clerical life. A number of lay people are in search of a transcendent-immanent style of life that gives meaning to a busy married or single life. They want to blend their spiritual longings with their home and work life and with the demands of art, science, administration, and technology without neglecting times of prayer in solitude as a source of inspiration and aspiration. This search kindles also growing interest in the holistic transcendence therapy I have developed.

The fusional-affective way of life, about which I spoke in the former chapter, seems weaker in the West. As I said, we must make an exception for descendants of immigrants from South America, Mediterranean Europe, Asia, and Africa. The fusional-vital coformant of life also shows itself more in Western women than in men.

The transformed human life neither gives up individual development nor some measure of affective fusion with people and nature. Spiritual transformation makes room for affective togetherness and individual effectiveness. Both are deepened by the call and by the mystery from which this call comes forth. A wholly transformed life would be a striking epiphany of the mystery, also in its vital-affective coformants. Transformation lifts vital fusion to a higher plane. It turns this fusion into transcendent consonance with others, with nature, and with the mystery that carries them.

I have distinguished two main types of traditions: the transcendent and the pretranscendent. These point to two opposite paths of life, though in transcendent people they come together. Their lower path takes on the wisdom of the higher. Because I look at the pretranscendent path in view of transcendent formation by the mystery, I call its guiding tradition not exclusively developmental.

Individualistic Traditions

Individualistic traditions—if not responding to their ignored formational orientation—keep as their goal pretranscendent self-actualization in and of itself. To strengthen this pretranscendent self, people look for social acceptance, conviviality, and security; vital well-being and pleasurable sensations; functional skill, power, control, and individualistic ambition. They develop mainly their lower, logical, analytical reason, sometimes using its power to explain away unpleasant facts and truths. We can turn to lower reason to devise clever plots and schemes to get power, standing, and possessions. We can abuse lower reason to reduce our orientation to formation in and with the mystery to merely its subordinated developmental aspect.

Sometimes the dawning of an awareness of the transcendence dynamic initiates the striving for what I call "functional-transcendent aims," such as meditative centering and relaxation, aesthetic and cosmic bliss. These higher aims, however, do not by themselves lift us to the path of formation in the fully transcendent life. These strivings are still too much motivated by the life directives of lower self-actualization and of lower self-esteem. Transcendent self-appreciation, self-reverence, and call appreciation have not yet fully filtered through the grid of individualistic self-esteem, elevating it to a higher plane. Self-reverence is awe for the mystery in ourselves and others, awe for our unique-communal life call by the mystery that grants us our deepest, distinctively human dignity.

Individualistic or transcendent traditions about our unique-communal call of life make us look at our formation field in different ways. Individualistic ones proceed from a basic separation between me and mine and what is not me and mine. This view gives rise to other splits, such as those between transcendence and absolutized pretranscendence, mind and body, spirit and matter, I and other, humanity and nature, earth and cosmos. The individualistic tradition also takes for granted that these splits cannot be overcome. They reduce human nature to mainly its pretranscendent potencies, ignoring its innate transcendence dynamic. As long as this happens, the splits cannot be reconciled; consonance with humanity and nature, earth and cosmos, cannot be regained. Such reconciliation can be facilitated by transtherapy, in private or in common.

Congruity and Consonance

The self-actualizing tradition holds that we should use our functional reason to work out systems of congruity instead of true consonance. In this context I use the term "congruity" to mean our practical adjustment to the outer appearances of people, events, and things, while we keep inwardly separated from them. Consonance means for me an inner loving flow with their deepest meaning as given by the same mystery that makes us be.

For example, I may make the material situation of a discriminated-against minority more congruent with material standards of my society that seem to be reasonable. This effort is worthwhile. It makes me look good; it lessens the threat of social upheaval that could put a stop to my own projects of self-actualization. At the same time, I stick inwardly to my secret feelings that the discriminated-against minority is not as good as I am. I live in ignorance of the call to formation by the mystery and of the transcendence dynamic we all share as the ground of our deepest dignity.

I need to rise in consonance above this separation. Systems of congruity outline practical and useful points of convergence between what we know, see, and use. Striving for congruity, we look mainly for working relationships between objects as we know them technically. We do not bring about an affective consonance with people, nature, and the environment. We may want only to master and control them in as nice and subtle a way as possible. We want everything to serve the self-centered self-actualizations of individuals, groups, countries, or the human race as a whole and, in the process, we still want to look good and gentle.

Such systems of practical congruence, while useful in some regard, do not help us to overcome the affective dissonance, distance, or separation between people. Neither do they heal the felt split between us and the universe, nature, and its mysterious ground. They only give us more explanatory and pragmatic concepts about the measurable aspects of their appearances in our environment. This power enables us to manipulate things more effectively, which, up to a point, can be desirable and even necessary. But if dominance of others is our main disposition, it will retard our growth toward a true, transcendent, affective binding of intimacy and consonance with people, events, and things in themselves. It would kill true ecological commitment, to say nothing of our commitment to uphold the human dignity of all people.

In transcendent traditions we seek knowledge and wisdom that help us to transform our life. We strive for affective consonance with people and with our surroundings. We want to flow with them wisely and lovingly in compatibility with our call and tradition. We look at human life as a unique and superior creation, a superb manifestation of the same mystery that creates and maintains the universe in which we live and move and have our being. We affirm "what is." We revere it as lovingly willed or allowed by this mystery. With all that is and comes to be, we walk in appreciative intimacy. We are in love with reality's all-embracing Source. We deepen this intimacy in prayer, contemplation, ritual, music, song, storytelling, poetry, painting, sculpture, or simply in silent wonder. This closeness inspires a cosmic sense that all that is, is a creation or, as some would say, an emanation of an all-forming mystery.

Time and Space in Tradition

Looking at the meaning of time, individualistic, developmental traditions posit a straightforward movement. For the future of humanity they draw not so much on past wisdom as on present sciences, technologies, and political projects. These are for them the sources of forward movement and progress in time.

Transcendent traditions, to the contrary, point also to the past. They draw on writings, symbols, myths, legends, parables, holidays, and rituals that remind us of the deeper meanings buried in the communal memory of traditions. They call for moments to remember the striking manifestations of the mystery of formation in history and evolution. These celebrations are ritual reenactments of what the mystery once did. Under most circumstances, they draw people into awed awareness of the mysterious presence always at work in and beyond cosmos, history, and humanity.

Musing on the meaning of space, self-actualizing traditions look at it as profane, homogeneous, neutral, and mathematical. Transcendent traditions do not reject this view, but they round it off and align it with transcendent-immanent wisdom. They call for an appreciation of the mystery that binds all that is in space and time. They point to the sacred aspect of space as preserved in such holy spaces as temples, churches, synagogues, sacred trees, towers, waters, burial places, and places of pilgrimage.

Artists inspired by transcendent traditions strive to awaken experiences of the "more than." They do not create beauty for its own sake or for individual enjoyment alone. They bring into the open epiphanies that are hidden in nature and humanity. By so doing they unwittingly reveal the deepest ground of their own inner life.

Traditions of lower self-actualization and mere development make artists and their works more individualistic, even if they use their imagination and intuitive reason poetically. Aesthetically, they bring out meanings that touch their vital or vital-transcendent sensitivity. As long as they live in the atmosphere of individualistic traditions alone, they are less likely to abide in the transcendent ground of their inner life. They seem less able to communicate to others transcendent meanings.

Transcendent traditions see human life not only as individual, collective, and developmental, but as unique and communal. The unique life call of each person is seen as interwoven with his or her place in community and society. The unfolding call of a person in history and society is experienced as linked— by some kind of preformation—with the communities within which a person has to make his or her call tangible in space and time. They look at the individual means of putting one's call into everyday practice as necessary but secondary; these means are used to serve one's deepest calling.

Individualistic traditions relate best to functional collectivities and developmental strategies of individuals. Transcendent traditions, however, turn these collectivities into interforming communities of unique people. Collectivities do not acknowledge a call that makes each person unique. They look at self-actualizing individuals as the basic elements of the collectivity. For them, they are wholly equal to one another. Individualistic, developmental traditions encourage people to outdo others within their groups. Differences in functional worth and developmental advantages guide this competition. Lower individualistic self-esteem, not deepened by call-appreciation, ties in with these differences.

Traditions and the Sociohistorical
and Vital Dimensions

Transcendent-immanent traditions respond in a special way to the sociohistorical and vital dimensions of life. They foster in their followers transcendent intimacy relationships within communities, the first of which is the family. From this viewpoint, the family or community, not the self-actualizing individual, is the basic unit of society.

By contrast, individualistic traditions are committed to lower self-actualization and development. Our pretranscendent needs are the focal point of their attention. They drive people to pursue security, conviviality, pretranscendent development, and social confirmation of individualistic self-esteem. They foster this way by conformity, manipulation, and competition within the collectivities in which people find themselves inserted. Within these collectivities they set up clever networks of acquaintances, colleagues, comrades, and team members. They become masters of political correctness.

Modern collectivities strike us as incredibly mobile. People are moved from one place to another. This fosters superficial collectivities instead of true communities. Ties of intimacy are apt to be temporary, unstable, and precarious. On top of this, a climate of constant competition in the marketplace and of merely developmental education breaks down trust, intimacy, and reasonable dependency needs.

To put it briefly, the basic views of what form human life should take are different in these two main types of traditions.

Effectiveness of Transcendent Traditions

We should transform our individualistic strivings by transcendent aspirations. We must complement developmental education with transcendent formation. This will make us more effective in everyday life. Transtherapy again facilitates this turn to transcendent living.

Self-actualizers diminish the full realization of their potential by the anxious intensity of their competition. Their shaky self-esteem is vulnerable. It depends too much on the approval of colleagues, peers, or superiors. Anxious concentration on achievement and avoidance of failure keeps us rigid and tense. These tensions harm our health and immune system. When we rise above coercive strivings, we gain in relaxed freedom and openness. We become less enslaved to coercive dispositions of achievement or avoidance of failure. We care less for material possessions, repute, and standing. Still, we appreciate these goods if they come as a gift.

Our view of reality becomes wider and deeper when it draws on the wisdom of transcendent traditions. Our senses, imagination, memory, anticipation, and reason open up. We spot opportunities for growth that a less transcendent person would have missed. In transtherapy sessions-in-common, this opening up in any participant leads to great joy shared by all. It hastens the transtherapeutic process in others.

Called to Wholeness of Life

I started this chapter on transcendent traditions with the assertion that they awaken us to our call by the mystery. Under favorable conditions our life call shows itself to us as coming forth from the cosmic and radical mystery of formation. The mystery calls us through this call. It inspires us to walk in its light in daily life. Over a lifetime, our deepest call becomes known to us bit by bit, but never wholly. The moments of unveiling are like spots of clarity in the night of unknowing. Every time we get in touch with the mystery, we sense our deeper calling. This mystery is first of all the hidden *radical* mystery as it is in itself. This mystery is called "God" in many traditions. It is also the mystery that manifests itself in its epiphanies. These are the veiled appearances of a mystery that slip soundlessly into our life, that show themselves in earth, universe, and their formational unfolding, in history, humanity, and in all fields of formation. This is the cosmic mystery set into motion with its laws and directives, its powers and dynamics, by the radical mystery.

Our own destiny comes across to us as a gift of transcendent love. Such awareness leaves traces of wisdom, joy, and peace in its wake. Our hidden call lights up for us as both unique and communal. It retains its distinctness from everything else. At the same time, it enables us to flow wisely with the forming movements of nature and history. Our call strikes us as incomparable with the calls of others. It grants us a unique responsibility and mission. And yet this call, as embodied, blossoms only briefly on earth. We are dropped for a fleeting moment in time among the countless other forms brought to life over the millennia before and after our arrival and departure from this world. We are a tiny crest on the wave of the formation of this earth and the life it carries. This wave in turn is only a minute ripple in the mighty ocean of formation of the universe.

At privileged moments, our own unique form of life heightens our awareness. It shows itself in its coherence with other forms in time and space. We get a sense of our consonance with the radical and cosmic mystery that is at work everywhere as it is in us.

Our pretranscendent life turns out to be an instrumental, merely developmental life. It is destined to serve and share in our transcendent mission. The call brings about its own unique embodiment in the enterprises to which we give form in our daily field of presence and action. With and through our transformed, pretranscendent life, our call draws its luminous path in our passing world. Our pretranscendent life gives tangible form to our aspirations and inspirations; it is transformed into a translation of our call. It turns itself into a concrete expression of our flowing with the mystery that calls it forth. Thanks to our vital and functional skills, we can transcribe the call into field-effective expressions of vital affection, of competent functioning, of social concern. At moments of crisis in this unfolding, transtherapy can be of great assistance.

Sub-"I's" of Our Pretranscendent Life

The call should reign over the many dimensions and articulations of our everyday life in a complex world. In the beginning these embodiments do not come together. We must bring them into consonance with one another, turning them into servants of our central inspirations. We cannot at once bring order to the dimensions and articulations of our life with its myriad acts, attitudes, and dispositions. We must take into account their numerous dispersions in the spheres, dimensions, regions, and ranges of our intricate field of presence and action.

First, we must single out the diverse facets of our life. We must look at our various sub-"I's", such as the functional, vital, sociohistorical, apparent, current, prefocal, and infrafocal "I's." Each sub-"I" strives to play the main role in life, to expand its empire. Each sub-"I" keeps trying to take control, making itself the central power in our personality. Doing so, it gets out of touch with the real centering call at the heart of our life. In their isolation sub-"I's" can turn into idols. They make our everyday life into a kind of plaything, into a competing club of idolized sub-"I's" that may tear us apart.

Any articulation of a dimension of our life can put itself forward as a new, all-dominating sub-"I." Take, for example, the vitalistic sub-"I" of the drug addict, or the functionalistic sub-"I" of the workaholic, the sociohistorical sub-"I" of the fanatic fascist or communist, or the repressed infrafocal sub-"I" of the abused child.

Some look at such an idolized sub-"I" as the true call of their life. In fact, it stands for only one of the possible limited channels of expression of our true life call if they are purged and transformed by the mystery of formation.

All these sub-"I's" bring about corresponding dispositions in the heart. They, too, should be placed under the canopy of our true call. Otherwise, our character or heart remains divided. When the division of our heart becomes extreme, we run the risk of taking on what I call a "multiformational" personality.

Becoming whole of heart is a lifelong endeavor. Often it demands the work of healing. The healed heart mirrors our unique life call. It reflects this call insofar as it shows itself in the here-and-now situation of our life and in the light of our faith and form traditions. Our healing heart turns in love and inspiration to our divisive sub-I's; it makes them compatible with its message; it gently orders their dynamics, dispositions, acts, and directives.

This wholeness, rooted in mystery, holds us together on our arduous journey. We cannot make the journey alone. We hunger for the wisdom of classic transcendent-immanent traditions. The forming mystery—through eras of graced human aspirations—inspired humanity to give form to transcendent traditions. These help us immeasurably along the way.

Pretranscendent developmental traditions show us the first steps on the path of healing the heart. In this preliminary phase of a hitherto-broken heart, pretranscendent traditions offer much help. However, they should not hold us back in the false faith that pretranscendent integration or individuation puts us at the end stage of our journey. In that case, a pretranscendent tradition would retard our search rather than lead us forward on the road to final peace and consonance. We need, above all, the completion of our integration in the light of transcendent traditions.

This chapter gave us a deeper insight into formative transcendent traditions by comparing them with developmental pretranscendent traditions. One of the main theses in this chapter was that transcendent traditions awaken us to our call to wholeness. I showed how we fall away repeatedly from our inner and outer at-oneness. We create dissonances between our many sub-"I's" if we do not turn them into servants of our central aspirations. We need to grow into a transcendent identity of heart that reflects increasingly the secret identity of our life call. This growth meets with many pretranscendent and transcendent identity crises. In the following chapter I shall address these crises and their solution whether or not transtherapy enters the picture.

CHAPTER 8

Transcendent Identity Crisis and Transtherapy

Populations are marked by their traditions. So, too, are the social scientists who study them. They mirror in their theories the traditions they observe in the people with whom they live and work. Consider Erik Erikson's concepts of self- and ego-identity. In his analysis of these ideas, he cannot help but be influenced by popular traditions shared in contemporary Western circles. These traditions manifest a strong belief in autarkic self-actualization.

Otto Rank's stress on the self-creation of the personality through will and individuation offers further proof that he, too, like Erikson, comes under the influence of a longstanding tradition of individual self-actualization as ultimate.

Pretranscendent and Transcendent Identity Crises

I do not wish to deny the contributions of these and similar theories of personality. I believe their main contribution is to increase our understanding of pretranscendent identity conflicts and crises. Large segments of the population are formed in and by such developmental traditions. The analyses offered by scientists like Erikson and Rank do not cover the whole story of human formation. They do not explain how crisis experiences of childhood, youth, and young adulthood can affect for better or worse our transcendent journey. Such experiences need to be considered also in the light of the transcendent-immanent dimension of life and of the special crises generated by our transcendence dynamic.

We cannot deny the existence of conflicts and crises of transcendence. They come into being with the maturing of our transcendent dimension. They bear on the transformation of our pretranscendent life. These experiences cannot be equated with those that go with crises of self-creation of an individualistic personality. The solution of crises of transcendence can complement, correct, and deepen the solution of conflicts associated with a healthy, pretranscendent, individual life. We are bound to face crises of interformation with our family and others with whom we share the same tradition. This brings us to the challenge of how to grow in fidelity to our own unique-communal call of life without giving up cordial relations with our communities. Such crises go with the territory of transcendence; but, I repeat, they are not the same as crises of individual self-development.

Compatible Pretranscendent Crises and Experiences

Does this mean that pretranscendent identity crises have no meaning at all for those who strive to live by a transcendent form tradition? The answer is clearly that they do have meaning. As my concept of the form-traditional pyramid makes clear, people in pluriform societies live not only by their own basic tradition. The latter certainly gives form to the deepest dispositions of their core form, heart, or character. But the heart is surrounded, as it were, by an outer layer. It draws on traditions borrowed from and combined with one's basic tradition. Such borrowing gives rise to conflicts between the foundational and the added traditional dispositions. The intake of elements from other traditions carries the seeds of confusion. Many of these elements come from individualistic trends in the Western world. A crisis sets in as one tries to grow in compatibility with the reasonable directives guiding life in our society without diminishing congeniality with his or her transcendent tradition. We must look carefully at popular styles of personal and social life. In what way are they at odds with or compatible with our basic convictions?

The chances of a major crisis developing lessen as we grow in the wisdom of selective compatibility without compromising our essential beliefs. This growth becomes complicated if popular pretranscendent traditions belittle everything transcendent. We feel a tension between our transcendent dispositions and our striving for reasonable, wise adaptation to the individualistic traditions prevalent in society. A denigration of our own transcendent tradition by others makes it even more difficult for us to come to cordial accommodation.

What must we do to withstand the mockery of our convictions by successful superiors, colleagues, friends, and neighbors, by the media, by admired authors, artists, thinkers, scholars, and scientists—a number of whom belong to our own faith tradition? Do they live their formation tradition only on the pretranscendent level of functional dos and don'ts? Admiring them uncritically may only serve to deepen our own conflict.

Resolution of Transcendent Identity Conflicts

I have seen the following three attempts to try to resolve this conflict:

1. We can choose to give up our own tradition and to go along totally with traditions of absolute self-actualization and development. The latter tradition moves from its secondary position in our life to the base of our pyramid. Soon we are inclined to think less and less of the style of life that flowed from our

former basic faith and formation tradition. To uproot the residues of earlier dispositions of our core form is almost impossible. We may block reminders of what was. The more disturbing the blocked dispositions become, the more intense may be our devaluation of our former basic tradition. We put down what we used to believe. Otherwise, the traditional dispositions we have rejected start to gnaw at us and create an undeniable conflict.

2. An opposite attempt to solve the conflict entails rejecting anything individualistic traditions have to offer us. We begin to idealize uncritically any and all elements of our basic formation tradition. We do not admit the imperfect ways in which a tradition manifests itself in the concrete life of its often-failing followers. We keep our eyes only on the best our belief system has to offer. We tell ourselves that we do not need the skills and knowledge given to us by the arts, by positive sciences, or by developmental education. We focus only on the theoretical assumptions of artists, scientists, technicians, or developmental educators that are at odds with our tradition. This kind of blind criticism makes us overlook their helpful insights and findings. Their empirical conclusions can shed light on how we can carry out effectively our transcendent ideals in everyday life. We should not shun the natural revelation of pretranscendent theories and data. Such a rejection of scientific knowledge is extreme and unreasonable. It stagnates our transcendent life. Transcendence is meant to be dynamic. It means growth in the life of the spirit. Our spirit is openness to anything consonant with the mystery's gifts of reason and reality. The moment we close our spirit arbitrarily to pretranscendent directives, we blunt its life. We no longer let our spirit be what it is: a universal, multidimensional openness to all that is.

3. There is a third way to lessen the tension between conflicting traditions. It begins when we take another look at our own transcendent tradition. What in it is only accidental or accretional? Turning to its sources, we see elements and practices that are not essential. We look at the life situation we share with others. We ask ourselves what light other traditions and disciplines shed on them. How far can we go along with them without dropping the foundations of our own tradition? Compatible insights thus gained can make our work of reappraisal easier. It helps us to spot what we believed falsely to be basic. We withstand the put-down of our own tradition without saying no to the good contribution of others. In this way, we do justice to innovations suggested by any source of knowledge, wisdom, experiment, experience, and developmental education without doing injustice to our own tradition.

Transcendence Therapists and Identity Crises

Many people cannot appraise their form-traditional problems by themselves alone. To help them, each tradition needs scholars, teachers, directors, mentors, transcendence therapists, or formation counselors. They should be well versed in problems that stem from crises in the traditional coformant of our identity.

In transtherapy, practitioners often face people caught between their upbringing as children in their original tradition and their later exposure to other traditions. They may have tried to brush aside their original tradition. They rebelled against their parents, who stood for it. Social status, success, and financial resources may have come between them and their former adherence. For a long time they seem at ease in their new life-style and position. Then, symptoms of inhibitions in their work and relationships, often accompanied by physical problems, anxieties, and tensions, begin to show up. Transtherapists and formation counselors can help people to see that various layers of tradition-based dispositions in their life can be at odds with each other. Dissonance may have broken up the traditional coformant of their core of life. This split has brought about their current symptoms. In despondency, they seek individual or group transcendence therapy or formation counseling. They vaguely sense that they have to heal in themselves the clash of warring traditional dispositions.

Interiorized Conflict between Transcendent and Pretranscendent Traditions

A crucial feature of this crisis is the opposition between the central views of a transcendent and those of only a pretranscendent, self-actualizing form tradition. Transcendent-immanent traditions instill the faith that everyday life is meant to be in tune with the transcendent direction of a loving mystery. Depending on the faith tradition that underpins a particular form tradition, one may see this mystery as either a personal God or a divine cosmic energy. The pretranscendent traditions of self-actualizers do not foster faith in a personal life call. People feel that it is up to them to make things happen. They look at events in their life as discrete happenings or mere coincidences.

Many therapists, counselors, and developmental educators are trained on the basis of pretranscendent traditions alone. They do not know how to respond to transcendent symbols that turn up in the minds of people who come from transcendent traditions. They look at them as disturbing, repressive fantasies or as signs of some kind of resistance to the real therapeutic enterprise of self-actualization and development.

Transcendence therapists accept the traditional feelings and dispositions of those who come to them for healing. They help counselees to dialogue with these emotions in a respectful, yet critical, fashion. They wait respectfully for the moment when a person is ready to reflect on them. Gradually, transtherapy draws disturbed people toward the insight that one cannot sweep one's past and present dispositions under the rug. They have become too much a part of one's core form of life.

Counselees begin to see that they have to opt for a basic form tradition. In the course of their therapy, it may dawn on them that they have to find the connection between their basic dispositions and the elements they took over from other traditions. They can do so only insofar as these elements are compatible. Moreover, this integration has to be congenial with the basic tradition to which persons are committed and with their unique-communal life call as illumined by that tradition. It also has to be compatible with their life situation.

In the course of transtherapy, people in trouble learn to take into account how their original tradition has already structured affectively the base dispositions of the core form of their life. The dispositions evoked by this tradition may have been internalized. This assimilation of form directives is due to an affective relationship with a family and with other authoritative representatives of one's faith and form tradition. If absent, it can be found by communicating with the faith and form traditions that one hopes to opt for or that one has already opted for as basic in one's life.

Authoritarianism and Formative Authority

Some form traditions emphasize proper deference and submission to authority. Excessive submission may lead, however, to a curbing of any direct talking out and working through of anger, hostility, frustration, or differences of opinion. Even in adolescence there may have been little effort to acknowledge and assert the beginning awareness of one's unique-communal life call.

A number of followers of authoritarian traditions have learned to idolize authority figures inside as well as outside the family. Such idolizing tendencies may be used as shields against their own angry feelings toward authority in any form. Often the angriest people feel an intense need for confirmation by the idolized authorities they meet in family or in later life. They hunger for authoritarian confirmation of their own heightened need for self-affirmation. An excessive need for confirmation by others could be the result either of early over-confirmation by doting parents or a lack of affective attention by parents who are self-preoccupied. Hidden doubts about the meaningfulness and worth of one's unique-communal life call within one's tradition easily arise as a result.

Insofar as traditions are truly transcendent, they are not authoritarian in the pretranscendent sense. Rather, they point to the mystery of formation as the deepest origin, author, or authority of one's life. Legitimate human authorities are called to be messengers of the mystery of formation. They represent the ultimate author of our transcendent traditions. Authorities are called to be humble coauthors with the mystery within us and without. They should not be idolized as if they were in and by themselves the ultimate authors of our unique-communal existence.

Transcendent Identity and Form-Traditional Accretions

A transcendent-immanent faith tradition should be embodied in our pretranscendent life. Faith is a power of transformation. The striving for compatible embodiment gives rise to numerous formation traditions within each faith tradition. Much can and often does go wrong in the transmission of form traditions. Usually, the family, other groups, and individuals unwittingly alter in some fashion the traditions they hand over. The resulting accretions can deviate from the original traditions. The main reason why this happens is a lack of purification of pretranscendent fears and desires. These are linked with coercive dispositions that spring from pretranscendent strivings.

I want to mention here, and in more detail later, that an important part of our vital makeup is what I conceived and defined as our organized neuroform. The neuroform oversees, so to speak, our autonomous nervous system. This system turns dispositions into automatic patterns of reaction. The moment these robot-like dispositions are triggered, they take off by virtue of an automatic chain of acts. Our coercive dispositions take on the conditioning given to them by our autonomous nervous system. Whole families as well as large groups of unrelated people, even if they adhere to transcendent form traditions, are subject to such conditioning. Fanatic dispositions, for example, can break the link with the belief system that undergirds any formation tradition. Coercions of this sort push people into conflicts. They foster wars between Christian denominations, among different groups of the same denomination, and among members of different religions. Here we glimpse something of the awesome power, for good or ill, of formation traditions and their accretions.

Traditional Coformants of Our Core Identity

Conflicts and crises between traditions in a pluri-traditional society are traceable to identity conflicts in our core form of life. Let me now summarize the traditional elements at work in this core form.

1. Ideally, the core form of our life should stay in tune with our life call. This call holds the secret of our ultimate identity. To fulfill this call, we draw on elements of traditions that appear in our formation field. For example, in America, people draw, among others, on elements of a capitalistic, democratic tradition.

2. To keep in tune with the call that identifies us uniquely, we should remain open to both our higher (transcendent) and our lower (pretranscendent) levels of life. Both carry elements of various traditions. To link these wisely

together gives unity and strength to our core identity. An Irish immigrant, for example, can retain consonance in the core of her personality by binding together her Irish faith customs and the compatible elements she finds in her American style of life.

3. Both higher and lower dispositions give direction to our search for identity. They make us draw on traditions that are at work in our past and present formation fields. A Buddhist from Thailand living in London will thus be directed by Buddhist, Thai, and English traditional directives.

4. These traditions pick up "side directives" that are typical of the families, groups, and individuals that make us aware of general traditional directives. How the Thai-Buddhist picks up the English tradition depends in part on the family or group that shows him or her the English tradition in its own particular way.

5. Transcendent form traditions also carry directives for the transformation of our pretranscendent by our transcendent life. Such transformation takes into account, it does not denigrate, our pretranscendent existence. We need pretranscendent skills and developmental education to make transcendent directives work in our everyday field of life. For example, Teresa of Avila transformed the use of her pretranscendent skills in the light of her mystical experiences. As a result, her functional organizational qualities were used to the full. She could fulfill her call to organize the Carmelite reform by founding and administering new convents.

6. In some instances we neglect to attune our life as a whole to our deeper aspirations. We allow only pretranscendent traditions and developmental education to guide us along the way.

7. Our core form or heart sets up an order by rank of dispositions from more to less basic. This ordering ties in with the place accorded to traditions in our pyramid. Followers of Islam, for instance, may put the Islamic tradition first, their family tradition second, their business tradition third, their sport tradition fourth, and so on.

8. The example of the basic Islamic traditions applies, of course, in their own way, to the basic traditions of all other religions and ideologies. In all of them, the foundational core or character dispositions of our heart make it possible for us to give form in daily life to the baseline of our pyramid. These dispositions also enable us to select the elements of other traditions that are compatible with our own. While superseding the base of our tradition pyramid, selections thus made are still in tune with it. In this way we can both serve and expand our emergent identity without causing conflicts and splits in our lives.

9. Identity conflicts arise if and when our core form or heart does not stay in tune with the different elements in our tradition pyramid. An Islamic entre-

preneur, for instance, may split his life in two: fidelity to his Islamic prayer life and commitment to the American way of doing business.

10. The failure to integrate our core form, including its continuous, lasting dispositions, with our basic tradition results in a fragmented character. A divided heart tears us apart. We fall into self-doubt because we cannot take into account in a balanced way the direction of our calling. A weak, uncertain core succumbs to an anxious, at times desperate, search for a unifying, energizing life orientation. For example, a Hasidic youth may agonize over how to bring together his formation tradition with his desire to become an actor in the style of the American theater tradition. He wonders if both styles of life belong to his unique life call or if they are diametrically opposed. He finds himself in a serious identity crisis.

Questions for Reflection on Our Identity Crises

I touched on the main elements that forecast an identity crisis. This overview now makes it possible for me to outline some questions that may lead us to disclose and begin to resolve a variety of tradition-based identity conflicts. Such healing strikes me as one of the conditions for the formation of a poised and assertive, yet relaxed style of life. If we trust the general direction of our life call and if we remain open to its disclosures, we may want to inquire about the following either on our own or in transtherapy:

1. Am I aware of any signs of fragmentation in my core form? Do I link to this fragmentation the feeling of having lost consonance? Do I keep track of my experiences of diminishment of formation energy and loss of faith in my life direction? Am I able to sense a waning of my love and hope for life. Do I notice an increase in feelings of insecurity, fear, and despondency?

2. Once I come to the insight that the fragmentation of my core form may be linked with these losses, I can take the next step. I pay attention to how I am moved by elements of various form traditions. Did I take in too many elements of other traditions without putting them in touch with my basic tradition?

3. Does my life reveal some basic direction? How does this direction guide my daily interactions? Does it strike me as pointing to the hidden call of my life? If this direction does not strike me as congenial with my call, what feels uncongenial? Do these feelings give rise to dissonances in my tradition pyramid?

4. Do I challenge myself enough to keep aware of the character dispositions by which I live? How do some dispositions set up the dissonances I begin to discover in my core? Do some of my formation dispositions and their directives lead to war with one another or do they stay compatible? Is my heart or character divided or united by them? Am I still unsure of my identity?

5. Can I catch some likeness between the dissonant elements of traditions I imbibe and the dispositions to which my heart gives form? Do I carry in my heart or its corresponding character a split between my basic traditional dispositions and those called forth by elements of other traditions?
6. Did I attempt to evolve and commit myself to some order of preference or rank between the dispositions of my character? Did I take time to foster a similar order between the elements of the traditions to which I adhere? Do my preferences strike me as congenial with who I am called to be? Can I show how my dispositions and their supporting traditional elements are compatible with my real life situation? Do they push or pull me in the direction of my life call and its basic underlying traditions?
7. Do I see more clearly how the form-traditional elements in my life have been imposed on me by family, friends, groups, neighbors, teachers, and the media? Am I aware of how they may have turned these traditions around by their own life direction, their mannerisms, quirks, and affectations, their own security directives, ambitions, ethnic, economic, and political affiliations? How did they in turn—within their own formation history—take on some of the peculiarities imposed on them by their own families and by the people around them?
8. Did their twisting of the form traditions, which I made my own, stir up dissonances in my life? How can I shake these obstacles off? How can I prevent them from interfering with my life call? Do they disorient my balanced appraisal of the elements I took over from different form traditions?
9. What changes do I myself bring to the traditions I cherish? Do they touch me as in tune or out of tune with my basic faith and form tradition, with my life call and life situation?
10. Does my transcendent life and its underlying or basic tradition give direction wisely to the pretranscendent traditions by which I also live? How is that direction touched by people who handed such traditions over to me? For example, a pretranscendent authoritarian tradition may wield its power over me as if it were an expression of transcendent, even divine, authority or authorship. In that case both pretranscendent and transcendent formation traditions may have corrupted the true meaning of authority.

Transcendent identity crises make us aware of the differences between transcendent and pretranscendent individualistic traditions with their mere developmental practices. Because of their effect on our life formation, I want to look specifically at some of these general differences in the following chapter.

CHAPTER 9

Transtherapy and Various Kinds of "We" Relationships

I depict in my formation science and my formative spirituality the ideal human community as one of mutually complementary "we" relationships. In such relationships the boundaries between the lower "I's" of the transcendent partners mellow. They allow for reverence and respect for each person's pretranscendent embodiments of any aspect of his or her calling in and by the mystery.

By contrast, I discovered and analyzed the dominance of the individualistic "I's" in many pretranscendent traditions. They encourage their followers to cling to the pretranscendent fences of rank, expertise, power, status, education, possession, and so on. I observed in my research that they label others as important insofar as they are proudly caught in the same confines. This individualistic ranking may supersede our appreciation for the transcendent nobility of each person's life.

Appreciation of each person's hidden dignity should be nourished continuously. My transtherapy helps counselees to experience that the transcendent dignity of each human person goes far beyond all secondary individualistic qualities. It fosters mutual love and cooperation for the good of all. By contrast, individualism lessens our availability for the intimacy we experience in transtherapeutic group sessions; it may interrupt the give-and-take necessary for mutual confirmation. People may adhere defensively to certain boundaries between their lower "I"'s, even when they meet each other in pleasant, albeit superficial, social situations.

The individualistic tradition retains what it calls the ego boundaries (or what I would call the lower "I" boundaries) between, for instance, counselees and counselors. It regards the ego as the ruler of behavior in the light of a pretranscendent superego. In transtherapy, however, we begin to experience that our higher "I" is rooted in our founding life form, that it exercises a central influence within our mature core or character form. This higher "I" does not attract much attention in individualistic theories of personality. Therefore, people often turn to transtherapeutic treatment after they have become relatively well on the pretranscendent level because of pretranscendent therapies of self-analysis, self-actualization, and educational development.

Transtherapy and the Differences between Boundaries of Transcendent and Individual "I's"

In transtherapy we begin to experience that our two "I's" show two opposite kinds of boundaries. The higher "I" turns for wisdom to its transcendent formation conscience. I explain in transtherapy that my concept of the transcendent-immanent conscience differs essentially from that of the superego. Our higher conscience reminds us of unfaithfulness to our unique-communal call of life. The call is not easily caught, nor can it be taught, by ourselves or others. Yet from it comes forth the personal nature of each one's transcendent-immanent life as enlightened by the mystery speaking inwardly in consonance with classical, time-tested faith and formation traditions.

The vulnerable uniqueness of our higher "I" makes us feel the need for its safekeeping and privacy. Our transcendent dimension of life responds to this need by drawing the boundaries of our higher "I" more or less distinctly. This enables it to retain its innermost secret. It communicates its mystery only indirectly, if at all. For this reason, I warn against careless crossing of such boundaries. I advise there against lightly communicating to others our inmost spiritual experiences.

People living a transcendent-immanent life keep the boundaries of their pretranscendent life more open than the innermost boundaries of their higher "I." Their lower individual boundaries more easily mellow in family and group relationships. They do not have to cling to them as the main or only protection of their deeper life. They do not have to safeguard them as cautiously as people do for whom the individualistic "I" is not only first in their hierarchy of values but also the only "I" of which they may be aware.

The inmost unique "I," its tentative unfolding, its transcendence crises, failures, affects, thoughts, and ambivalences, are kept private by transcendent persons. In more intimate relationships, they may give away something of who they most deeply are, but often only indirectly, by subtle innuendo. This caution safeguards their privacy from meddling outsiders, who show no understanding.

I tell my transtherapists and counselors to draw on their empathic intuition, creative imagination, memory, anticipation, and experience. Then they will be sensitive to the veiled messages of these counselees, messages that touch on the mystery of their inmost life. Once they feel really understood by such therapists, they may let something of their deeper life shine through.

Transtherapy and the Living Out of Fusional Traditions

A transcendent tradition may be lived by counselees who happen to be fusional in temperament. As I have shown in my anthropology, a fusional tradition disposes people to merge their pretranscendent life with that of others around them. Whether or not they maintain a fusional disposition may depend on other traditions in their internalized pyramid of traditions as well as on their temperament or temper form. If the form tradition they live by is fusional too, its boundaries in their individual life are diffuse and permeable. To outsiders, the fusional person may seem almost lost in family and community, in business and leisure. He or she strikes us as an open book everyone can read. The same does not apply to those people living on the transcendent level, who also may happen to be fusional. Outsiders and even transtherapists initially may not always be aware that such persons show fusion of this sort only on the lower level of their life. Beyond that, their transcendent tradition has formed them in a deep inner life protected by a transcendent privacy disposition. They live in the light of a deeper inspirational life with well-defined inner boundaries.

Because of their at-homeness in a deeper "I," persons at home in the transcendent feel less defensive about the boundaries of their lower individual "I." They can share it with others without losing themselves. In this way, transcendent traditions help fusional-transcendent people to keep their often-surprising calm. I observed in my research of fusional-transcendent people, as distinct from other fusional persons, a deeper peace and poise in the midst of their lively participation in groups of family members and peers as well as with school, company, church, and business associates.

Transcendent persons who happen to be also fusional by temper or background look for warmly nurturing "we" relationships. Their open, diffusive individuality is by no means the mirror of their far more reserved inner life. They often feel displeased by curious explorations, interpretations, and questions that touch on their deepest experiences. They may experience such inquiries as intrusive or insulting. Indiscrete remarks about their most private life interrupt even their usual "we" relationships on the pretranscendent level. Such probing may make them withdraw momentarily, at least inwardly.

Transtherapy and Followers of Transcendent Traditions

Some people who come for transcendence therapy adhere to communities with transcendent traditions. Still, they themselves may be out of touch with their own transcendent uniqueness. They may vaguely follow the general directives of their tradition, but only in a pretranscendent way.

I discovered also that a block to the personal living of our traditions is too much fusion with others. I saw that some of my fusional subjects paid so much attention to others that they forgot to attend to their own needs and feelings.

They were so taken up in fusional compatibility that they were no longer in touch with how they themselves really felt.

Transtherapy aims to put us in touch with ourselves at this deeper level. We must give up excessive attachment to a fusional "we." Otherwise, neither our transcendent nor our pretranscendent life allows us to maintain sufficient distance from others. It then becomes difficult to stay in touch with the subtle disclosures of our life call.

Transtherapy and Followers of Authoritarian Traditions

Faith traditions enter our everyday life through the door of our form traditions. They give practical meanings and directives to our faith. Such form directives may be more or less balanced. For one thing, awe-struck adulation of authoritarian figures by fanatic followers of a cult may lead to a haughty authoritarianism intolerant of any expression of differences of opinion. Victims of such intolerance may grow fearful themselves when they feel angry with authoritarian leaders, parents, teachers, or other superiors. They do not dare to admit to themselves or their transtherapists how upset they are. Because of their distorted form tradition, they suppress their awareness of any feeling of anger as if that awareness in and by itself alone would already be sinful. Either that or they vent it on people less powerful than they are, for example, on foreigners or minorities. Some turn their anger against themselves. Often, it comes out in bodily symptoms like despondency or nonclinical depression, or in a proneness to accidents and failure.

Many followers of authoritarian form traditions tell their transtherapists that they fear that they will suffer condemnation or punishment if they show fury toward parents or persons above them. This expectation carries over to people who are their peers or to those under them or even to their transtherapists. They expect rebukes from anyone to whom they show the slightest sign of irritation.

During a recent interview in Europe with Dutch supervisors of groups of laborers from Germany and the Netherlands, it struck me that incidental forgetfulness on the part of supervisors to greet them cordially brought anxiety to many German employees. Coming as they did from more authoritarian traditions, they feared that they might have angered the supervisor in some way. The Dutch, who live by less authoritarian modes, either did not notice the apparent rebuke or remarked, "That's the supervisor's problem, not ours."

I distinguish in my formation science between authoritarian form traditions and authoritative faith traditions. Authoritarian form traditions make people fear that the authorities will turn against them. This fear gives rise to the deformative disposition of coercive pleasing. Transtherapists must help them to disclose and to overcome this tendency. This coercion makes them believe that they will displease any person whom they perceive as in some way more important than they are. As long as they have not sufficiently recovered from this tendency, transtherapy cannot be effective.

Transtherapy, Socio- and General Interphobia

Our counselees may be circumspect or overcautious with superiors, be they parents, teachers, chairpersons, administrators, physicians, supervisors, or transtherapists and counselors. In their company, they become overly accommodating, pleasing, apologetic, and self-blaming. They do not dare to bring up in a credible, circumspect way reasonable demands, questions, complaints, and critiques.

In social situations these counselees may adopt an apparent life form of shyness and withdrawal. When I observed this phenomenon in group transtherapy sessions, I defined it as *socio-interphobia*. I mean by this an abnormal fear of meeting with social groups. The underlying fear is that a group or some of its members will in some way act superior or authoritarian toward me. The sociophobic person thinks, "They may be offended by me. I may unwittingly blow my cover. They may see through me, condemn me, or think less of me. They may get me."

Socio-interphobia is related to, but different from, what I call *general interphobia*. The latter fear touches not only on meetings with social groups but on all relationships, even those that are meant to be intimate with one or a few other persons. I observed this sometimes in private transtherapy. There it interfered with the free and candid communication between transtherapist and counselee.

Many anxious people take on a style of more or less withdrawn politeness or make-believe charm in meeting with others. This, too, can seriously hinder the transtherapeutic candor of exchange. What seems difficult, if not impossible, for them is to come to true interformation through spontaneous exchanges of thoughts and feelings. True maturity enables one to be businesslike and reserved, functional and distant, affective and close to others at the right time and place. I observed that the persons to whom I could apply my new concept of general interphobia usually feel coerced by their disposition to assume a distant stance all the time with all people. They do so even if another or the transtherapy situation itself does not call for it. This phobia may be so strong that they cannot surpass it, even if they feel bad about the outcome of their own coercive disposition and would like to change it.

I realized and described frequently how authoritarian form traditions call forth in susceptible people a real fear of ever showing anger toward authority. Even the slightest wave of anger fills such persons with dread. This anxiety carries over in the formation conscience of one's pretranscendent life. This lower, fear-filled conscience picks up—like radar does an enemy signal—any anxious feelings other people in authority happen to show. Of course, authoritarian formation traditions should never be confused with reasonable authoritative traditions, notably faith traditions.

The Difference between Transtherapy
and Functionalistic and Transcendent Traditions

I found in my research that functionalistic traditions may give rise to what I defined and described in Europe as "functionalistic consciences" in our counselees. Often, they seem driven by ideals of achievement and success, poise and control, skill, acquisitiveness, competence, and performance. My concept of the "managing me" as manifested in these counselees sets up its own idealized self-images of successful functioning. This creates tensions between their achievement-driven conscience and their actual performance. As anxious overachievers they are caught in the trap of comparing themselves constantly to other competing functionaries. Transtherapy has to assist them in making this lower type of conscience subservient to their transcendent life call. When this happens, it calms their fears and enables them to continue their spiritual journey less dependent on popular standards of apparent success.

Some followers of functionalistic form traditions may not make any effort to reform their excessive functionalistic norms of successful life. They tend to feel uncertain about the worthwhileness of their functional performance. They are tyrannized by the need for perfection. They seek constant assurance that they are doing well. They may conspire to get others to confirm them by praising any functional achievement of theirs, no matter how nondescript it may be. A character like "Ted Baxter" on the *Mary Tyler Moore Show* could be seen as a striking example of this need-for-assurance compulsion.

While many communities are at least publicly committed to transcendent traditions, their followers may actually fall in line with the functionalistic trends they are exposed to in their pluritraditional formation fields. They cannot give up their obsessive hunger for praise, status, and fame, but they do not dare to show it. The transcendent form tradition in question makes them feel as if they ought to maintain in public a stance of modesty and humility. In front of others, they may try to suppress their push for confirmation, but it consumes them all the more. I once knew the manager of a large organization who tried to remember all the names and actions of those whom she had to confirm for fear that anyone overlooked by accident would hold it bitterly against her.

Final Caution

Please remember that all I have been saying refers in my formative spirituality to form traditions, not faith traditions. For a faith tradition to uphold true authority, it does not need to be *authoritarian,* only *authoritative.* A form tradition is different. As I have shown, its task is to help us carry out the foundationals of our belief system by means of practical "how-to's" developed and handed over by groups and individuals. In the process, they often have to adapt certain aspects of their formation style to changing situations. They may interject into the foundations of a form tradition elements of other traditions toward which they feel a personal or group affinity. This can give rise to a contamination of their transcendent traditions by fusional, authoritarian, and functional form traditions. The original matrix of such a form tradition is transcendent faith; its deformation draws on contaminated pretranscendent formation traditions.

To grow in transcendence, we must be able to detect and reform the wrong accretions to which any form tradition is amenable. We must ask: Are these at odds with our unique transcendent life call? Are they out of tune with the foundationals of the faith and form traditions to which we are committed? Do we perhaps need private or group transcendence therapy or transtherapeutically inspired formation counseling?

Transtherapists in Relation
to Adherents of Other Traditions

More aware now of some of the differences between our own and other traditions, I asked myself further in my transtherapy theory: how can I teach my transtherapists to approach the adherents of other traditions with more understanding, especially when they come to them for my transtherapy? I offer them in my theory the following points for consideration:

1. Become familiar with the expectations and anticipations that people of other traditions as well as with what we ourselves bring to our togetherness with one another.
2. Take note of the misunderstandings that come up in meetings between people of different traditions.
3. Take into account the concept in my formation science of the "tradition-modulation coformant." I mean by this any influence of other cultures and traditions that modulates our own tradition by coforming it. How does such a coformant change or modulate somewhat the form of a tradition? For example, American Jews who adhere to the Jewish faith tradition allow their American situation to modulate the European way in which their Jewish ancestors in Europe for generations gave form to their faith.
4. How does the way in which a family, group, or individual hands over traditions to its children modulate their meaning? Are such changes in tune with our own or their original basic faith and formation traditions?

5. How do changes in fields of life affect the traditional dispositions and sub-. sequent attitudes we ourselves and others hold?
6. How do these already-changed dispositions and/or attitudes change even more through meetings among people who represent pluriform traditions? For example, how do changes in policies against racial discrimination in one Christian church affect such policies in others?

Such questions sensitize us as transtherapists to the formational meaning of changes in the sociohistorical dimension of the traditions of our counselees. Important for effective transtherapy is a refined perception of the deeper coformant of the unique-communal life call of our counselees. Its dormant power awakens and makes itself felt in a life-call crisis. This crisis brings about a disclosure of their own form potencies and needs. We can help them to appraise the opportunities a crisis may open up for them. They may see possibilities to give new form to their call in their changing situations.

For instance, adolescent counselees may discover that a basic aspect of their unique life call is musical creativity. To give concrete form to this aspect, they must take into account their sociohistorical situation. Their opportunities will be different if they live, for instance, in Kampala, Uganda, or Paris, France. Wherever they live, it is crucial that they live their call in the light of their transcendence dynamic. Otherwise, a life-call crisis may again occur.

For example, a tradition of respectful docility for admired teachers may have been paramount in the sociohistorical setting of a zealous student. Suddenly this history changes. The student, who happens to be especially creative, finds herself in conflict with the teacher she venerates. This conflict points to a deeper underlying crisis. The dynamics of the transcendent call to originality compel her to pursue her autonomy. She fears being absorbed in the destiny of her teacher. Becoming a teacher may not be the way the mystery meant for her.

To superficial observers the conflict seems unreasonable, but not to those who understand the dormant dynamics of her call. This sensitivity enables transtherapists and counselors to help the student approach a solution to the conflict she feels that she herself may not yet fully understand. Finding the answer to her dilemma is crucial. I introduced in formative spirituality my maxim that the way to transcendence gets blocked when we are unfaithful to the intimations of our call. The same is true when we refuse to look for a solution, even when it becomes clear to us that we should try to do so.

Transtherapy and the Life-Call Crisis

Subjective feelings of our counselees as related to their personal life-call crises do not explain in full the objective facets of their conflict, especially if it is not shared with others. The call, together with its crises and conflicts, not only reveals something of the uniqueness of these counselees; it also can disclose to us the demands of the community on them. Their call is interwoven with the calls of others. They share their field of presence and action. They are touched by similar opportunities and limitations.

A violinist in a chamber-music ensemble is called to make musical performance an important part of her life. The unfolding of this facet of her call fuses with the performance of others. The other participants give form to their music in interformation with her performance. Their cooperation allows the unique talent of each performer to shine; it also lights up their ability to stay in tune with the entire orchestra and its conductor in respectful harmony. A domineering conductor can kill off uniqueness in the artists under him. Each one of them may feel a life-call crisis emerging. Conflict follows. They protest. The dictatorial conductor plays a role in these individual feelings of crisis, too. Dormant emotional complexes, related to one's personal history of call crises, are awakened by his imposition. The behavior of the conductor obviously affects the esprit de corps of the offended artists and may arouse the sympathy of the public with their condition,

An alert transtherapist takes such objective coformants into account to understand what is happening. In the midst of these dynamics of conflict, he or she realizes that the logic of subjective feelings of crisis is operative. This logic differs from yet should complement wisely the detached logic of pure reason. Every irrational change in the history of a tradition, individual or communal, has to be examined by the transtherapist case by case. Our counselee must take into account, yet also go beyond, individual feelings and personal emotional complications. The transtherapist must turn the counselee also to the objective constellation of the field, to the facts at hand, and to the actual formation history of the protagonists concerned.

One source of these objective factors can be found in my observation that form traditions have generated their own representative institutions. In regard to one or the other counselee, these institutions may have their own life and power, their own observable form directives. Therefore, transtherapists cannot presuppose that each traditional deformation in their counselees can be fully appraised by resorting only to their frustrated personal feelings. Needless to say, their affections play a significant role in their complex form-traditional character unfolding. We must not overlook these as a possible explanation when behavior has become patently unreasonable, when conflicts are unsolvable, and when the formation process stays stagnant. However, we must also pay attention to the impact of the objective, external factors embedded in form-traditional institutions that impact on their life.

Transtherapy and the Sociohistorical Interformation
of Culture and Traditions

I trust it is clear from my examples that there is an interforming relationship between the sociohistorical dimension of a culture and that of its traditions. I developed my concept of this dimension of culture in my formation science. In my thinking, this dimension mirrors among other things the fundamental affective dispositions, directives, and attitudes of a period of history. The question for my unfolding formation science was: In what mode and measure is the sociohistorical dimension of a culture reflected in its form traditions? And how do these culture-reflecting traditions affect in turn one's counselees? I developed this thought of mine in 1944 in Holland by careful observation of and reflection on the form traditions of the people hiding with me. I asked myself: how do they mirror various sociohistorical dimensions of the subcultures from which they are coming? I extended my reflections to people elsewhere in the world.

Take the story of the Boers in South Africa. They had to defend their lands against marauding tribes. This led historically to the emergence of fundamental affective dispositions to perceive the black population as inferior servants of the whites. These popular cultural feelings were reflected in the local form tradition of the Dutch Reformed Church of that time. The interpretation of the Hebrew writings of the Bible mirrored the form-traditional feelings in such a way that one could read the story of the Promised Land and the fight against its original inhabitants as the story of the Christian Boers in the promised pagan land of South Africa. Locally, it changed the sociohistorical dimension of the Dutch Reformed formation tradition. This change was reflected in turn in the sociohistorical dimension of the culture of the South African republic, leading to the laws of apartheid. Presently, the sociohistorical dimension of the same culture is changing again. This emergent change is reflected, too, in the historical dimension of the Christian form tradition. Christians began to perceive that their interpretation of the Bible had to be changed in such a way that it no longer demanded apartheid as if it were a Christian formation directive.

This example illustrates my contention that there can be a powerful connection between warped cultural dispositions and the historical deformation of traditions. Many of the Boers, their ministers, government administrators, police, and soldiers seemed driven by a compelling need to keep the blacks in line by any means possible. One could compare this with the obsessive-compulsive deformation of the core form of certain individuals and their consequent compromises, ambivalences, hysterical outbursts, rationalizations, and hidden anxieties. This is only a comparison, nothing more. I do not wish to imply that all Boers suffered from a personal obsessive-compulsive character deformation. What I want to point out is that the adherents of a formation tradition may share in the core deformation of that tradition while their own personal character in everyday interaction may not manifest such a deformation. The twisted traditional coformant of their life may only come to the fore when they speak and act in unison with other adherents of the form tradition.

They all share in what I would call the public expression and implementation of the core form of their tradition. In that case, the shared deformation is not due to personal obsessive-compulsive mechanisms going back to childhood or to later traumatic experiences. It is based on one's faith that the directives of a tradition are reflections of the divine will and predestination, even if one's personal limited creaturely wisdom cannot understand and perhaps does not sympathize with such directives. Unfortunately, this makes the public expression of the warped traditional core form seem more convincing and reasonable to its participants.

I conclude that we cannot explore fully the obstacles to transcendent formation if we neglect to examine the impact of traditions and cultures on their adherents. It is crucial for sound transtherapy to distinguish between dispositions that are merely initiated socioculturally and our personally rooted deformative dispositions. The transtherapeutic approach will be different in each case.

Transtherapy and the Collusion of the Core-Form Deformations

The deformation of the historical dimension of a form tradition may have started out or been reinforced by powerful or high placed individuals. These may have suffered already in their own personal core form similar deformations. They may have persuaded other adherents of their tradition to change their biblical interpretations accordingly.

The deformed core form of a formation tradition is a privileged ground for the emergence or deepening of already-existing, individual core deformations. Such deformations may be obsessive-compulsive, hysterical, excessively ritualistic, superstitious, schizoid, masochistic, sadistic, paranoid, paternalistic, authoritarian, and so on. Problems are compounded when there is a collusion between traditional character and personal character deformations. Such collusions may produce extremists who serve fanatically the regimes or institutions set up by adherents of twisted ideological or cultic traditions. Examples are the Nazi, Communist, and some South American oligarchic regimes. Such extremists become the infamous executioners, death squads, prison guards, torturers, and instigators history records. They are the monstrous products of the deadly mix of dissonant personal and twisted traditional core forms. They give deformed transcendent traditions an odious name. They camouflage their own pathological deviations with the deviations of the core form of the formation traditions for which they claim to stand.

The collusion of the two core forms can happen in thinkers, artists, teachers, politicians, playwrights, journalists and others like them that history names. They express their warped vision in art works, thought systems, news selections, editorial comments, and the like. Their position enables them to infect many others with the same deformity. This is an illustration of the mirroring of traditional deformations in the culture at large.

In the light of my formation science and my theory of transtherapy, one can explore objectively the historical dimension of any form tradition. This research will usually disclose some influence of twisted sociohistorical attitudes at certain periods of that form tradition. In some measure, this can happen at any time. No form tradition, no matter how sublime, is immune to this happening. Therefore, my stress on caution in the appraisal of traditions. Look carefully for any deformity of the core form of a form tradition. Watch also for any collusion between deformed traditions and deformed personal character dispositions. Are certain individuals predisposed to such deformation?

Without due attention to the hidden coformants of any tradition, my students and readers could misinterpret a significant part of their data. We should always stay alert to the possible contamination of our transcendent strivings by pretranscendent sociohistorical deviations in our own life and in our form traditions. The question is, How do these traditions affect our human life personally and communally?

CHAPTER 10

Transcendent Formation and Interformation

In my thinking, interformation is universal because it occurs continuously between all forms in cosmos, humanity, formative evolution, and history. Because of its universality it comprises also the interactions between the various forms that make up our own life and its field of presence and action.

The formation phases of prehuman unfolding of the cosmos, of our shared human history, and of our personal life are outcomes of this always-ongoing interformation. For example, the formation phase of primitive life on earth could evolve only after the cooling phase of our planet in interformation with the sun. Primitive life, in turn, could only emerge by the interformation of gasses and chemicals. To put it briefly, all forms and energies in time and space and in our field of life are always and everywhere interforming with one another. Therefore, one of the assumptions of formation science calls to our attention that all formation is interformation. This ties in with another assumption of mine that the absolutely independent development of any form in the universe is a fiction of our imagination.

Personal-Communal Interformation

I call the interformation between people "personal-communal" to set it apart from other forms of interformation in the universe. This kind of interformation only takes place between people. Our interformation with others touches and shapes our life in a special way. Therefore, I put it into my paradigm of the human formation field as one of its five essential spheres. In this diagram it represents our personal-social interformation with others. For brevity's sake, I have shortened the phrasing to the "interformational sphere." It is the most sublime form of universal interformation known to us and, as such, it is essentially different from other forms of interformation. I use the term "interformation" for all of these forms in keeping with my principle that all the ways of human development and interaction should be seen as formational because they are connected with the formation mystery and/or with transcendent human formation.

Human formation is, by definition, interformation with others; it goes on between generations. For example, the animosity some Palestinians and Israelis felt toward one another stems from the forming and deforming influences of generations before them. Interformation happens also all the time between people of present generations. For example, parents interact with one another, with their children, their neighbors, the members of their church or synagogue. By the same token, the suspicious mood of Israelis and Palestinians is shaped not only by former generations but also by the contemporary uprisings and clashes between them. Because interformation plays such a central role, it influences not only transcendent formation but also the process of transtherapy.

Fusional Interformation

Personal and social interchanges can become fusional, as I earlier indicated. Take, for example, the emotional intimacy expressed between members of a tribal family. They flow together and merge in an outpouring of feeling at such shared moments of intimacy as births, deaths, illnesses, battles, victories, and defeats. They fuse into a oneness of passionate purpose, mutual care, and empathic commiseration.

A highly charged level of vital-affective intensity runs through such fusional interformation. It fosters strong ties within certain populations, notably the Mediterranean and quite a number of African and Asiatic populations. They love to live and work together in affective fusion.

Generally speaking, women appreciate networks of affective connections more than men do. Within such bonds of affection, the drift toward fusion can happen. Today this might be less so because of the functional emancipation of an increasing number of women.

Fusional interformation calls forth a special sensitivity to one another. It brings warmth and care to relationships. It draws people into a vital "we-form" experience; it carries them beyond a more withdrawn "I-form" stance toward life. The fruits of fusion are, among others, closeness, thoughtfulness, and intimacy. Fusional people are easily drawn into emotional exchanges. The novelist Nikos Kazantzakis gives us a striking example of fusion in *Zorba the Greek*. Fusional persons love to give and receive symbols that show concern and affection rather than coldness and indifference

Vitalistic Fusionism

Fusional interformation may stay imprisoned in the pretranscendent realm of life in only its vital aspect. It may then deteriorate into fusionism. To keep fusion healthy, we must temper its vitality without destroying its lively animation. Transcendent wisdom side by side with functional reasonableness should keep the vital dimension in touch with the inspirations of the mystery and the practical needs of everyday living. Otherwise, we risk getting caught in a sentimental vitalism that would interfere with our phasic journey.

Vital charm can be an expression of vital fusionism. It can be exploited for selfish aims. One can abuse vital charm to obtain results without work. Charm can be turned into a tool of seductive manipulation that takes advantage of the fusion needs of people. The vitalistic charmer senses that the overdependent, the lonely, the less mature, the weak and wounded are likely to fall for this seductive magic. Interformation turns into deformation. Those who become his or her emotional captives may already be prisoners of their own unpurged lower fusion drives. It is all too easy for charming seducers to take advantage, for instance, of a lonely widow or a single person seeking a suitor. These victims of vital charm may be left in the cold the moment they entrust their savings to unscrupulous escorts.

A charming spiritual director may even collect a number of directees to fulfill her own need for fusion and veneration. Jimmy Jones and David Koresh, who seduced their followers into death, offer striking symbols of taking people off the path of true transcendent formation while pretending, or even themselves believing, that they are leading them to the "promised land."

Shared Vitalistic Fusionism

Shared vitalistic fusionism can drive us into anxious enclosure within an emotional "we form" of life. One pushes aside all outsiders. The members of the "we group" run down anyone among them who strays from the vitalistic group conscience. Obvious examples are Mafia families, Nazi groups, and certain cults. Traces of clannish fusion can be found also in fundamentalistic subtraditions that can emerge in any ideological, scientific, clinical, religious, or managerial belief system. In our personal life, shared vitalistic fusionism is a hindrance on the road to transcendent uniqueness. Vitalistic fusionism breeds confusion. It is the parent of dissonance. It blocks the awareness of our unique-communal call. In a vitalistic community, we do not look for our own life call; we let the emotional demands of vitalistic togetherness run our life. Not real community but an emotional crowd, sometimes deceptively called community, drives our moods and feelings.

The disposition of fusional interformation, once it will be tempered by wisdom, can be an asset on the way to transcendence. It can help us to resist the opposite danger, that of being caught in the rampant individualism I sometimes call the scourge of our age.

Fusional Form Traditions

Some traditions are fusional; others are not. Within the many form traditions that spring from the same faith tradition, some fusional ones strike us as both reasonable and wise. They offer a way to put one's belief system into practice. For example, some of the charismatic form traditions in various religions draw a number of participants from among fusional people. They strive to develop affective ties between themselves and God as well as among themselves. Not all of them foster sufficiently the rational and volitional aspects of the spiritual life. Sometimes reasonableness seems of little or no concern. Feelings that are out of control may at times take over. The vital-affective aspect of fusion starts to guide fusional group appraisal one-sidedly. Superiority feelings toward those who show less emotional pietism may come to the fore. People may push the idea that their way is the best way for everyone. They may even question if people who do not feel at ease with their spirituality are really faithful to the faith they claim to share.

Another sign of vitalistic fusionism, raised to the level of a formation tradition, entails a drop in attention to one's personal calling. A deaf ear is turned to the inspiration to unfold and use as well as possible one's unique and individual gifts in service of one's own transcendent formation and unique-communal life call.

Fusion and Basic Form Tradition

A fusional form tradition can become so particular that it strays away from the basic formation tradition of its supporting religion or ideology. Basic form traditions are different from basic faith traditions. They also differ from secondary form traditions that are not as foundational as the basic form tradition of a belief system.

A general basic form tradition unfolds over time within each specific belief system. As such, it goes beyond all particular form traditions of the same faith. It stands between the faith tradition and its mushrooming particular form traditions. An example is the basic sacramental formation tradition of some Christian churches.

The basic form tradition strives to do justice to all the common foundationals of formation that have become known to the followers of a faith tradition over the centuries. They are the outcome of the empirical formation directives found effective by many particular formation traditions within the same faith tradition. Over centuries and generations, they have gained, by means of repeated critique and general agreements, the classical status of formation foundationals. This status is based not on faith systems alone, nor merely on their informational theologies or ideological philosophies. The basis of this more universal form tradition is the empirical experience of what has proven over generations to work best for putting a belief system into practice.

An example might be the classical liturgical prayers used, for instance, in Catholic, Episcopalian, Orthodox, and Lutheran communities of faith. If a movement away from these classical foundations becomes commonplace, it may point to the necessity to reappraise such a controversial aspect of the foundational form tradition. An example of such reappraisal is the change in Catholic liturgy from Latin to the national language of the faithful.

The basic form tradition is not the same as the faith tradition itself. Therefore, we can change it more readily, though not as easily as particular form traditions. For example, the form of the basic ancient liturgy in the Russian Orthodox Church cannot be changed as readily as the forms of peasant devotions practiced by its faithful.

Transformed Fusion

Many charismatics as well as revival groups and movements in a number of religions and ideologies can give rise to form traditions that are helpful for fusion-prone personalities. They can answer the need for transformed fusion in those who are temperamentally and sociohistorically inclined to live their affectivity in vital ways. They may also be a response to a longing for affective fusion in those who ignored this aspect of their particular makeup under the pressure of a functionalistic society.

I chose already as an example charismatic formation traditions. My findings apply as well to other special form traditions. For example, the traditions of specific religious or ideological communities are not immune to vitalistic fusion. They, too, can fall into the arrogant conviction that their form tradition is the best one for all people, no matter what their life call, temperament, character, individual form potencies, and formation field may be.

Regardless of how emotionally enmeshed we are in a fusional community, we must hold on to an inner life that is reasonably and volitionally rooted in our presence to the mystery, in our basic faith and formation tradition, in our life call, and in the formation field in which we find ourselves. Without this depth of a freely chosen volitional and reasonable realism, it will be difficult for us to walk unscathed the path to transcendent immanence.

Hierarchical Interformation

Human interformation can be more or less fusional; it can also be more or less hierarchical. Hierarchy means order of rank. When two or more people affect the formation of one another's life, there is usually some order of influence in this process: one may be more dominant, the other more receptive.

In parent–child interformation, the parent is usually more dominant, the child more receptive. However, the child, wittingly or unwittingly, gives some form to parental life, too. Parents have more power to refuse or change the form given to their life by children than children do in regard to the form given to their life by parents. When the parents age, suffer infirmities, or are in need of aid from their now adult children, the hierarchy of interformation turns around. It is now the child who exercises formation dominance. Yet aged, feeble parents can still give some form to the life of their grown-up children. They may do so by the way they ask, take up, and accept aid from their children. The life of their adult children themselves would take on a somewhat different form if they would not be formed by their responses to the reasonable needs of aging parents. Similarly, the life of young parents would have taken another form if they would not have to care for their children.

To put it briefly, hierarchy does not do away with mutual dependency. The more extensive the interformation between people is, the more intricate their hierarchical relationships will be. Complexity can cause misunderstanding, manipulation, crisis, and conflict. For example, members of a complex governmental structure may experience more conflict than the owners of small stores with few employees. Therefore, it is important to appraise the hierarchical relationships that are fostered by a formation tradition.

I am interested in such relationships from the viewpoint of transcendent interformation, especially in view of transtherapy. My main questions are the following: How do form traditions differ in various interformational hierarchies? How can the style of hierarchical relationships be integrated, transformed, and made consonant in groups and persons? And, most important for this volume, how does such integration or the lack thereof affect the problems encountered in transtherapy?

Hierarchy of Formation Control
and Hierarchy of Formation Competence

Speaking of hierarchical traditions, I make a distinction between what I call a hierarchy of formation control and a hierarchy of formation competence. For example, the hierarchy between communist authority and its subordinates was a hierarchy of sheer political control. The hierarchy between a true teacher of formation and her or his directees is one of competence. People let themselves be formed by teachers because of their acknowledged competence. Students in turn help their teachers' own ongoing formation. Their research, questions, papers, and feedback add to the body of knowledge all draw upon. Students' love, appreciation, and confirmation can deepen teachers' affirmations of their own life call and its mysterious source. Mutual confirmation helps them and their students on the path to liberating transformation sustained by sometimes unexpected moments of transtherapeutic healing.

I see different anticipations in either the control hierarchy or the competence hierarchy based on certain dispositions and attitudes. These expectations are internalized. I want to limit my remarks here to those one can observe in a hierarchy of control. Afterward I will consider those that are typical of the hierarchy of competence.

Dispositions in Hierarchical Control Traditions

In hierarchical control traditions, the subordinate members are trained in dispositions proper to their position. Docility, obedience, deference, and subordination in relation to the dominant partners are deeply ingrained, at least in the more form-receptive partners. The ideal dispositions for those who are in charge, who are the dominant participants in a hierarchy of control, are different. For them, concern, confirmation, patience, understanding, sensitivity, wisdom, prudence, knowledge, example, and responsibility are taught by transcendent traditions.

These two different internalized sets of anticipations match one another. The more receptive participants are, the more they anticipate that the dominant participants will use their power of control to fulfill certain responsibilities owed to those under them. For example, those who enter a community in any religion or ideology expect those in control to care for them, to assist them in their adaptation to this new life, and to respect the gradual disclosure of their unique-communal life call. They feel hurt if their superiors or their directors of formation do not respond with concern, consideration, and confirmation while they themselves are asked to live in docility, obedience, and deference to them. If they are disappointed repeatedly, they may come to the conclusion, "I have to look out for myself since no one else will." This mentality is the opposite of the original anticipations fostered by consonant formation traditions.

The hierarchical relationships set up by transcendent traditions set their course on the basis of the aims of formation in a family or community. The controlling hierarchy and the tradition for which it stands call for solidarity and cooperation, for holding on to the norms and customs of the hierarchical family or institution.

I distinguish between overt and covert hierarchical control. In many macho traditions, for instance, men have overt power of control, but it may be balanced by the covert hierarchical control of women, especially in the area of child rearing.

Hierarchy of Formation Competence

Formal hierarchies of control are complicated by informal hierarchies. The latter draw their power from the particular competencies of persons who do not speak from a formal position of control. In a hierarchy of competence, respect, idealization, and even veneration are shown for competent persons. For instance, an outstanding football player gifted with strategic insight may be listened to in spite of the fact that he is not the coach who stays on top in the hierarchy of control.

Hierarchy of competence can fall together with hierarchy of control. The most competent person can be in the leading position. This is not always so nor is it necessarily desirable. Often, someone without any position in the hierarchy of control has competencies that are more appreciated than those of the leading person in a hierarchy of power. It can happen in a family, for instance, that the wife or, in some cases, the older son has certain needed competencies that are lacking in the husband or father. What if a wife is more competent than her husband in running the finances of the family? Often we see a similar division in competencies in communities and institutions. This holds true especially for transcendent traditional institutes. Commitment to the tradition is a first requirement for a leader of the tradition. Sometimes this need brings people to the top who lack gifts, talents, and skills in some other practical or sensitive areas of leadership. A subordinate, competent person should then defer to the person in charge, because he or she is responsible for the basic form to be kept alive in the community in tune with its tradition.

Prudent leaders, in turn, respect competent persons who happen to be subordinates in the traditional hierarchy of control. They let them assist them as a kind of unofficial, limited "hierarchy-by-competence."

Different people within the hierarchy of competence have different competencies. That is what makes it so complex. An intricate web of relationships arises between people in the hierarchy of control and those in the hierarchy of competence. Ideally, they give form to what is at best an attainable, if not a perfect, consonance. Sometimes, either a controlling hierarchy or a competence hierarchy carries a family or a community. Much depends on their form tradition. A tradition may be reasonably authoritative. Under the influence of other traditions, however, some become authoritarian. In some instances an authoritarian hierarchy of control may put an end to any hierarchy of competence.

Competence in this context includes, but also goes beyond, functional or administrative abilities. It touches also on competencies of the mind, the heart, and the spirit rooted in inner dispositions and affects. Marriage, succession, appointment, or election pushes some people into a hierarchy of power. Sometimes they suffer from dissonance between the public comportment now demanded of them and their own core dispositions and affects. To be credible, they must hold publicly to the popular traits of their form tradition. Some of these may not be in consonance with their own dispositions.

Subordinates within an authoritative institute may show the same dissonance. Some, for instance, hold on to angry feelings about superiors in the hierarchy of control. At the same time, the apparent form of life (the way they appear) of these subordinates stays polite and deferential. Publicly they conform to the tradition, but a closer look at their behavior shows that only their apparent form is deferential. Their inner feelings and outer actions are less than cooperative with the authority of those responsible for the tradition.

All members of an institution may speak the language of their shared tradition, but some among them maneuver indirectly for what they personally prefer. All of these attitudes delay our progress on the way of transformation together. Private and group transtherapy can assist in the healing of such tensions.

Transcendent Transformation
and Pretranscendent Individuation

Central to the thinking of many people today about pretranscendent individual growth are the developmental schemes proposed by the social, clinical, educational, and managerial disciplines. These schemes are limited by the preferred focus of attention of such disciplines, which, as I have shown, is pretranscendent self-actualization. We can be enriched by some of the useful insights and findings of these pretranscendent approaches. However, we should complement and, if desirable, correct these with transcendent formation insights.

For instance, one of the assumptions of the psychoanalytic tradition is that character formation comes about through conflicts and deficits in one's childhood. While this insight is true in part, it bypasses the mighty influence of transcendent formation traditions in Western countries, if they are truly "lived" by the family.

Significant in this regard is the assumption of many representatives of the orthodox psychoanalytic form tradition that character formation is determined fully by the particular events that take place in the psychosexual and psychosocial formation phases of early childhood. These phases are seen as applicable to children in all possible formation traditions. Were that true, the sociohistorical formation patterns of any given tradition anywhere in the world would be determined by the effects of Western psychosexual and social development.

A rigid attachment to such prescientific assumptions makes the study of many form traditions reductionistic. In the extreme, it could reduce a wholly different form tradition to only the psychoanalytic tradition. Psychoanalysis would then begin to function less as a science and more as a proselytizing ideological tradition or formational belief system in its own right. Such an approach would clash with the integration of some formationally critiqued contributions of psychoanalysis into the body of transcendent formation science and praxis. It would also hinder the particular articulations of psychoanalytic theory in different form traditions.

To get to know the formation scheme of any distinct tradition, we must look at that tradition in and by itself. This holds especially for transcendent traditions. Social, clinical, educational, and managerial disciplines, as I have shown, are for the most part based on observations of Western pretranscendent traditions of individualistic self-actualization. Their formation criteria are invariably weighted in the direction of pretranscendent form directives. Followers of these traditions appraise other traditions in the light of these one-sided, absolutized criteria. Often they reduce transcendent traditions to immature or pathological ways of life.

Therefore, one of the responsibilities of formation science and its articulations in various traditions is to unmask such reductions and distortions. People whose path is significantly influenced by such pretranscendent views of life usually lose the sense of the holistic, transcendent way. Some may reduce their transcendent tradition to a dull collection of coercive dos and don'ts. What I have written about transcendent ascendance may be for them a closed book. My transtherapy aims at assisting them in the awakening of a critical awareness of how ideological, religious, scientific, popular, or clinical formation traditions may have affected their character unfolding and the dissonances in their form-traditional pyramid.

CHAPTER 11

Disciplines and Dynamics
of Transtherapy

In my study of the dynamics, conditions, and transition crises of transcendent formation in pluritraditional functionalistic societies, I have often asked myself, What, if anything, can counseling, therapy, and direction do in this regard?

A momentous shift in our appraisal of the phases of character and personality formation happens if we look at them in the light of our transcendence dynamic. This shift transforms our approach to all forms of counseling, therapy, and direction, especially of people who find themselves in a crisis of transcendence. Our usual ways of offering help and guidance ought to be complemented by formative counseling, transtherapy, and spiritual direction in the light of the dynamics of transcendence and of the classical formation traditions. Attention would then be paid to the deepest meaning of ongoing formation, reformation, and transformation as operative in crises of transition. Such care giving goes beyond clinical symptoms, diagnostics, and analytical treatments while still appreciating their relative usefulness and value. Transtherapy focuses mainly on the distinctively human. This focus precedes, complements, and corrects our attention to clinical labeling, testing, recording, and prescribing.

A first condition for transcendence therapy is that one be engaged in his or her own transcendent-immanent life formation. Only then can we assist others in their times of crisis. While learning these dynamics is important, it is vital to live them through personally. It is not necessary to have arrived, but at least one has to be on the way to transcendence. After all we never arrive but always ought to be arriving in some way. Dynamics of transcendence need to be experienced to be understood. Learning about them supports this understanding, but it cannot replace our lived experience of them in the light of our classical and classics-compatible transcendent-immanent traditions.

It goes without saying that we should take into account the insights and approaches of all schools of counseling and therapy while not allowing ourselves to be taken over by any one of them exclusively. Our insights into the formation crises of counselees come not only from tests and diagnostic tools but from their own experiences as illumined by the wisdom of transcendent traditions. We must accept our counselees or directees as they are here and now in their life's journey. Such ease of acceptance ties in with our coming to accept crises in our own life and from the experience of coping with them formatively. In the preparation I have done of formation counselors, trans-therapists, and spiritual guides, I try to turn their attention to their own formation by always asking them to describe formative events in their own life. To learn and practice the counseling methods of psychological, clinical, and educational disciplines is helpful, but, by itself, it does not guarantee effectiveness in our assistance of others in their transcendence crises.

Formation scientists, counselors, guides, and teachers are called to make people ready for a new era. In service of the possible dawn of a new age, they put the wisdom of formation traditions in touch with the compatible insights of the arts, disciplines, and sciences. Together they give form to a science of transcendent formation. This science can assist people caught in transcendence crises. Often the true nature and purpose of such crises are obscured for them by their formation ignorance. A transcendent change in intraformation has to take place in a sufficient number of people. Only then may they effect a transformation in the interformational and outer spheres of their formation field. They may reform or replace collapsing functionalistic institutions. Communication in depth, mutual confirmation, collaboration, concelebration, social justice, peace, and mercy then become cherished ideals for many to be pursued with courage and competence.

Transcendent Constancy and Phasic Formation

Transtherapists and formation counselors, faced with the crises of their counselees, move beyond their lower personality and its corresponding apparent forms. They focus on the founding form as mirrored in the core form, heart, and matching character of their empirical life. This form remains constant in the midst of current formations. It is never fooled by popular pulsations or anxious attachments. Formation crises are opportunities to become aware of the temporal, fragmented, dissonant quality of the lower personality in isolation. A formation crisis opens us to a dynamic of centering. We gain a deeper awareness of the directives of our founding life form or unique-communal life call. Crises can enable transcendent directives to take precedence over functional ones in our life's formation. They give us the openings through which our founding form and its grounding mystery can flood our lower personality with transcendent meaning.

Formative counseling, transtherapy, and guidance assist us in aligning our socio-vital-functional personality with the transcendent directives disclosed to us during the accelerated formation flow of phasic crises. Alignment lessens the vague familiar feeling of dissonance between what we most deeply are and our actual form of life. This process of alignment is moved by the dynamics of consonance.

Transtherapy and the formative counseling allied with it appreciate deeply the indispensable socio-vital-functional personality in which current formation dynamics initially manifest themselves most obviously. This appreciation leads to dialogical consultation of the biophysical, clinical, and social sciences. It is through the phasic development of this lower personality that we can express human life in its multidimensional totality. Through the service of our functional dimension, our founding form becomes more empirical; it expresses itself uniquely and individually in our concrete field of life. Our well-developed lower personality—now formed and illumined by our founding form—becomes a unique epiphany of the formation mystery in action. Transtherapy and formation counseling can thus unblock the roadblocks to transcendence. They can set us free for the great adventure of listening to our unique-communal life call.

Pluritraditional Society and Effective Transtherapy

Transtherapy, as I conceived and developed it, sets us free for transcendent formation by rescuing us from the tyranny of unappraised traditions pulsating in our society. In pluritraditional societies, we are exposed to competing traditions that confuse us even as they beg for our allegiance. At times, they turn us into skeptics about the value of any tradition. They may uproot us from a tradition that has worked well for us over many years.

A transcendent wisdom of life directives flows from a coherent system of beliefs, symbols, and dispositions that go beyond yet are consonant with one's basic faith tradition. Originally, such formation systems were rooted in monotraditional communities, such as those of groups of people that were Jewish, Islamic, Christian, Hindu, humanist, socialist, or tribal. Today we see more and more that such monotraditional societies are coming to an end. The surviving traditions must help their followers to live compatibly in societies that are pluritraditional. A pluritraditional society gives form to common symbols that are for the most part pretranscendent. Examples are the symbols put out by science, by a mixed and watered-down national culture, by public education, entertainment, and media-driven information systems. Thrown in with them are symbolic remnants of group traditions. Within this ever-changing field of public symbols, each person or group of persons selects or creates a constellation of symbols, meanings, and form directives.

Problem of Scientism

To me, scientism (not science) is one of the central problems of modernity. When positive sciences are made the only source of all truth, we fall into scientism. They may seem to present people with a full-fledged formation tradition that by itself can save them. Such quasi-scientific form traditions are laden with prescientific presuppositions and directives presented to us as the ultimate conditions for the good life. At the heart of their message is the personality ideal of the rationalistic individualist. Corresponding with this idolized image is a depreciative disposition toward transcendent traditions and their image of the ideal form of life.

What transcendent-immanent traditions communicate goes beyond merely rationalistic and scientific life directives. Yet, they do not deny their real contributions. To the contrary, transcendent traditions encourage people to listen respectfully to reason, science, and functional intelligence. Their formationally relevant contributions are carefully scanned and, if desirable, reformulated, by experts in transcendent formation. They are made use of gratefully yet cautiously. One puts them into dialogue with higher transcendent reason and consults the wisdom of classic formation traditions. The point is, we can and should profit from the blessings of positive science and technology without becoming captives of the prison of lower reason alone. Sober, critical dialogue with higher reason should set us free for the transformation of our life as a whole.

Self-Actualization and Militant Individualism

One of the common beliefs in Western societies has been that of militant individualism. This individualistic trend has been strengthened by the increasing mobility of people. People lost touch with the circle of their own familiar, locally celebrated form traditions. Many turned into lonely self-actualizers. They felt thrown back upon themselves. No longer able to draw on their traditions, they collapsed inwardly.

At times, we all feel overwhelmed by the weight and diversity of traditions that try to force us to align with them. Often we are like lonely soldiers in a world of crumbling supports.

In such a climate of confusion, social, clinical, managerial, and educational disciplines are a help, but we ought not to expect from them more than they can give. Pretranscendent facets of life and world should not be mistaken for full-fledged transcendent-immanent traditions. They cannot guide the whole of our life nor fulfill all of its aspirations. In our search for direction, we should not expect that such disciplines can provide the missing wisdom we need for transcendent living. By themselves, for example, they cannot redeem us totally from a symptom like low-grade spiritual depression as distinguished from the clinical variety. It is possible, of course, that in some instances both kinds of depression go together.

Transcendent-immanent traditions as consonant encourage us to listen creatively and critically to what such disciplines have to teach us about life and world on the pretranscendent level. How we use their findings depends on our ability to lift them cautiously in the light of our higher or transcendent reason. It always takes into account the wisdom of classical traditions. It lets us see how to take advantage of the blessings of positive science and technology without becoming their captives. Transcendent-immanent traditions leave us free to foster the transformation of our life as a whole.

Some representatives of clinical, social, educational, and managerial disciplines look at transcendent traditions and experiences depreciatively. They are inclined to appraise them in terms of hidden pathologies, compensations, regressions to oceanic childhood experiences, sexual sublimations, and emotionally exalted fusions with others and nature. They treat spiritual encounters among people as mere repetitions of earlier childhood relationships, even if that is not necessarily the case. Not all scientists go so far. Many of them do not fall into the temptation to turn their scientific or scholarly disciplines into the basic formation tradition that governs their own life as a whole. They are already sufficiently rooted in traditions of their own. For them the path to a peace-filled life entails the transformation of their pretranscendent "I" by their higher "I." This occurs over and above the aid they can receive from their pretranscendent disciplines for their and other's pretranscendent problems.

In the light of a transcendent tradition, they look at this transcendent "I" as carried by the mystery of formation. They draw wisely on social, clinical, or educational knowledge and practice. They look at the latter as helpful in bringing together various aspects of their life, or, in other words, of integrating their pretranscendent "I" into their transcendent "I." An already integrated lower "I" is most ready to be taken up by the higher "I," which can use it as a necessary means to put its aspirations into practice both in one's own life and in the marketplace. The integration and consolidation of the lower "I" is a prelude to the deeper consonance to come. In severe specific problems of lower "I" integration, the transtherapist refers the counselee to a trustworthy pretranscendent therapist specializing in the problems of pretranscendent disintegration. After this has been cleared, the person may be ready for transtherapy.

Overreaction to the Claims of Pretranscendent Disciplines

Some representatives of pretranscendent disciplines make spurious holistic claims. They talk as if these disciplines themselves are full-fledged faith and formation traditions. Such claims in turn trigger an unfortunate overreaction in some followers of transcendent traditions. It may take the form of rejecting these pretranscendent disciplines altogether. Often this truly regrettable reaction seems to parallel an anxious need to reaffirm one's own threatened identity. What may be missed is the fact that one's own transcendent tradition, insofar as it fosters the universal openness of the human spirit, does not cast aside proven scientific facts.

We should critique any overexalted image of health, happiness, and wholeness that some pretranscendent traditions place before us. We should unmask the promises of lasting peace, joy, effectiveness, and prosperity that "will be ours if only we take up their guidelines."

The best image for a life whole, healthy, and happy is not that of a rationalistic, fully autonomous, and self-actualizing individual. Transcendent traditions offer us instead the image of persons centered in their higher "I." This "I" is attuned to one's life call by an indwelling, all-surrounding mystery. The transcendent "I" lets us see the possibility of peace amid the stresses and pulls of a splintered and confused society. We should take seriously the insights that come to us from the disciplines of the pretranscendent life. At the same time, we should look critically at statements that may turn out to be less than scientific. These unvalidated presuppositions may have been added to the scientific data when these were reworked into theoretical explanations. We must also ask ourselves if what they tell us is in tune with our transcendent form tradition.

Transtherapy

I drew on the science of formation to give form to the discipline and practice of transtherapy, my therapeutic approach that gives priority to the transcendent dimension of life. My question is: How does the transcendence dynamic reveal itself in people in different situations? How does it flow with or push against the dynamics of their pretranscendent life?

The transcendence dynamic is the power in us-as-distinctively-human to go beyond mere pretranscendent living. This concept of mine is an empirical-experiential, not a philosophical, concept. Transtherapy works with people who want to avail themselves of this power. As the founder of the transtherapeutic approach, I seek to complement the good effects of other types of therapy that sustained counselees so far. Unlike some other therapies, the strength of transtherapy lies not mainly or not only in cognitive processes, such as interpretation or in the process of transference. Its real power lies in a relationship that is not only pretranscendent but also transcendent. This keeps both the therapist and the counselee sensitive to the experiential transcendence dynamic. What counts most here is person-to-person encounter on the transcendent-immanent level.

I teach transtherapists that they should start out from the trust that a hidden deeper "I" is waiting to be awakened. All happenings in one's pretranscendent life, its struggles and victories, its hopes, dreams, depressions, and disappointments, are acknowledged. I teach them to encourage people to view them also from the perspective of their own transcendent formation traditions. It may well be that the problems of their pretranscendent life are so complex and particular that one has to refer them first or simultaneously to therapists who specialize in pretranscendent therapies that touch on these problems.

Once the pretranscendent "I" has become more whole and healthy, it can be lifted into the light of the higher "I" and of the transcendent traditions to which it is committed. I explain to transtherapists why and how the transtherapeutic relationship goes beyond transference and countertransference. These processes are shown to be helpful in certain pretranscendent therapies. At times, transference does happen in transtherapy itself, but it is not turned into one of the main tools of the therapeutic process, as may be appropriate in other types of therapy.

When I speak to transtherapists about a personal mode of presence in transtherapy, I want to avoid misunderstanding. What I mean to say is that transtherapists should not focus primarily on pretranscendent symptoms of distress. Neither should their main concern be with the symptoms of only the pretranscendent dissonance of their counselees. Concentration on such experiences can be crucial in pretranscendent therapies. In transtherapy such concentration can be abused to circumvent the exploration of deeper dispositions of dissonance. It is precisely these that may feed and sustain the transcendence problems of the counselee.

I advise my transtherapy students to examine with counselees also the influences of their form-traditional pyramids. How have these traditions coformed the core dispositions of their life? One should realize that such factors can be internalized in both counselees and transtherapists, especially when the respective tradition pyramids of both tend to overlap. The patterns of formation traditions do not reside exclusively *out there* in society. They have been assimilated *in* the intraformational tradition pyramid. This constellation of insufficiently appraised traditions may be so confusing and divisive that transtherapeutic treatment becomes necessary or highly desirable.

Fear of Offending the Transtherapist

A special problem may emerge in people committed to transcendent ideological or religious form traditions. For a number of them, it is difficult to express anger openly and directly to a hierarchical superior within their own tradition and community. This fear of offending hierarchical superiors can be carried over into the therapeutic relationship. Some counselees may almost never express anger, frustration, irritation, disappointment, or other ambivalent feelings. In that case, transtherapists must become sensitive to possible indirect ways in which counselees may express ambivalence and dissatisfaction. For example, they may talk repeatedly about things that seem to them at variance with what the transtherapist claims to be hearing; or they may express the desire to terminate the sessions; they may not show up for it or arrive too late; they may resist irrationally the suggestions of the therapist; they may transpose anger from the therapist to someone else or to their tradition, and so on.

Post-therapy Dependence on the Transtherapist

In pretranscendent therapies, the counselees are expected to become independent of the therapist. The same is aimed at in transtherapy. In practice, this is not always the case. Both the counselee and the therapist may share the same particular transcendent faith and form tradition. This tradition may be marked by a profound emphasis on formational idealizations and by subsequent identifications with outstanding examples, teachers, and authorities of that tradition. This pattern may be transposed to the transtherapist.

Transtherapists are only familiar to their counselees in the therapy hour. During this period, therapists show their best side. They are perceived as healing and caring, as exemplary representatives of the transcendent traditions of humanity. Such perceptions may give rise to a process of post-therapeutic idealization of the transtherapist. It may leave some counselees with a disposition to identify closely with him or her long after the therapy sessions have ended. Obviously, this can harm the disclosure and implementation of one's own unique-communal life call as different from that of the transtherapist's. The working through of this identification is a necessary part of transtherapy.

Adoption of Means of Pretranscendent Therapies

I teach my transtherapy students that they, as a general rule, should be cautious when adopting certain aspects and methods of pretranscendent therapies. Such adaptations must be made within a transcendent setting. The situation with which transtherapists deal may be different from those dealt with by pretranscendent therapy. One of the tasks of transtherapists and formation practitioners is to shed light on the form-traditional relationships of counselees. How have the people who approach us for guidance internalized these relationships in their life? How may these internalized relationships influence the transther-

apeutic relationship? Do we make a distinction between the particular formation traditions of our counselees and their foundational faith tradition? Do we
keep in mind that the form tradition of counselees is only a particular, limited
implementation of their faith tradition—one that can be consonant or dissonant
with the basics of the faith and formation tradition they are already committed
to?

Individualism and Pretranscendent Traditions

Certain facets of pretranscendent therapies are incompatible with transcendence therapy. They are too exclusively oriented toward the absolutized autonomy of the individual. Counselees in pretranscendent counseling may actually
learn how to create meaning in their own life, how to become free from traditions, how to set up and clarify their own values. Such learning may conflict
with the basic directives given by their transcendent formation traditions and
communities.

People who live by the truth of a transcendent tradition want to remain
embedded within its teachings, customs, rituals, and relationships. They, too,
may experience depreciative feelings toward certain aspects of their traditions,
especially toward their distortion by insufficiently informed or transformed
teachers and parents. Transtherapy helps them to become aware of those feelings. It enables them to see the distortions. They may also feel resistance
toward the foundationals of their tradition. Transtherapy enables them to deal
wisely with these resistances. Its answer is not to reduce these foundationals
through excessive demythologizing. Such reductionism would rob faith and
formation foundations of their dynamic power and meaning. It would
seriously disrupt the cohesion of the internal map one has formed of one's
tradition. It could also diminish one's compatibility with the community that is
also rooted in the same foundations.

Fractured Core Form

I am aware that people may turn to transtherapy when they are more or less
in a state of desperation. They suffer due to a clash of warring "I's" and sub-
"I's." The symptoms of dissonance make their lives less effective. They are in
despair because their call identity is badly fractured. Their internalized form-
tradition pyramid lacks integration. Their heart is divided. Conflicting directives tear them apart.

When people stay mainly on the pretranscendent levels of life, they experience events as discrete happenings or coincidences. Transcendent traditions,
by contrast, approach all happenings as epiphanic. They see them as formation
events or as formation opportunities. Epiphanic means that they are given or

allowed by the formation mystery for one's deeper transformation. The mystery of formation hides under the cover of everydayness. It calls for unconcealment by faith, hope, and love. As I have said before, coincidences are really providences (see volume 6 of this series).

Transcendent traditions help us to experience how the mystery reveals itself in everyday situations. They foster belief in a profound consonance, a veiled interwovenness, between the pretranscendent and transcendent dynamics of human life. Those who ask for transtherapy sense that this consonance has been broken. They feel that the interflow between transcendent and pretranscendent living has been disrupted. They come with the hope that consonance may be restored because they have come to believe in a personal destiny. A unique life call begins to unveil itself to them. They want to trace this call through its particular turns, twists, and cycles as well as through the formation traditions they cultivated in their life. Faith in the mystery enables people to believe in all events as formation opportunities.

Pretranscendent traditions make people feel that it is up to them alone to bring about the fullness of peace and joy. By contrast, my transtherapeutic approach points to the assistance given to us by the mystery and by transcendent formation traditions. Transtherapists help counselees to regain their lost epiphanic appreciation. Once this transcendent appreciation has been recovered, the flow of consonance may be restored gradually in their divided life. They begin to live again, or for the first time, in the faith that everything that happens to them can be related to the disclosure of their unique-communal call of life.

Transcendent Reading Direction

One of the means I advise my transtherapy students to utilize to foster transformation in their counselees is transcendent reading direction. The therapist recommends at the appropriate phase of the therapy slowed-down meditative readings of transcendent texts, preferably from each one's own tradition. I teach prospective transtherapists how to select readings that tie in with their counselee's personal capabilities, problems, and affinities. A portion of the sessions can be used for dialogue about these form-traditional readings. The reflections they evoke can be recorded in the counselees' reading journals. Dialogue may clarify how counselees have incorporated in their form-traditional pyramid dissonant elements of other form traditions in various ways and to varying degrees.

Special attention should be given to incompatible aspects of popularized ideological faith and form traditions, be they social-scientific, managerial, or educational. The task of a transtherapist is to assist counselees in the process of bringing these elements to focal consciousness. They must learn to appraise the compatible and incompatible elements of other traditions assimilated in their own form-traditional pyramids. Many sessions may then have to be spent in reforming their pyramid as well. The response of my transtherapists to their reflections in this regard should be more empathic than cognitive. One must accept and emphatically discuss what counselees present as well as the level on which they present it, showing profound sensitivity for their feelings at this juncture of their journey. One must know where and how these reflections tie in with the basic patterns emerging in a person's field of life.

Family Twisting of Form Traditions

Parents often distort traditions when they communicate them to their children. They may foster an exclusive "we community," dominated by their own one-sided and possibly distorted view of their traditions. A too exclusive we-form of life impairs one's power of personal appraisal in the light of one's authentic tradition. The appreciation of one's own life form and its guiding traditions may be too closely interwoven with the perhaps warped identity of one's family or community. This deformation misdirects one's conscience. It makes it emotionally impossible to deviate from any appraisal, right or wrong, offered by one's family or community.

This clash between form traditions of the family and newly emerging insights may undermine one's sense of self-appreciation. It creates uncertainty and anxiety. The attempt to contain this anxiety about inner fragmentation generates enormous inner stresses and strains. New form-traditional images arising from one's pluritraditional society may be overidealized precisely because they are at odds with the older, shattered ones that came from a distorting family or group.

The result of this process is a seriously fractured core form. A person may be semiparalyzed in her or his functioning. The familial deformation of the foundationals of one's faith and form tradition has to be worked through. This is what led to a deficit or arrest in one's early formation. The reaction to this deficit may have been a frantic search for new idealized models of traditional living. Pretranscendent form traditions, presented as new or perfect, become models of other enticing forms of self-actualizing individuation. My transtherapy offers a necessary corrective. It points to one's unique transcendent life call, which includes as a basic ingredient one's authentic faith and formation tradition.

In the beginning of the reformation process, one may need idealized figures that model, if not one's unique-communal life call, then at least fidelity to that call as lived in the light of one's chosen, basic tradition. The more counselees grow in fidelity, the more their call will be disclosed to them. This will lessen in turn their need for overidealized or idolized models.

It is my contention that certain contributions of various personality theories and therapies can be relevant to transtherapy. All of them, however, have to be altered to fit the context of transcendent formation in a pluritraditional, mostly pretranscendent society. It is now time to ask ourselves specifically, how does transtherapy work and why is it so necessary today?

CHAPTER 12

The Bases
of Transcendence Therapy

Transcendence therapy is a process that assists people before, after, and especially during a transcendence crisis. Transtherapy is illumined by the tradition to which both transtherapists and their clients are committed. Their enlightenment is sustained by the insights they bring to their encounter from the directive disciplines necessary for the study and practice of transtherapy.

Transcendence means "going beyond." Transtherapy helps people to surpass wisely former ways of life. It is rooted in the art and discipline of foundational human formation. This discipline emerges out of reflection on the consonant classics of spiritual transfiguration.

Transcendence means to be raised beyond the form one has given to life so far. It is liberation from historical, vital, and functional fixations. This transition is usually initiated by an experience of crisis. Many people can handle this experience by themselves. Others need assistance to bring it to a head. Assistance during this crisis helps people in need to clarify and deepen their life direction. Their basic orientation is nourished by their religious or humanistic tradition. They may be pledged to this tradition wholeheartedly, halfheartedly, or hesitantly at this moment of their life.

Transcendence therapy can be effective only if those who share its blessings are committed to the search for the pearl of wisdom of continuous transcendence. This pearl is hidden in forming, reforming, and transforming traditions of humanity that are nourished by the light of the always forming, reforming, and transforming mystery. The therapist must experientially grasp this wisdom tradition in its power of transfiguration for each unique person. He or she has to be able to sympathize with a person's attempts to transcend to a more congenial form of life guided by this wisdom.

Past and Present Experiences Supporting This Project
In the late 1950s and early 1960s, I was consulted by people who were formed by religious or humanist wisdom traditions. Their problems generally

were not of a neurotic or psychotic nature. If they were, they had usually been dealt with in pretranscendent and functional-transcendent therapies.

Now they manifested mainly symptoms of what I later identified as a transcendence crisis. In their prefocal aspiration for a deeper transcendent lifestyle, they experienced, among other problems, difficulties in integrating their wisdom traditions with their longing for a more deeply seated form of life. While the symptoms of their crisis might seem similar to those rising from neurotic conflicts, the usual therapeutic approaches proved helpful only to a point. This experience inspired me to complement these standard approaches with a special kind of therapy based on my theory of distinctively human character and personality formation.

I discovered that my principles of transtherapy could be utilized, with the appropriate modifications, by any of the great formation traditions. I applied these principles in Holland in 1944, the last year of the war. I did the same in my transtherapeutic counseling sessions with students of the Dutch Life Schools for Young Adults.

From 1954 to 1963, my research, teaching, and publication in this field took place within the psychology department of Duquesne University in Pittsburgh. By 1963 my approach was sufficiently developed to warrant the foundation of a separate graduate institute at the same university. Initially called Institute of Man, its name was changed to the Institute of Formative Spirituality in 1978. The program I founded offered, until its closing in 1994, M.A. and Ph.D. degrees in Formative Spirituality mainly within the formation tradition of Christianity. It accredited over seven hundred students, some of whom occupy leading positions in spiritual formation in a wide variety of formation institutes in many countries. Now this work continues under the auspices of the Epiphany Association, cofounded in 1979 by myself and Dr. Susan Muto.

Bases of Transcendence Therapy

Transcendence therapy is based on two essential characteristics of human life. The first one is "form-ability," which refers to the human ability to give form in some measure to one's life.

The second is the dynamic of the ongoing formation of our distinctively human character and personality. The human person is always trying, mostly implicitly, to give form to his or her life. This formation process is *holistic* because it tends to give a unifying form to life as a whole. Holistic formation is based on the unique capacity of the human being to rise above his or her separate, particular experiences in an appraising and integrating overview. The capacity to do so is rooted in our human spirit. As I have tried to show, our spirit is our potential openness to all that is. Therefore, our spirit can also open up to the formation mystery as speaking in our personal life as well as in the formation traditions of humanity. Holistic formation can, therefore, also be called spiritual formation.

Unfolding and Formation

People, like plants and animals, unfold spontaneously. People, however, are able to reflect on their unfolding. They can observe the direction of their development. Animal life unfolds spontaneously, programmed by instinct and drive. Animals do not complement their spontaneous development by self-awareness or spiritual reflection. Not so for human life. Our life is marked by a tension between spontaneous self-unfolding and transcendent formation. This tension shapes our human character. It is the fruit of such enlightened unfolding. At certain crucial moments, this tension can increase to such a degree that it becomes a crisis of life direction. The solution of this crisis implies "going beyond" the form that life has assumed so far. What we have here is a transcendence crisis; the therapy concerned with it is what I have called "transcendence therapy." This crisis is generally known as *an identity crisis*. I initiated the term *transcendence crisis,* because it emphasizes the transcendence dynamic. I discovered this dynamic at the heart of any crisis of human identity.

Human development thus implies two poles: spontaneous unfolding of life and transforming transcendence of that unfolding. If either is neglected, human growth will be hampered or falsified.

Differentiation and Integration

The transformation of our life implies two movements: differentiation and integration. Differentiation of our character may follow the disclosure and implementation of new directives for our life. They are responses to new experiences. They result in new character dispositions. Integration complements this differentiation; it reintegrates the part of our character that was temporarily split off by the process of differentiation.

Wholesome integration depends on our transcendent view of life, our rising beyond disparate experiences and observations. Our view of transcendence is colored by our life call and the way in which it assimilates the traditions of our culture. We do so in silent discourse with the basic tradition to which we are committed.

Vitalistic View of Self-Unfolding and Formation

There is a spontaneous movement of growth in every human being. Holistic transformation should always communicate with this spontaneous, vital unfolding of our life. Formation is an ongoing dialogue or a creative tension between our transcendent life dimension as transformative and our spontaneous self-unfolding. A purely biological view of human unfolding would deny that there is a tension between vital unfolding and reflective character formation. In this view, anything new in human development is not owing to reflective character formation; it is simply the result of a vital unfolding of a kind of blueprint laid down in our biological organism. This theory of unfolding would not deny that the environment of the child has something to do with his or her growing up. But from the biological perspective the environment is utilized by the unfolding organism only in accordance with its innate biological blueprint. The environment merely offers useful matter for the preestablished unfolding organism.

Holistic transformation holds that indeed the innate laws of the organism have a basic influence on the unfolding of the person. One certainly utilizes the environment in service of organismic needs and perceptions. But the environment also contains wisdom directives expressed in the thickly woven webs of cultural symbols, languages, and customs. Cultural values and traditions have a directive influence on the life of the person. In dialogue with biological influences, they become transformative of the person as a whole in both his or her biological and transcendent abilities.

If self-unfolding were only a question of autochthonous biological growth, it would be impossible to give any form to it from a cultural wisdom perspective. The biological perception of self-unfolding in the human person is deduced from the organic growth seen in vegetative organisms. A plant's unfolding can only be influenced partially. By manipulating temperature, light, and humidity, one can affect the plant's growth. Such influences cannot change *essentially* the basic form the plant will assume once the growth process has taken its course. My holistic view of human formation holds that we in some measure can disclose and shape a unique character of life that goes beyond exclusively biological determinations. Biological determinations of development are always there; we must respect them and take them into account; but the way in which we do so depends on the distinctively human wisdom directives that we enlist in the higher unfolding of our character and personality dispositions.

If growth or unfolding were only a biological process, no transtherapy would be possible. By contrast, certain behavior therapists would argue, the only meaningful aid to growth would be the effectuation of favorable conditions that facilitate the already predetermined biogenetic form the human organism should assume. However, this kind of help would only be of minor importance. It would not offer any possibility of creative transformation of the process of biological unfolding; it would remain exterior to it. The only assistance such a behaviorist could offer the unfolding organism would be care, protection, and sustenance of the already fully determined growth process.

There would be no creative direction for any transformation in the holistic sense which my transtherapeutic approach proposes.

Transcendence Crisis

Transcendence is one of the fundamental dynamics of human formation. Each person approaches his or her full potential by transitions from lower to higher forms of life. Each transition is accompanied by a transcendence crisis.

When the climate for formation is favorable, crises of transition begin early in life. Stages of development succeed one another gradually and smoothly. Such gradual succession is unlikely in cultures that neglect spiritual formation. In these cultures, during the first half of life, people have little time or space for reflection. In midlife, however, some people come to acknowledge the limits of their vital and functional powers. Because of earlier denial or unconcern for such limits, the crisis of transcendence may find them unprepared. Striking psychological problems may result from this delayed breakthrough of a first experience of contingency.

The resulting panic in a number of people has made the transcendence crisis—for the first time in history—the focus of study for sciences other than my discipline of human transformation and transtherapy. Specialists such as anthropologists, medical researchers, psychologists, sociologists, usually refer to this phenomenon as the "midlife crisis." In my view, it is only one of many possible transcendence crises. Its aim is to foster human formation in depth. Midlife crises have emerged in Western cultures in such intensity that they have become a focus of psychological concern. For me, the midlife crisis serves only as a paradigm of all transcendence crises that serve our distinctively human emergence and participation in a life fully lived. It demonstrates the dynamics of transcendence in our human character and personality formation as a whole.

Crisis: Danger and Opportunity

Crisis, from the Greek *krineo,* literally means "a parting of the ways." The transcendence crisis denotes a parting of life directions. A person's options lie between a less or more transcendent direction of character and personality unfolding. Crisis implies stress and uncertainty. A transcendence crisis may make us tense and anxious: it means the loss of a life form with which we felt at home and the option to grow into another form as yet still foreign to us.

The Chinese have two characters for the word crisis. One character means danger, the other opportunity. A transcendence crisis gives rise to many dangers. First, there is the danger of becoming fixated, out of fear, in a no longer life-giving dimension of our existence. The reverse danger is one of overreacting against the former formation period, leading to a rejection of its authentic gains for our character growth. Second, there is also a danger of opting for a false form of life. Third, there is the danger of past unsolved problems and neuroses reappearing. Fourth, there is danger either of escape in defensive overactivity or of withdrawal to escape the crisis.

Yet any transcendence crisis means also opportunity: the opportunity to grow in our humanness, to discover more of our unique-communal life call, to integrate increasingly our life, to grow in wisdom and inwardness, to come more in touch with our deepest self.

Main Questions of a Transcendence Crisis

What does life mean? Where am I going? What form should I give to my life? Can I find help for my life direction in the formation tradition to which I am committed? These questions express human aspirations for meaning, direction, transformation, and belonging. When they are worked through effectively, they become thematic in a transcendence crisis.

To transform our life, we need to know in what direction we should go. To find that direction we should find out what life means to us and what we can learn uniquely from our chosen formation traditions about the meaning of life in general. Logically, therefore, questions concerning the meaning of life should come first; those of direction, formation, and formative tradition should follow.

In practice, the questioning of the direction arises first in a transcendence crisis or during transcendence therapy. We look into the past. *Where have we gone? What direction did our life take? Why is this direction disrupted? We look toward the future. How should we direct our life from now on?*

Detachment Crisis

Detachment is indispensable on the journey of transformation. It can be passive and external, or active and internal. Passive detachment involves the deprivation of something that has been a lively part of the structure of our character and personality. It seems to have lost its animation and inspiration. This is structural deprivation. Active detachment is a personal giving up of the inner attachment to what we have been deprived of. I call this a transforming, character-renewing deprivation.

The transcendence crisis is initiated by unavoidable deprivations owing to radical changes in life. The "letting go" of active detachment is a necessary condition for an effective solution of a transcendence crisis; it demands a working through of our feelings about structural character deprivations. Working these through on our own, sustained by transcendence therapy, consists of three phases: a phase of mourning; a phase of redirection of our thoughts, feelings, and perceptions; and a final phase of reintegration of relevant former and present life directives into a new set of character dispositions.

Transcendence therapy, therefore, implies facilitating a detachment from structural deprivations. We may have invested years of self-exertion in the structuring of our character. We found security in the familiar dispositions of our personality. Therefore, detachment may be difficult. It often leads to conflicts that give rise to psychic and psychosomatic symptoms. The detachment process during therapy entails a detachment from past emotional investments. It involves a divesting that sets us free for an investment in deeper transcendent wisdom directives.

Direction Crisis

The direction of our life is partly chosen, partly imposed. Many life directives are imposed on us by our finite life situations. They limit our possibilities of change. Our capacities are also limited; they pose another restriction on us. Initially, we tend to be unaware that our life follows directives. They are implicit as we interact daily with people, events, and things that coform our life situation. As long as effective directives flow spontaneously over into daily living, things are not problematic. Deeper reflection on where we are going seems a hindrance rather than a help in a life of functionalistic stagnation. As Socrates said, the unexamined life is not worth living. Yet many people do not examine their lives.

A special source of life direction is the directives of classical human wisdom traditions communicated by parents, teachers, preachers, friends, colleagues, political parties, school acquaintances, neighbors, and the media. They present a fund of sedimented consonant life directives. We have, as it were, a stock of transmitted life directives at hand. Out of this stock we fashion spontaneously our daily life activities. Each time we meet a challenge, we fall back, often prefocally, on this stock of directives to help us meet life's crises. Every time a directive meets a given situation consonantly and effectively, it is confirmed as part of our life direction.

Sooner or later, however, we will meet problems we cannot solve with these confirmed directives. The taken-for-granted effectiveness of our life direction is interrupted; the unproblematic now becomes problematic. If this questioning of our life direction is accompanied by stress and deprivation, it may give rise to a transcendence crisis. Shocked by the insufficiency of our guidelines, we may turn to others for help. Transcendence therapy can be helpful for people in this predicament, especially when they cannot find wise and sympathetic listeners to relieve their lonely search for appropriate directives.

The problem of a halted life direction can be solved only by taking a stand that transcends both the familiar stock of directives already available to us and the stress and deprivation of the crisis situation.

We must distinguish between the "raw material" out of which the transcendence crisis is made and the "formative focus" of this crisis. The various deprivations and stresses comprise the "raw material." The turning to a more transcendent form of life is the formative focus of this crisis. It can thus never be solved satisfactorily by isolated solutions to each distinct stress that accompanies each structural deprivation. We would be dealing with symptoms instead of with the crisis itself. What is needed is an integrated, holistic solution.

Continuity Crisis

The reorganization of our current life form does not mean that our previous life direction will be eradicated. Our core remains intact. Let me explain. There is a distinction between our lasting core form and our periodic form. A well-formed character and personality is an integrated structure of various dimensions and articulations of human living. I identified them earlier as the sociohistorical, vital, functional, functional-transcendent, transcendent, and transcendent-functional dimensions. They are differentiated in various substructures or articulations. These dimensions of the human life form and their articulations do not develop equally all at once. Each attains to a fuller development at a different period of our life. These periods of special development and dominance of a specific dimension are temporal or current phases of our unfolding personhood. They are distinguished from lasting or core dispositions embedded in our core form or basic character.

In a transcendence crisis, the dominance of past periodic forms of life is more radically questioned. As a result, our periodic and current personality may be strikingly transformed. Yet our basic character may stay relatively the same. We may come, however, to a deeper awareness than we had previously of this core of our personality.

The collapse of a periodic and current life form leads to a temporary loss of balance. Hesitantly, in the midst of trial and error, a new aspiration begins to emerge. Our heart and its corresponding character begin to open to a differentiation of dispositions. Then a process of integration sets in; wholeness is slowly restored. Our new life form—more transcendent in nature—is gradually integrated with the sediments of our previous forms of life. These sediments may enrich our continuous core, heart, and matching character. The condition of enrichment is that these sediments are compatible with our unique life direction. In the course of this process of reintegration, we become more at home with the deeper core of our existence.

Aspects congenial to our unique life form gained in former periods of growth are thus not necessarily abandoned; they receded temporarily in the background. When the new dimension—or any one of its articulations—has been sufficiently formed in us, the residues of the former dimensions and artic- ulations emerge, only to be reintegrated again into the new, more transcendent dimension. They will now be subordinated more explicitly to the transcendent dimension of human life.

The task of transcendence therapy thus implies a relativizing of former periods of self-formation; the acceptance of detachments such relativizing entails; the appraisal of our current life direction; the decision to deepen cer- tain aspects of that direction while abandoning others; the appraisal of the task of transformation in the future; and the reintegration of past and present con- genial directives. Much now present in the current direction of life may have to be abandoned during and after therapy. Still, there is much that can be retained as a basis for the formation of a new form of life. In case no transcendence therapy is needed, much of this process evolves spontaneously and prefocally without analytical deliberation. In that case, the spontaneous process is illu- mined mostly by the implicit wisdom of our unique-communal life call and of our faith and formation traditions.

Idealized Life-Directives Crisis

Our transcendent life is a life of aspirations, just as our functional life is a life of ambitions. Aspirations stimulate us preconsciously long before they appear in the foreground of our formation awareness. Early in life, our innate aspirations manifest themselves in our inclination to set up ideal life directives. Our tendency to idealize is a symptom of our distinctive human transcendency.

An ideal life directive is a wished-for event. This wish reveals a hidden awareness that we should not be satisfied with any current or periodic form of life as ultimate. A vague sense of being called to an ever more transcendent life direction gives rise to an idealized vision of what we should become. The dynamism of our transcendent aspirations—as such still unknown to us— lends color, excitement, and elation to our ideal directives. The functional real- istic dimension of our human life is still underdeveloped in our youth. At that time, the preconscious transcendent aspirations can give rise to idealized or even idolized life directives, for they are not yet modulated by the sense of concrete incarnation in daily life. A realistic appraisal of idolized directives is one of the functions of a transcendence crisis and of transcendence therapy. This appraisal should not paralyze idealism but should harmonize it both with the unique life form we are called to unfold and with the demands of daily life. If idealized life directives are not made consonant during transcendence therapy, they may simply die, and with them dies our sense of aliveness and purpose.

As children, we may be misled by our innate but untested aspirations. We believe that we can make things come true by our wishes alone. This magical deformation of childhood aspirations is partly remedied by the incarnational aspect of human life. This aspect of reasonable realism asserts itself during the periods of more functional character formation. Ideal directives are tempered by the demands of reality.

A transcendence crisis—and, respectively, transcendence therapy—tends to purify radically our idealized or idolized directives. Our formation attempts are then released increasingly from their magical component. In therapy we observe often that this rebirth is preceded by a temporary regression, marked by a feeling of insecurity. Control of life seems lost. Praise or blame of the therapist does not help. Praise is easily taken as a reassurance that the participants can still realize their unrealistic life directives. Blame may tell the opposite—that clients should feel guilty because they cannot live up to their exalted self-expectations.

Crisis of Appearances

Life-in-formation must adapt itself to its surroundings, for we live not only with ourselves but with others. This adaptation implies a guarded yet relaxed self-revelation—guarded in the sense that our inmost heart and character are vulnerable and easily misunderstood. If manifested unwisely, it might evoke disbelief, irritation, envy, ridicule, and suspicion. Moreover, an unnecessarily powerful manifestation of our uniqueness may overwhelm others, hurting their vulnerable sense of independence and self-reliance.

There must thus be a difference between who we are for ourselves and what we look like to others. Our apparent form of life should not reveal totally our unique deepest aspirations. Each current life form we develop maintains this apparent form, the way we are genuinely present to others, the limited but true face we show in daily life.

In transcendence therapy, participants become more aware of the appearances they developed in their interaction with others. They look at them more critically, realizing that some impressions they make are deceptive. They then seek to drop or replace them. In other words, they try to overcome the separation between apparent form, current form, and inmost form of life.

Therapeutic teaching and dialogue about their crisis make them gradually aware that a congenial apparent life is a selective expression of only those true aspects of their life direction relevant to the situation at hand.

The beginning of transcendence therapy is often a period of ambivalence and uncertainty. Ambiguous about their inner turmoil and desirous to hide it from themselves and others, counselees may begin to wear masks foreign to who they are. This trying out of false masks is part of the process of finding appearances that fit the more congenial life form that emerges during this crisis. If the therapy fails, participants may spend the rest of their lives in tiring attempts to keep up false appearances. Others, distraught by the disclosure of their deceptive appearances, go through a period of neglect of appearances; they may look sloppy, unsettled, unreliable, eccentric, and out of touch with their daily situational reality. In a later phase of therapy, many begin to try out new, considerate ways of presence to others, faithful to the more syntonic life form that emerges.

Clarification of Dialectics and Dynamics

Transtherapy-in-common should help clarify the common elements of formation and how they are responded to in the formation traditions to which the group is committed. The sessions should help participants to discover experientially how a personal assimilation of these foundations can be facilitated by an effective utilization of the relevant contributions of the arts and sciences. The transtherapist then assists the group in making explicit the implicit dialogue between the basic wisdom of their formation traditions as enlightened by contemporary knowledge and their personal formation.

Clarification implies a "conscientization" of the dynamism of each individual's current form of life. The dynamism of human personhood is coformed by pulsations, impulses, ambitions, and aspirations; these can be in harmony or disharmony with one another. Human personhood is sociohistorical, vital, functional, and transcendent at the same time. It becomes clear to group members how the historical dimension gives rise to pulsations, the vital to impulses, the functional to ambitions, the transcendent to aspirations. Participants should be helped to see how their current life form modulates these dynamic orientations, their hierarchy and interaction. This facilitates for them an understanding of why a particular modulation of life can become problematic in a transcendence crisis. They should realize experientially that any modulation of the dynamism of life's unfolding can be congenial or uncongenial; it is congenial in the measure that the modulation is in harmony both with the unique life form clients feel called to and with the current form their life must assume here and now. They should discover and accept the fact that nobody attains perfect congeniality, that they themselves and their transtherapist can only strive to be on the way to congenial living.

Subsequently, counselees are encouraged to clarify the cause of possible uncongeniality in their present life. This cause is self-alienation; it ensues from the structural deprivations that initiated their transcendence crisis and brought them to this kind of therapy. Reflection on alienation should make them question any excessive dominance of pulsations, impulses, ambitions, or aspirations. By implication, the structure of their current life form—its underlying attitudes, perceptions, feelings, and motivations—can become the focus of therapeutic clarification.

Clarification should be deepened by what I call in this context transcendent or formative reading therapy. The group is exposed to classical and contemporary formation writings, preferably from their own tradition. Formative reading therapy introduces them, in a contemporary and personally meaningful way, to the formative wisdom accumulated by generations.

CHAPTER 13

Process and Principles
of Transtherapy

My aim in this chapter is to propose some working principles of transtherapy that are eminently practical

Principles of Resourcing and
of Relief of Accretional Anger

A number of participants discover that their humanist or religious directives
of formation are more a result of acculturation than of a personal assimilation
of the sources of their formation tradition. Correspondingly, they realize that
the life directives obtained this way contain accidental cultural accretions.
Certain accidental accretions—now seen to be at odds with their unique life
call—were formerly communicated as essential. Sometimes such quasi foundations of formation were imposed under threat of punishment and of failure
of life. This imposition gave rise to false guilt feelings and to a deep-seated
anger, often repressed and denied. This anger tends to come to awareness during the therapy sessions. So do the deformations to which such false guilt and
repressed anger give rise.

Transcendence therapy deals with this guilt and anger by the application of
its principle of formative resourcing. This technique entails an experiential
reclaiming of the very sources of the counselee's faith and formation tradition.
Resourcing thus facilitates a working through of false guilt, of one's feelings of
betrayal, and of one's anger about superfluous traditional accretions.

Principles of Resistance-Resonance Identification
and Their Appraisal

Therapy sessions must develop the art of resistance-resonance recognition.
They should heighten the sensitivity of the participants to their own reactions
to the communications of therapist, group members, and formative readings.
Participants learn to appraise the inner sources of their resistance and reso-

nance reactions and what meaning they may have for their life direction. The therapeutic method suggests that they write down those experiences and their subsequent reflections on them. If a directive keeps drawing them and if appraisal has purified it from excessive one-sided determinants, they should be encouraged to try this directive out in daily life and to discuss the consequences of their attempt.

The spontaneous resistance or resonance reaction may be vivid or faint, depending on the temperament and character of the participant. What matters is the final effect of the appraisal. Does it make a sure and lasting impression on one? In what way is a certain directive significant for this unique person at this moment of life? Is this directive in consonance both with the fundamental wisdom of one's chosen formation tradition and one's unique-communal life call? Counselees should learn to accept that they may not yet fully grasp the meaning of a directive that touches them. They must allow the directive to disclose itself further in its own good time and in its own unique fashion.

Principle of Illusion Identification

The transtherapist dialogues with the group about the danger of illusionary resonances. Group members should become aware how self-alienating pulsations, impulses, ambitions, and aspirations may lead them to pretend that they experience the same resonance they admire in the therapist or other members of the group. This can lead to the adoption of willful life directives that make people the captives of an anxiety-evoking web of dos and don'ts. Not formation, but obsessive-compulsive deformation may be the result. Because the false self-image is a product of the ambitious ego, it may lead to envious competition. Such image envy usually betrays itself in the group discussion, creating an opportunity to work this problem through by means of experiential dialogue.

Principle of Facilitation of Self-Direction

The atmosphere fostered by the transtherapist can facilitate or stifle the participants' life direction. Participants should always be treated with dignity; they are considered people attempting to find and unfold their own form of life. The transtherapist's attitude communicates itself in subtle ways. It is perceived preconsciously by participants. Often it influences the unfolding of a participant's direction more than anything else the therapist does. The transtherapist should aspire to be a facilitator of the unique transcendence process in the participants. He or she should respect their unique-communal path of inmost becoming. At times, therapists may fall back into the gray area that includes respect and goodwill, but also a tendency to impose on others certain aspects of one's personal expression of the formation tradition shared with group members. Insofar as this is the case, the solution of participants' transcendence crises will be delayed.

Transtherapists must work through their own flights from transcendence. They should discreetly help their clients to distinguish between what might be mainly a reflection of the transtherapist's own life and what is universal and foundational for all, because of its being rooted in the mystery of formation. The mystery's loving will for them has to be implemented by each recipient of transtherapy in the light of the disclosure of their own unique-communal life call and consonant traditions.

Principle of Clarification of the Fusion Impulse

During transcendence therapy, a desire for fusion with the therapist or group members may manifest itself. This impulse is a distortion of an emergent aspiration for union with transcendent wisdom directives, symbols, and realities. This accounts for the participant's striving to lose him or herself in the idolized therapist, group member, or group. Some clients may seek desperately for the legendary guru who will save them at once from the emptiness the crisis entails. To avoid friction and to foster fusion, participants may flow with every thought and feeling of the therapist or the group without regard for their own direction. Prefocally, they try to fit their emergent life form into the contours of the life form of the therapist or of significant group members. Their praise entices them to still greater compliance; their blame signifies a break in fusion that they patch up by still greater submission. This distortion of the aspiration for transcendent union explains the magic hold of certain cult leaders. They are spellbinders for young people driven by our one-sided functionalistic culture into a transcendence crisis with which they cannot cope sufficiently.

If the fusion impulse is deep-seated or reinforced by cult leaders or others, the person should work this distortion through in private transcendence therapy before being allowed to continue the group sessions.

One means to lessen the fusion impulse is the use of sessions guided by different therapists, each representing a different style of transcendent life. This may counteract the tendency to identify transcendence with the unique mode of transcendence characteristic of only one of the therapists.

Principle of Clarification

The principle of clarification can be applied effectively if group members overcome their self-deceptions. A too-direct attack on their illusions may enhance their defenses and entrench them more deeply in their outmoded forms of life. Sensitive to their defensive self-perceptions, the transcendence therapist begins where the participants are, allowing ample time for dialogue and questions. The therapist may establish a question box in which participants can deposit anonymously some of their questions and objections. In service of right timing, therapists should read carefully progress notebooks and integration papers entrusted to them. It is essential that participants know that the therapist realizes what they are going through; the therapist must show an understanding of their feelings, an empathy with their guilt, anger, resistance, anxiety, and uncertainty. The transtherapist unveils as much or as little of their illusions and deformations as they seem able to bear at any given moment. He or she does not compel the admission of their deceptions; admissions may come long after the session, in later sessions, or in between sessions. The therapist's formative role consists mainly of creating opportunities for awareness of the real and illusory facets of participants' self-formation.

As I have said, the first step toward the solution of the transcendence crisis is an awareness of an alienation from one's current form of life. This discovery is unsettling for many. The pain of momentarily losing one's bearings cannot be prevented, even by the most understanding of therapists. It may express itself in tears, angry resistance, patterns of fight or flight, veiled attacks, or hostile questions to catch the therapist or to make him or her feel uncomfortable.

Paradoxically, all these eruptions of open hostility may be signs of progress. They signify that the implicit crisis has become explicit, that the first phase of awareness has been initiated. The therapist's behavior at this time should be marked by respect, equanimity, compassion, and empathy. Therapists should understand that the attacks are not directed at them but at what they symbolize: the inexorable demands of the unique-communal life call to be disclosed and implemented.

Principles of Transcendence Therapy and Resistance

The concrete application of the method runs, of course, into the problem of resistance. Resistance occurs not only because of the defensive self-perception, just mentioned, but also because of the newly emerging transcendent aspirations. Transcendence implies an aspiration to union with transcendent wisdom directives, symbols, and realities insofar as they invite each participant to live them uniquely. This appeal to transcendent uniqueness can be distorted by the still-dominant functional ego. This ego may tempt the person into a warped striving after absolute independence. This distortion may manifest itself in an obstinate inner closure to any appeal of the transcendence teacher. Resistance often reveals itself in slightly veiled hostile questions, in aggressive one-upmanship, or in withdrawal. It may also lead to a defensive inner focusing on any idiosyncrasy of the therapist that seems to justify the rejection of painful self-insight engendered by his or her communications.

One client, Jack, tried to defend himself against change by becoming so upset by my *way* of saying things that he became unable to hear *what* I wanted to communicate. He was so busy upbraiding me inwardly that he protected himself against any challenging directives that might have penetrated his antagonistic heart. He became caught in internal scolding. He confused transcendent self-direction and ego-direction, transcendent uniqueness and ego-centered individualism. Experiential dialogue during the sessions is meant to foster, among other things, the insight that there is only one way to preserve and enhance beneficial ego strength, while at the same time growing to union with the transcendent and its manifestation in self, people, world, and nature. That way is to analyze one's resistances and to disclose how they are rooted in a still too exclusive dominance by the sociohistorical, vital, and functional dimensions of one's character.

A special resistance may be expected in anyone in the group who has been liberated from the effects of brainwashing by cults to which they belonged. The same resistance can be found in group members who have been shocked by the dire effects of cultic brainwashing they observed in others. The sessions should clarify the nature of authentic solutions of the transcendence crisis. Such solutions grow slowly from relaxed self-insight fostered by therapeutic dialogue about one's life and about the foundations of one's formation tradition. They should be distinguished from changes that are the result of manipulative words and actions of certain cult leaders that play on affective needs, false guilt feelings, and distortions of transcendent aspirations. Their manipulations are based on a too-limited special or personal spirituality instead of being based on one that is foundational.

Resistance-Resonance Identification Principle

An effective application of this principle of identification presupposes that the participants come to recognize any affinity reaction they may experience during their therapy. The resistance or resonance reaction occurs because of an experienced affinity between, on the one hand, the communications of the therapist, of the group or the formative readings, and, on the other hand, the directives or needs for directives that play a role in one's life. The affinity reaction can be negative or positive.

The negative reaction points indirectly to one's affinity insofar as it is a defense against any directive that is rightly or wrongly experienced as a threat to one's current or deeper life direction. The need for affinity makes people yearn for affirmation in the communications of the therapist. When it does not come forth, frustration and resentment will be felt. Resistance results.

Positive reaction is the result of an experienced affinity—rightly or wrongly—felt between therapeutic communications and emergent selfhood. The participants should be helped to move from reaction to response. The affinity response may be different from the original affinity reaction that gave rise to it, for it has been transformed or affirmed by the therapeutic process of appraisal.

Formative Appraisal Principle

A responsible application of the appraisal principle requires attention to the various dimensions of appraisal. I name these fundamental, adaptive, situational, vital, functional, and transcendent.

Fundamental appraisal discerns if the negative or positive affinity reactions point to a fundamental affinity. It signifies an attunement to what the person is basically called to be and become. Adaptive appraisal discerns how the directive—to which the person does have a fundamental affinity—can be adapted to the empirical character he or she has already developed in life. Situational appraisal ponders how the new, current self that emerges can most effectively appear in the concrete life situation here and now. Vital appraisal evaluates the organismic implications of one's newly emerging form of life. Functional appraisal estimates the practical implications of the same. Transcendent appraisal discerns which transcendent directives, symbols, and/or realities can serve effectively a new form of life more in tune with one's life call and formation traditions.

This prolonged process of appraisal, fostered during the dialogical sessions, enables participants to grow from a blind affinity reaction to an enlightened, free affinity response.

Formation Exercises

The practical application of transcendence therapy includes the keeping of a progress notebook that traces how one is implementing the appraisal process. This exercise can be expanded by the use of a so-called formative reading notebook. In it the counselee records the experiences evoked by formative readings suggested, assigned, or freely chosen. An additional means to transcendent-immanent life direction can be the writing of special papers about one or the other formative life experience.These notebooks and papers enable the therapist to take into account the needs of the participants. They warn the therapist when some participant needs personal contact with him or her or another transcendence therapist. It makes the therapist aware, moreover, of symptoms of pathology necessitating other kinds of therapy.

Idolizing and Demonizing
of the Transcendence Therapist

When the phase of the explicit experience of alienation from the current form of life is worked through, a phase of anxious search for a new form follows. Initially, the participants look for this form as embodied in living persons after whom they can model themselves. The transcendence therapist often becomes the target of this search. Some may identify the therapist as the *embodiment of transcendent living, the* model of the "ideal" form of life. Such idolizing cannot be maintained indefinitely. The devotees are bound to discover the limitations of the therapist's way of life and presence. Disappointed, they may fall into the opposite exaggeration. They are tempted to demonize the therapist. In their mind and heart they begin to stress one-sidedly the flaws of his or her style of transcendence. This phase of the process, when moderated wisely, may liberate them from an excessive binding to the therapeutic teacher. It may create more room for direction by the formation mystery itself.

The therapist should realize that different participants may be at different stages of the transcendence crisis. Accordingly, he or she may be the target of a variety of projections. Some newcomers, for example, try to keep their crisis at a safe distance by attending the sessions in a state of affable, intellectual interest. They may reduce their perception of the therapist to that of an amusing, interesting, or arrogant teacher. Others, already beyond this stage, begin to experience an explicit alienation from their current form of life; they may feel lost and desperate, tearful, and anxious. They alternately hate and love the therapist for what he or she does to them. A number of them will resist the therapist stubbornly to maintain the life form with which they were at home before the crisis. Those who enter the next stage of a positive search for a more transcendent form of life may idolize the therapist, while the ones who move beyond that initial enthusiasm may perceive him or her as a fake who disappointed their expectations, a person with feet of clay who cannot live up to what is communicated.

When participants grow beyond these latter idolizing-demonizing stages of the crisis, they begin to recognize that both they and their therapist are limited, unique persons called to grow by a succession of increasingly transcendent forms of life, none of which will grant perfection to either them or the therapist. Once this stage is reached in therapy, the positive work of disclosure and implementation of the new current form can progress unhindered. Defenses and projections that prolonged the crisis no longer stand in the way.

The therapist should learn how to lessen the intensity of the feelings projected by the participants. By discussing the transcendence crises of people in general, he or she may make them ready for these experiences. By pointing out from the beginning his or her own limitations ("I am only a person who is also always in ongoing formation"), the therapist may lessen the intensity of the positive and negative projections.

Therapeutic Reading Principle

The practical application of reading therapy demands that the readings selected have proven to be helpful to persons in a transcendence crisis. The group is initiated in the art of formative reading, taught to ask themselves questions that do not emerge from literary or intellectual criticism but from the aspiration for transcendent illumination. Questions might include the following: Is there something in this text relevant to the crisis I find myself in? Do I feel reactions of negative or positive affinity, of resistance or resonance, when I am reading reflectively? How do I appraise these feelings in accordance with the kinds of rules of appraisal discussed in the sessions? How can a text that touches me be assimilated uniquely so that it begins to direct my emergent form of life?

Fostering the reading of classical formative writings, such as Thomas à Kempis's *Imitation of Christ, The Confessions of St. Augustine,* and Pascal's *Pensées,* lessens the danger that the person in crisis become the victim of passing fads, the devotee of incidental cults, or the captive of totalitarian movements. The transcendence teacher introduces the participants to the classical texts. He or she fosters an attitude of inner availability to any word of the writer that may be relevant to the search for personal transcendence. Evoked in one is a readiness to appraise such words in careful reflection. Participants are asked to note such texts in their reading notebook, along with their experiences of resistance or resonance, and to add to these their own reflections.

Therapeutic teaching makes them see that writing as a mode of self-expression tends to clarify and deepen the experiences they have to cope with as a result of both the teaching and the readings. They are encouraged to reread their notes; this may reawaken in them reverberations of the original experience and give rise to deeper understanding of why the struggling person is this way. These personal reading notes, like those in the progress notebook, provide a kind of log of the inner journey of counselees that is helpful to them and their therapist.

One important task of the formation sessions is to help people in them to shift from informational speed reading to slowed down formative reading, interspersed with pauses for reflection. They are taught to read with ease of mind, to dwell on the text leisurely, to muse about it—not to become strained, tense, or willful but to keep quietly open to sudden associations or flashes of insight. They are encouraged to maintain the inner freedom to close the book when a thought strikes home and to take time to dwell on it, sitting quietly or walking in nature. Soon participants experience that formative reading mellows the ego, not by sapping its true strength but by diminishing its arrogance, its false exclusiveness, its pretense of ultimacy.

Any diminishment of the ego's arrogance makes one more available to the transcendent life direction hidden in formation writings. The power of this direction does not depend on how much but on *how well* one reads. A single page of a book that *really* speaks to them, dwelt upon reflectively and perhaps discussed with their therapy group, gives more inner direction than whole chapters devoured eagerly but in a superficial manner. A page that resonates for a person in crisis may be of such profundity at this moment that he or she keeps receiving light and direction every time it is dwelt upon. The therapist's experience—nourished by personal interaction with people alone or in a group and by the reading of their notebooks and papers—enables him or her to advise them on literature that may be especially relevant for one at certain stages of a crisis. The formative directives disclosed this way are not necessarily new and bright ideas. The ideas may be familiar. What is new is that they light up in a personal way because of the dynamics of the transcendence crisis at work in them.

Coping with Vital Tensions

Effective application of this approach requires that the participants lessen excessive bodily strain while reading or attending the sessions. Strained functional reading, listening, or discussing does not occur just in the brain of the participants; it establishes itself in muscles and bones. This tautness reinforces in turn the tension already present in one's mind. Tight lips, clenched teeth, frowning forehead, or rigid posture may betray the tenseness of achievement-oriented people when they are reading, listening to, or discussing something. When people are tense and taut, they cannot dwell on the written or the spoken word; they are not ready to receive in gentle equanimity any directives relevant to their struggle. Hence, dialogue is encouraged about how to engage in progressive bodily relaxation, in gradual emptying of the mind so that one may unwind and feel comfortable and at ease. Participants are asked at the same time to keep in mind any text they may have found to nourish their emergent life direction. The deeper their relaxation and receptivity, the emptier their heart and mind in regard to things unrelated to this personal transcendence crisis, the closer they will be to the disclosure of directives that may carry them beyond it.

Therapeutic Limits

I have developed transcendence therapy to bring to a head a transcendence crisis, to facilitate the solution of its conflicts, and to heal in this process its psychic and psychosomatic disturbances. Transcendence therapy does not solve serious neurotic and psychotic conflicts; it presupposes their earlier solution for its own final effectiveness.

For example, a second generation of Muslims growing up in the West—without symptoms of neurosis or psychosis—may manifest psychic and psychosomatic distress that upon examination cannot be traced to a character neurosis but only to an intensified transcendence crisis.

Fiercely committed to the formation tradition of their people, averse to humanist or Christian traditions in the realm of their character formation, they still experience at a later age a conflict between the formative customs of their families with their accidental cultural accretions and their need for a cultural and personal adaptation to Western ways of formation. The structural deprivations later in life deepen their need for a more transcendent outlook on reality, but they cannot find it in family customs whose accretions veil their deeper formative meaning. When such problems seem unsolvable and the disturbances unbearable, they may find relief in a transcendence therapy group with others who share similar needs, conflicts, crises, and traditions. In the therapy sessions, they are encouraged to return creatively to the formative foundations implied in the Qur'an and elaborated experientially as wisdom of living in the formative writings of the Muslim tradition, such as some of the Sufi classics. Relevant insights of the arts and sciences help them to integrate the rediscovered foundations of their tradition with their cultural and personal formation demands.

In case their Muslim tradition as such has become a question, transcendence therapy by itself cannot answer it. Other professionals—theological, philosophical, and spiritual counselors—are the experts to be consulted then. Similarly, if serious neurotic or psychotic conflicts are the main source of their disturbances, other kinds of therapy must solve these problems before transcendence therapy can be effective.

A Case in Point

The following case presents some data on one specific group. To protect its anonymity, all indications that could lead to an identification of the group or its participants will be avoided.

The group under consideration consisted of twelve participants cared for by three collaborating transcendence therapists, each one conducting two successive periods of about fourteen weeks. These coincided with the two-semester span of the academic year of the university that employed the therapists. To enhance the probability that the participants were at least in an implicit or potential formation crisis—instead of suffering mainly from deep neurotic or psychotic disturbances—they were selected by means of personal interviews by each of the staff members. These interviews were given after the staff discussed the detailed, lengthy essay required from each applicant, which explained why he or she wanted to participate in the sessions. In this essay they were asked to tell as much about themselves as they could: family; personal and professional history; educational background; current work and future task orientation; personal motivation for coming to the sessions; and how they felt this therapy could be meaningful at this moment of their life. After the personal, separate interviews by the three staff members, a follow-up discussion by the staff of the results of the interviews led to a decision to accept or reject their application. By means of this method some serious cases of neurosis or psychosis were eliminated; these people were advised to look for other kinds of therapy. In two cases in this group, therapists failed to detect severe neurotic problems before acceptance.

As usually happens during the therapy sessions, when the potential transcendence crisis became acute, minor traumatic and neurotic problems of the past reemerged and were intense enough in five of the participants for them to be referred for appropriate treatment to a psychiatrist. This outside treatment did not interrupt, rather it complemented their participation in the group therapy. Because of this experience it has become standard procedure to inform the participants of the availability of outside therapists and to encourage them to contact them the moment they feel the need for this assistance.

Because of the therapeutic work of integration of one's formation tradition with one's unique formation history, participants of a group are selected also on the basis of their sharing in the same tradition. For this specific group, people committed to a Christian formation tradition were chosen. The results of the therapy were mixed: the two wrongly admitted, seriously disturbed people needed prolonged private therapy after finishing the sessions; of the ten remaining participants, two avoided therapeutic change by fixation on a past ineffective form of life; two others entered but did not surpass the negative phase of the transcendence crisis, as became clear in a yearly follow-up meeting of former participants. Six participants were able to bring their implicit transcendence crisis to a head and to initiate an effective solution during the therapy.

In follow-up studies a few years later, resistance participants who did not reach a full crisis awareness and its solution during the therapy admitted to having learned "a lot." It is not impossible that these lasting impressions may play some role later, in case life makes it difficult for them to avoid the transcendence crisis entirely. Staff experience with successive groups and with the failing, resistant participants in the yearly follow-up meetings increased their skill in selection and therapeutic approach. While the effectiveness of the therapy—dependent also on the free cooperation of the participants—can never be one hundred percent, the number of successful participants may increase over the years.

In this group the main obstacles against a therapeutic awareness and solution of the transcendence crisis were a lack of contact with their own experiential life; a failure of personal experiential penetration of the theological and ethical abstractions of their religion, combined with unfamiliarity with its formation tradition; a postponement of the solution of adolescent authority problems; an overdependency on affection, praise, and assurance by significant others; and self-alienation because of a somewhat hysterical or compulsive identification with social-religious slogans in regard to contemporary social or political issues.

They were invited to write so-called play papers about a significant life experience. The dialogue about these papers made participants aware of their experiential estrangement. One tragic case was that of a participant who had an extensive professional knowledge of psychology and had complemented that expertise with studies in information theology. He was so totally alienated from his own experience that it was impossible for him to report on any personal experience in his own words. If he could not use general psychological or theological categories, he panicked. The patient experienced the same blocking in the keeping of a experiential progress and reading notebook and had to be referred to private therapy.

When participants were able to come in touch with their own experience, they went through a crisis, facing for the first time feelings and conflicts they had always covered up with theological, philosophical, ethical, or psychological abstractions and generalities. Part of this crisis could be solved by bringing them in touch with the more experiential writings of their tradition, until then unknown to them, and encouraging dialogue about them. Another result of this first experiential self-awareness was a becoming conscious of an authority conflict not solved in adolescence and expressing itself now in an emotional negativity, slightly veiled in "rational" complaints about the therapists. On the other hand, their need to maintain a childlike, affective dependence made them try to seduce the therapists to parental manifestations of warmth, love, acceptance, praise. When the therapists were able to resist this seduction, some insecure participants became hostile and angry. In some failed cases, this childlike hostility syndrome would remain, as became clear in the yearly follow-up meetings. The more anxiety was evoked through the emergence of the crisis, the more some participants tried to escape change by flight into intellectual discussions. The more intellectual and academic the participant was, the more often he was tragically alienated from his experiential life. When finally the intellectualistic defensiveness did break down, the "learned" participant often became the victim of severe sexual problems. Having repressed his experiential life for so long, he did not know how to cope wisely within his formation tradition with urges he had been unaware of for so long.

An anxious clinging to a religious-social slogan was for some a last defense against facing themselves and their formation crisis. To avoid this confrontation, they would try stubbornly to replace the discussion of the inner problematics with a discussion of social problems and their solutions. It was also threatening for them to face themselves as responsible for their own choice of life instead of following blindly a slogan that pointed to a valuable social enterprise but one perhaps not valuable for them in terms of their own uniqueness. By wise application of the methods described earlier, at least six members of the group were able to break through their compulsion for praise and affection, their self-alienating social slogan identification, and their intellectualistic defenses; they were able to grow in openness to their experience and to the deeper life meanings of their tradition, to make explicit their formation crisis, and to find a solution of this crisis in a more mature and open form of life.

CHAPTER 14

An Illustration
of Transtherapy

I want to illustrate form-traditional conflict, its disclosure and transcendence, in the life of one of my counselees, a woman who came to me specifically for transcendence therapy.

Formation History

Mary had been raised in a modern American family by sophisticated Catholic parents, both of whom were college professors. While being committed to a Catholic formation tradition, they also completely identified with the artistic and scientific form traditions highly regarded in the state university systems in which they were teaching. They sent Mary to a Catholic boarding school to make sure that the Catholic formation tradition would be instilled in her. Mary was reared in this school in a simple, devotional life-style. Her father came from an Italian American family with a radical conservative form tradition marked by a paternalistic, authoritarian life-style. As a result, the father's guiding core disposition was law; unquestioning obedience was prefocally linked in his mind with divine authority. This made the father, in relationship to his wife and children, domineering, critical, and inconsiderate.

Mary, who was bright, reflective, and well read, was subjected at the same time to strong rationalistic-progressive and radical-conservative dispositions both in her family and in her boarding school. Later in college and graduate school, her exposure to equally rationalistic and scientistic formation traditions served to make the corresponding dispositions dominant. Conflict between the two sets of dispositions was unavoidable. It was compounded by the radical-traditional father–daughter relationship. Questioning the father's style would be tantamount to giving up her strong identification with her father that had become part of her own vulnerable core identity or character form. Rather than having to face this threat, she lived for a long time in the refusal to acknowledge the inner conflict she felt prefocally between formation traditions.

Mary's mother went along with her dominant husband's life directives. Mary herself had internalized a radical-conservative formation tradition. Hence, there was in her none of the typical adolescent's rebellion against parenting or against the directives of other authorities. Neither did she attempt to find herself by searching for her own life call and its subtle announcement in some of her own hidden character dispositions.

To understand Mary's predicament, we must realize that her parents' secondary traditional dispositions were contemporary, scientistic, and rationalistic. At the same time, their primary traditional dispositions were radically conservative. These permeated the structure of the father–daughter relationship. Throughout childhood and adolescence, Mary, in faithfulness to the radical conservative tradition of her family, had been deferential, overly obedient, and submissive. She tried to please her parents in order to gain their love and confirmation. She felt also compelled to be a good reflection of the family among other adherents of the same conservative formation tradition. For Mary, these were essential elements of her "familial interform" to be mirrored in her own core or character form.

Multilayered Core Form

Thus, a multilayered organization of the core form developed in Mary. The secondary dispositions and directives of her heart and corresponding character belonged to a rationalistic and scientistic form tradition. The problem is that at the same time the affective structuring of her basic traditions remained strongly radical-conservative. These latter dispositions had become internalized. The affective structuring of the radical-conservative father–daughter relationship had deeply affected her character.

In this type of parent–child interformation, the father tends to be somewhat distant and aloof. He may appear to his children as an authoritarian disciplinarian as well as a man responsibly concerned.

Mary manifested in turn the deference and submission to her father that was deemed appropriate by their kind of tradition. The same internalized tradition directed her to curb any direct expressions of anger, hostility, irritation, or frustration. Neither did she, even in adolescence, try to give form to a more personal assertion of a unique, individual communal life call. At that time, in keeping with this tradition, she tended to idolize her parents. Such idolizing protected her prefocally against secondary form traditions taking over; it prevented her from acknowledging the pain of anger she felt because of the absolutized parental dominance of her life. Idolizing also served her heightened need for continual confirmation by her parents—a need that was intense because her own inner core affirmation of her life was weak. Affirmation should come from one's own belief in one's unique-individual communal life call.

The radical conservative tradition can give rise to an apparent parental life form of dignified distance and a certain aloofness. This made Mary strive even more to gain evidence of her parents' appreciation and confirmation. The parents' appreciation became the fragile foundation of Mary's self-appreciation, their confirmation the shaky ground of her self-affirmation.

Collapse of the Core Form

Mary might well have become simply one more member of a class of women with an advanced education rooted in a radical-conservative way of life. For Mary this was not to be. A few years into graduate school, while she was studying psychology, the secondary layer of core dispositions, also initiated by her parents, began to surface. She broke through the prefocal refusal to face her latent anger, frustration, and hidden ambivalence. She began to delve into the difference between three types of tradition: an extreme radical-conservative, a less conservative, and a liberal one.

Mary's core form fell apart. All that the parental tradition stood for came into question. Her whole sense of having a life direction went up in smoke. Her idolized parental figures fell and broke into pieces. Mary's sense of self-appreciation, which had been linked almost absolutely with parental appreciation and confirmation, became shaky. Her power of appraisal was thrown into question. An inner sense of failure and loss swept over her. She felt rage at her parents for not having left her enough space for self-unfolding. She felt that they had sowed in her heart seeds of ambiguity. She realized that they had initiated her at the same time in a strong radical-conservative and an equally intense rationalistic-scientistic tradition.

False Identification of Faith and Form Traditions

Mary tried to reintegrate her core form first by rejecting outright her radical-conservative tradition. She chose not only to eradicate these feelings but also to dismiss the underlying faith tradition in which they were rooted.

During her transtherapy sessions, she began to realize that she was not experientially aware of my distinction between an underlying fundamental faith tradition and its numerous possible formation traditions. Rejection of one of these form traditions should not necessarily imply rejecting the underlying faith tradition. Neither should it mean that all other possible form traditions within the same faith tradition are equally unacceptable.

During the period when Mary rejected her original tradition, she substituted for the idolized parental figures new idolized figures, such as philosophers and psychologists. Their ideological traditions with their underlying assumptions or belief systems represented for her the secondary dispositions of her core form. This constellation of her secondary dispositions had now become the primary or baseline of her changing tradition pyramid. By internalizing these figures as part of her core form, she tried to bolster her shattered sense of self-appreciation. She was especially fond of authors who like herself rejected everything religious or transcendent and became completely absorbed in secular aestheticism, philosophism, and scientism.

When she came for therapy, she was under enormous strain. She tried to contain the anxieties evoked by a growing awareness that in the long run her new basic dispositions did not seem able to heal her inner core or character fragmentation. She felt threatened by the suspicion that the absolute dominance of her core form by these new idolizing dispositions would once again lead to profound disillusionment. She began to fear that her turn to pretranscendent secularism had been extreme. She was soon confronted by the question of whether or not any tradition could give meaning to her life. If not, where was she to turn? How could she escape despair or utter cynicism? So depressed did she become that she experienced fleeting thoughts of suicide.

In the meantime, Mary became semiparalyzed in her functioning as a graduate student. I helped her to focalize and vocalize what she was going through in terms of formation dynamics. Mary began to realize that she had sought the healing of her broken core form in pretranscendent secularistic traditions only. She acknowledged that her newly idolized core dispositions, directives, ideas, symbols, affects, images, memories, and anticipations were still at war with the old shattered traditional forms by which she used to live. This conflict revived in her the awareness of the seriously fractured core form she thought she was on the way of healing.

By the same token, she had no illusions about returning to her parental form tradition. She saw that she had mistakenly identified it as the only possible form-traditional expression of her underlying faith tradition. As yet, she was not sufficiently aware of the other possible form traditions emerging from her original faith tradition and lived by significant numbers of its adherents.

Healing of the Fractured Core Form

Prolonged transcendence therapy enabled Mary to heal partially the fracture in her core form. The basic strategy of the therapy was to assist her to enter the path of gradually going beyond the absolutized "either-or" she felt between two differently appreciated formation traditions and their corresponding core dispositions. This process gave her a transcendent vantage point. It enabled her to look in a more detached manner on the two traditions she had learned to appreciate, at least in part, but not to integrate.

Form traditions are handed over in a process of interformation. In that process the giver and the receiver are influenced by the particular affective tensions and dynamics that accompany each relationship. In early sessions, Mary had to explore the prefocal interforming relationships she had with her parents. She had to face her angry, resentful feelings about the distorted version of the radical-conservative form tradition she had absorbed from them. She had to ask herself what limitations resulted from this absolutizing of one out of numerous possible formation traditions? What additional distortions were owing to the idiosyncratic modulations of this group tradition by her parents, by their community of adherents, and by herself?

Mary had to do the same in regard to her new set of exclusive formation traditions and the corresponding core dispositions. The distorting changes were initiated by idolized teachers, friends, and authors who handed them over to her. She had to examine what her life call seemed to disclose at this moment. She had to ask herself if and in what way she could harmonize these traditions and dispositions with the present disclosure of this call.

In later sessions, Mary explored these questions: If and in what sense could she discover and appreciate fundamental and lasting truths, dispositions, and directives in any of the traditions she had internalized? How could these be harmonized in some measure with one another and with her life call experientially? Then she had to ask herself how she could integrate the mutually compatible elements of different traditions and of her life call in an internally consonant core form or character at whose center would be a less divided "I."

Consonance between Strivings

In our final sessions, Mary had to deal with the issue of consonance between pretranscendent and transcendent strivings. She was now able to realize that the distorted version of the formation tradition handed over to her was fraught with pretranscendent facets that were insufficiently transformed by the transcendent dimension of life. Neither were they fully consonant with the foundations of the underlying belief system. She also saw the bad effects of idolizing her parents. She came to acknowledge that later, in overreaction to her past, she had also idolized representatives of the opposite form traditions. She had almost coercively espoused excessively liberal teachers and authors as ideal representatives of secularistic form traditions. This move proved to be an obstacle to her free, open presence to the mystery of formation and its actual and potential messages.

Coercive Neuroformational Dispositions

Mary could now relate her semiparalysis, her fractured core form, and her divided core "I" to her coercive neuroformational dispositions. I use the term "neuroformational" in my personality theory to point to the "formational" or "forming" influence of our autonomous nervous system on the automatic, repetitious facet of our formation dispositions and directives. This influence can be either coercive or under the control of our insight and freedom. To the degree that neuroformational dispositions are coercive, they block, among other things, our path to empirical-experiential transcendence.

Such compelling dispositions and their directives are programmed into our autonomic nervous system. They can be activated by certain triggers. Among these are the distortions of the formation traditions that inserted these dispositions in our core form or character in the first place. This happened usually early in life. Once they are prefocally activated, they compel us to execute routinely their form directive patterns. They represent dissonantly our form traditions and their underlying belief systems. They masquerade as paths to a peace and happiness that only transcendent freedom from idol making would render possible.

Here my concept of the fantastic or phantom "I" comes into play. This phantom "I" is rooted in the self-centered, quasi-foundational life form. In this case, it gives rise to only fantasies of peace and happiness. These quasi forms of peace are marked by exaltation, instability, fleetingness, pretentiousness, and repeated interruption by spiritual, not necessarily clinical, depression.

In my formation theory of personality, four dimensions of the human life form—sociohistorical, vital, functional, and, now I would add, functional-transcendent—are pretranscendent. Every time Mary felt caught in one or the other of her neuroformational patterns, she tried to find its origin in the four possible obsessive strivings emerging from these dimensions. These strivings are the absolutized security and conviviality striving of the sociohistorical dimension; the absolutized gratification and sensation striving of the vital dimension; and the absolutized satisfaction, control, power, and self-actualizing striving of the functional dimension. The fourth striving, that of the functional-transcendent dimension, is to control and manipulate in a self-actualizing fashion the satisfying side benefits of the beginnings of a more transcendent life. Mary tried to pinpoint the distortions, selections, and rationalizations of the formation traditions that she had used prefocally to justify any or all of these coercive strivings and their dispositions in her neuroformational system.

Gnostic Interlude
Many people on the road to transcendence may be able to identify with Mary's first steps, for they were dominated by the functional-transcendent dimension. This dimension represents a compromise between the transcendent, traditional dispositions of the core form, which are basic, and the secularistic dispositions inserted in one's heart through pretranscendent

self-actualizing traditions. This compromise is attractive. It is clothed in spiritual symbols and effective techniques. It offers a quasi integration of true transcendence and the pretranscendent life. It has effective results. A certain peace, relaxation, and equanimity can be attained on the lower levels of transcendence by self-actualization techniques. Seduced by these symbols, by pretentious abuse of traditional language, and by relaxation techniques and their effects, one may stay at this lower level and subsequently block the path to higher transcendence.

Mary found herself caught in the tendency to make gnostic transpersonal psychologies, such as those of Carl Jung, Joseph Campbell, and Roberto Assagioli, or aspects of New Age spirituality, the be-all and end-all of the transcendent life. By subtly idolizing them, she silenced the unique call of the spirit in her life. This kind of gnostic transcendence blocked the way to ultimate transcendence. It took many sessions of transtherapy to help her to escape this powerful and insidious trap and to convert to the truly transcendent path. She had to catch herself every time she became ensnared again in either popular functionalistic or gnostic transcendent formation traditions.

Closure of Transtherapy

Mary herself knew when it was time to bring her transcendence therapy to closure. In the light of her now purified tradition pyramid, she felt ready to continue on the road to an increasingly consonant core form and to an integrated transcendent-pretranscendent core "I." She had regained confidence. She felt a resurgence of renewed formation energy. She knew she had attained a wiser appraisal disposition in regard to the formation traditions that might influence her life.

Of course, each transcendence therapy process has its own unique demands and rewards. For one thing, Mary was not only intellectually but also aesthetically and artistically gifted. This prevented the formation in her of what I call a one-sided functionalistic "I," yet it tempted her to adopt what I term a gnostic "I."

In contrast to Mary, most Western people who feel the need for transcendence therapy have been influenced prefocally by functionalistic form traditions that emphasize the bureaucratic, quantitative, and unimaginative. As a result, the core "I," the "I" of the heart, has been poorly formed. In some, this "I" at the center of the heart may seem to be almost absent. Insofar as they still have a core "I," it is heavily influenced by the functional coformant of their lives and traditions.

In such cases, transcendence therapy implies that the counselees make focal in their conscience the prefocal domination by functionalistic traditions. It calls for the awakening of the latent need for the "I" of the heart to be increasingly consonant with the transcendent "I" of our unique-communal life call. The functionalistic "I" is the "I" of only one dimension. Because of its dimensional one-sidedness, it cannot be integrated as such into the centering "I" of the integrational core or heart of human life. People must unmask the functionalistic directives of their life. The coldness and thinness of their core "I" must be thawed and expanded by personalized directives of traditions that foster a warm, many-sided openness to their field of presence and action without falling into gnosticism. Only then is their heart in the right mood and disposition to open up to the deepest transcendent "I" of the life call.

Mary's literary bent proved to be a great help on her further journey. She began to write about her struggles with her internalized form traditions. Artistic creativity enabled Mary to give form to new core consonances in her life in the act of communicating and articulating her own search.

Many people are coping with similar crises. Most of them have been exposed to the same significant traditions in their shared formation field. Readers of stories like Mary's benefit profoundly because such sharing makes focal what they may be coping with in a far less alert manner.

CHAPTER 15

The Goals of Transcendence Therapy from the Viewpoint of Formation Science

People seek transtherapy because they feel as if something is missing; they are dissatisfied with life; their existence seems dreary, meaningless, without verve and inspiration; they may have been in trouble with people around them in the family or in their place of work. Within themselves, they may suffer from disturbing symptoms, which diminish their effectiveness.

I can briefly summarize their feelings and symptoms by saying that they have lost the ability to appraise and implement the unique call of their life within their here-and-now situation. Therefore, I need to create an atmosphere that will enable them to understand themselves as called within their surroundings to face and accept their personal responsibility for transcendent formation.

Openness to Consonant Guilt

Guilt is consonant when it is in tune with all the spheres and dimensions of one's field of life as appraised in the light of one's transcendent faith and formation tradition. People must recognize and work through their consonant guilt. They should be liberated from guilt that is dissonant because it is not in tune with reality; it is rooted in despair and in a false perception of the divine. During this process of growth, I as transtherapist should be careful not to burden the other with my personal feelings of guilt, with my own expectations, or with norms that dominate the special form tradition to which I have personally committed myself.

Consonant guilt, responsibility, and commitment must grow out of the true, tradition-enlightened experiences of counselees. They must find their own personal response to lived reality and its myriad traditions, independent of my response to my reality and my tradition. They cannot become "whole" if they do not discover their own decisive answer to their own life, if they strive instead to incorporate personal answers of mine that may be alien to their own unique-communal life call and tradition. If they would blindly adopt my style of life, it could foster in them a harmful split between their own unclarified calling and tradition and my superimposed call and tradition. They can reach wholeness only if they discover their own consonant guilt, which may be covered over by layers of dissonant guilt. They have a right to their own true guilt in dialogue with their faith and form tradition. Transcendence therapy should enable them to discover their personal and social guilt insofar as it is linked with an experience of responsibility for their own becoming in the light of the transcendent formation tradition to which they are committed.

Acceptance of the Transcendence Dynamic

Transtherapy will enable people not only to discover their own true guilt and responsibility but also to experience that life is animated by a transcendence dynamic that fosters formation, reformation, and transformation. The transcendence dynamic may liberate them from the paralyzing influence of a one-sided mode of life, or it may lead to the formation of new consonant modes. This dynamic also inspires the integration of old and new modes of being into a more happy and harmonious style of life.

Liberation from obvious dissonance is characteristic of the initial phase of transtherapy. The discovery of hidden sources of dissonant modes of being and the development of new consonant ones are prevalent in the second period of therapy. The integration of newly emerging with past consonant dispositions of life into a new life form appears more clearly at the end of the therapeutic process. Of course, these three movements of growth are not mutually exclusive. On the contrary, they coincide. We can say only that one or the other is more dominant at a certain stage or moment of the process.

The Goals of Transcendence Therapy

People's experience that life is dynamic, growing, and becoming implies acceptance of the fact that their personality will never be "finished" or "totally understood" or ever "without mystery or problem." They begin to realize that they will always be on the road, always travelers, adventurers, pioneers, people who never reach the far West of their full existence. The final aim of transtherapy is, thus, not a state of static well-being but the full acceptance of a dynamic life opening up continually to new horizons.

Such therapy will enable people to adapt themselves to their emerging possibilities and to realize these in their lives. Neither therapist nor counselee can predict the appeals of tomorrow. But such therapy can create an openness toward the transcendence dynamic as well as a readiness to listen to any challenges that may announce themselves. This readiness implies the insight that one's actual life form is not fixed but truly changeable.

Faithfulness to the Infrastructure,
Flexibility toward the Superstructures of Human Life

When I use the term "actual life form," I mean the structural totality and specificity of the dispositions of life that people have formed up to this moment. They may mistakenly assume that their personality is fixed forever. They may perceive themselves as a thing molded once and for all. They may use this belief in unchangeability as an escape from the burden of becoming.

Transtherapy should enable them to become aware of what is consonant and dissonant in this view of themselves. Various dispositions of life are possible. They compose the core of one's being, its character. These dispositions should be in tune with one's life call and tradition as well as with the various life situations and transitions in which persons have to disclose and implement this call. For every person is endowed with a unique potential infrastructure of life which can be realized in a wide variety of superstructures.

The basic shape or infrastructure of one's life cannot be changed without violating one's unique-individual makeup. What can change, however, is the concrete realization of this hidden structure. People suffer because of their failure to express in their character or core form what they fundamentally are. The constellation of their actual form of life and their dispositions is dissonant. They may have internalized elements of popular incompatible traditions that are at odds with what they basically are. This disconnection makes it impossible for them to be who and what they should be.

A constellation of adopted dispositions may cover up the unique style of being that is meant for one from the start. No therapy, to be sure, can give people an exhaustive understanding of all that they are called to be. Transtherapy, however, may enable them to discover and realize themselves increasingly in the plurality of encounters that comprise their daily life in the world.

One of the bases of the unique style of each human life is that each person has a typical constellation of drives, impulses, and basic motives characteristic of our species. These fundamental forces are present in every human being at least potentially. Their relative strength and actual intensity, their mutual relationships and fundamental configurations, differ from person to person. I do not speak here about differences because of environment, formation traditions, and personal life situations, but about those more basic differences given from the outset as the raw material of human personalities.

It is true that every person must eventually decide on the fundamental orientation of his or her own life in the light of one's successive life situations and formation traditions. Yet the specific style of one's life, or the concrete embodiment of one's call, may in part emerge from each one's given constellation of forces or strivings. I have identified these in my formation science as pulsations, pulsions, ambitions, aspirations, and inspirations. Openness to both the life situation and the configuration of these forces is meant to lead one gradually to a more consonant and unique style of life.

For this reason, every theoretical simplification or reduction of the complexity of human life is potentially harmful. This does not mean that scientific theories are useless. On the contrary, each scientifically acceptable hypothesis enriches therapists with a new possibility for understanding certain realms of experience in their counselees. It expands their arsenal of tools of appraisal. The transcendent disposition in transtherapy, however, implies the use of these tools and acquired sensitivities within an infinite variety of possibilities of transcendent-immanent human formation.

For example, a counselee's preoccupation with study can be an expression of sexual curiosity, a compensation for a feeling of inferiority, an escape from social life, sheer pleasure in the intellectual dedication to a cause, or a form of obedience to parents, school, or other institutions. This involvement in study may also be the result of an irreducibly unique predisposition. In the latter case, it is a natural expression of the unique personality structure of this counselee and not merely a reactive phenomenon. Of course, many such motivations may be potentially or actually present in a counselee. In this case, they may influence one another. Such influence of a motivation does not mean that I can a priori consider one motivation and its contribution to a subsequent mode of life as merely derivative of another motive, which gives form to yet another facet of life. For example, sexual curiosity may contribute to a more generalized intellectual curiosity and influence its development. This does not mean, however, that one can reduce intellectual curiosity to mere sexual curiosity.

Liberation from Psychologism, Public Image, and Scientism

Persons who come for transtherapy today are frequently influenced by certain reductive concepts of fields such as psychology, psychiatry, sociology, anthropology, social work, or education popularized by the mass media. They may not realize sufficiently that these various theories reveal only certain possible sides of human life and by no means all possible aspects. Neither may they be aware of the underlying assumptions that may be at odds with their call and tradition. As a result, they may begin to see themselves almost solely in the light of one or the other clinical, sociological, or educational theory. Such a narrowed consideration will lead necessarily to a blind spot for those possibilities of character unfolding that are not emphasized by the particular theory in question. Many people are crippled in their formation by the influence of pop-ularized psychology, psychiatry, sociology, and education. Therefore, one of the long-range aims of transtherapy is to liberate people from the tyranny of popular concepts which in some instances, like a thick fog, may render wise self-perception impossible.

Another purpose of my transtherapy is to enable counselees to free them-selves from what I refer to as the despotism of the public image. Contemporary civilization makes people strongly aware of their public image or apparent form. Government and industry, schools and social institutions, the worlds of entertainment and even of religion are overly conscious of how to appear win-ningly in the eyes of others. The promotion of an attractive appearance can become a coercive concern, an anxious preoccupation. People overconcerned in this way may cease to be themselves. They care more about how they look to others than about what they are. They are more sensitive to the preferences of bosses, peers, and competitors than to their own feelings. They are inspired by the ideals of the majority rather than by those that are in harmony with their own deepest calling and tradition.

If the demon of public image takes possession of persons, they may be unable to distinguish between their own feelings and the urges of the crowd. Counselees may have risen to the heights of administrative, academic, or polit-ical success by cleverly catering to collectivities or to those who wield power. They may not be consciously aware that they have paid a high price for this popularity—their own priceless life call. The more intelligent, creative, and idealistic they are, the deeper they will be disturbed by this prostitution of their talents. Their most profound self may be compared to a call girl available to the best-paying patron and obligingly conforming to his every wish.

Preoccupation with public appearances has become a cultural disease, one that has led many potentially creative persons to a well-paid, apathetic, impov-erished life of quiet desperation. Many men and women who suffer from living a meaningless existence, high in status and possession, low in value, present themselves for transtherapy. Its overall aim should be to help them to discover their own life call and the wisdom of their tradition under the mask of their public apparent form.

Danger of Scientism

I consider another aim of transtherapy to be the gradual growth of a disposi-tion I would call "patient self-presence." Many people come into therapy with the fantasy that they will enjoy flashes of insight that will lead to sudden changes in their lives. This expectancy of swift improvement as a result of therapeutic manipulation is owing not only to magical thinking but also to the scientistic attitude fostered in our civilization. Physical science, the exploration and manipulation of physical objects, is desirable in its own realm. But scientism, or the expansion of the methods of physical science to nonphysical subjects such as human life and its mysterious call, is most undesirable. This type of reductionism is not a clearly formulated doctrine but an all-pervasive formation tradition assumed especially by those who know little about science itself. This form traditional scientism leads its victims to manipulate their lives as if they were physical objects, algebraic equations, or experiments in chemistry.

Such people may come into therapy convinced that their main problem is that they have not yet found the efficient method or technique for successful self-manipulation. Their scientistic disposition of life leads them to expect a fast diagnosis and an effective "recipe" for a swift metamorphosis of their personality. One of the chief things they have to learn is that one cannot deal with a dissonant disposition as with a diseased leg or liver, that an attempted equation of spiritual with physical healing is misleading.

In the long, sometimes tedious, process of transtherapy, counselees experience that an unwholesome life disposition is usually formed by an accumulation of insufficiently appraised experiences over a long period of time. They realize slowly and gradually that the manifold experiences which gave rise to this unsavory disposition were not worked through at the moment they were internalized. They were not freely and wisely appropriated. The counselees now gain insight into the complex structure of their core or character form of life. They begin to realize that to grow beyond incompatible core dispositions requires an arduous and patient dialogue with the myriad ways such dispositions are manifest in countless concrete situations.

Transtherapy fosters the development of the ability for persevering dialogue with the disclosures of one's call in daily life in the light of one's transcendent formation tradition. Another one of the long-range aims of transtherapy, therefore, is to prepare counselees to be patiently present to their dispositions as manifested in their formation field. This art often remains unlearned in our technological society.

Acceptance of Conflict

I do not believe that transcendence therapy can solve all conflicts and problems of counselees. This therapy helps people to uncover their unique fundamental structure and life call in the light of their freely accepted and practiced transcendent formation tradition. They learn to commit themselves to the implementation of this structure. They begin to transcend the spurious and dissonant structures that superseded their life call. This strengthens them against both the demon of the public image and their scientistic inclination to self-manipulation. They develop from mechanics of life into living persons, but this does not prevent contradictions and conflicts within their personality.

Contradiction and conflict are potentially present in the basic given structures of human life. People can develop a wide variety of dispositions of compatibility with their formation field. They should do so on the basis of their founding life form and chosen tradition. But these dispositions must be balanced and integrated with one another. The aim of transtherapy is not to solve all conflicts that may emerge during this work of integration. It is to help people to see and experience these opposed dispositions more clearly within themselves. Transtherapy brings to light what one is and sets one on the path of becoming what one is called to be. It changes neither the unique and fundamental structure of one's life form nor its inherent or acquired conflicts and contradictions.

CHAPTER 16

Core Dispositions at the End of Transtherapy

The end of therapy is the beginning of new conflict. Once one has come to be more oneself through transtherapy, one is able to discover, maintain, and restore the balance between the opposing forces characteristic of one's unique personality. A counselee may discover, for example, a disposition to overdependency which may not be reducible to any other "cause" in one's past or in one's present environment, but which is truly inherent in the very structure of one's pretranscendent life form. One must take a stand toward this inclination and learn how to live wisely with this particular expression of oneself in one's formation field. In this sense we may say that it is an aim of transtherapy to initiate consonant conflict to replace the dissonant conflicts of a counselee's past.

Having stated these general aims, I want to turn to a few specifics that will help transtherapists to recognize the main core dispositions their counselees may manifest after effective transtherapy.

Formative Candor

I consider it one of the long-range aims of transtherapy that counselees will have developed the disposition to be true to the formation mystery, to themselves, to their life call, to their chosen tradition, and to others. Counselees should be able to recognize their own transcendent and pretranscendent identity. They should know what they think and feel about the various aspects of their formation field and how it ties in or does not tie in with their call and tradition. This does not mean, of course, that they take into account only their own perceptions. Ultimately, only they themselves must make the final decisions in dialogue with their own well-appraised experiences. But perception should be enriched, deepened, and tempered by a personal appraisal of the insights of others, understood in the light of the basic formation tradition to which one is committed.

Candor implies that one has learned in transtherapy to abdicate all dispositions, attitudes, actions, customs, words, and expressions that are experienced as untrue. It is a readiness to diminish in one's life the tight hold of security systems one has developed in anxious self-protection. This task is never finished. The oversensitive security systems of a fear-filled human life form always remain available in the personality. They are triggered when the person feels threatened. So long as one does not develop this fundamental and courageous candor, one will not be able to achieve a consonant human life, free from excessive fear.

Why is it so difficult for us to abdicate all that is not truly us? I think that a deep formation anxiety makes us hold on desperately and tenaciously to our oversensitive security dispositions. Deep down, we are aware that up to now our real transcendent life form could not express itself, smothered as it was by the powerful security dispositions of our pretranscendent life. We cling desperately to apparent forms that hide our unacknowledged deficiencies. Prefocally we fear somehow that the loss of our "borrowed feathers" would reveal us in the ugly nudity of a deeply dissonant personality.

On a profound level, this perception gives us the anxious feeling that we are entering an emptiness in which we will lose all our moorings and certitudes. Thus, our resistance to candid self-appraisal is not so much a matter of bad will as of anxiety at seeing and revealing ourselves as small, limited, weak, and insufficient. Everyone wants to be somebody, a person who really counts. We are most afraid perhaps of the possible discovery that we are really not that important. It would be easier, perhaps, for us to accept ourselves as bad than as insignificant. Frequently, our disposition to attract the attention of others arises from a coercive need to be confirmed as somehow important in spite of our secret self-doubts. We want the approval of others to ward off the anxiety that we might discover our own insignificance. Our need for praise may not come from a real belief in our own importance. We may feel prefocally so unimportant and meaningless that we are overwhelmed by the constant fear that others may see us in the same way if we surrender our make-believe dispositions, attitudes, and behavior. Our secret perception of ourselves as small and worthless opens up for us a formation field in which people are constantly on the verge of discovering us. It is understandable that this fear leads us to a forced, spasmodic concentration on our own apparent behavior, words, and expressions.

Therefore, when we begin to give up our dissonant apparent form, our consonant apparent form becomes immediately free, more relaxed and natural, less tense and guarded. This breakdown of the old dissonant apparent form is already in and by itself an expression of our new form of life. It is true that at first we may appear less forceful and certain than before. However, the strength we now show, no matter how little, is truly the force of our own foundational life form. This small but true vigor is far stronger than our forced, artificial, self-conscious apparent form of the past. Our make-believe strength may indeed have seemed impressive to weak people in our environment. This new consonant strength, when we maintain it after therapy, will gain in depth. It will be free from the anxiety that invested so much energy in former supersensitive guardian dispositions in which our deceptive apparent form was rooted. Sooner or later, the consonant strength, which is truly ours, will influence others far more than the former show of force or cleverness. It will be more attractive and effective than our past pretense of power and unshakable self-reliance. The moment we no longer fear to look small, worthless, and unimportant on the pretranscendent level of life, we begin to blossom in the light of our uniquely important transcendent destiny. The courage to believe in who we most deeply are as rooted in a loving mystery endows us with the radiance of a significant, inalienable life call.

The basic candor gained in transtherapy also enables us to admit our own mistakes easily and swiftly. In the past we were afraid that any mistake we made or admitted would jeopardize our existence. We feared that it would destroy our esteem in the eyes of others. We were inclined to identify our whole personality with our success in society. If anyone attacked our work or devaluated our contribution, we experienced it as an attack on our personality as such. We felt threatened in the core of our being.

It is one of the long-range aims of transtherapy to make it possible for counselees to appraise their mistakes and failures as formation opportunities, as signposts of improvement and growth. They must be able to risk mistakes and to accept the consequences of these mistakes without anxiety, bitterness, and resentment. One direct result of this newly acquired core disposition will be a gain in courage, creativity, and productivity. For creativity and effective presence in one's formation field are frequently blocked by fear of failure. Creativity can flourish only when a person feels free to be found imperfect. Many people lead ineffective lives because they feel compelled to give in as soon as they blunder and are blamed for their failings.

Of course, it will take a lifetime to make concrete in daily endeavors this basic candor that people have developed in transtherapy. In the realization of this candid self-awareness, they will discover time and again pretranscendent resistances in themselves. Transtherapy should have established a transcendent readiness to cope with these resistances, a willingness to be neither more nor less than one really is. It should enable one to be faithful to the task imposed by one's formation field, one's life call, and one's basic faith and formation tradition.

Consonant Commitment

The readiness to listen to the appeal of the formation field in the light of one's formation tradition implies commitment. Consonant transcendent commitment means that we have given up our self-centered, autarkic outlook, that we have put ourselves at the disposal of the demands of our founding life form and our unique life call. This does not mean that we surrender ourselves blindly to others; rather, it means that we are willing to live a project of life that, according to our best appraisal, is in tune with the demands of our formation field and tradition. Instead of saying, "I decide what I like to do," we now say, "I personally decide on what is asked of me by my formation tradition in my formation field." What we give up is not our own judgment, insight, freedom, and responsibility, but our pretranscendent self-centeredness. We refuse to make pretranscendent concern the last and only criterion of our life call and subsequent project. Rather, we respond freely to the tradition-enlightened formation field in which we find ourselves. We do so in harmony with our own life call. This implies the experience that there is something higher than we are. In other words, there is a suprapersonal element in our surrender. This surrender liberates us from our pretranscendent prison. It integrates us within reality, cosmos, history, community, and transcendent tradition.

The commitment at which transtherapy aims does not find its source in a greater confidence in one's isolated self. On the contrary, consonant self-confidence is more the outcome than the source of consonant commitment. Free and relaxed self-confidence is rooted in the experience of one's integration in life, in culture and society, in nature, in the world of a suprapersonal tradition, in one's founding life call and its mysterious ground. If counselees are religious, they may experience self-confidence because of their rootedness in the mystery of the Divine. Consonant commitment diminishes dissonant anxiety. Consonant freedom is based not on belief in one's own strength, but on joyful surrender to the life call and its mysterious source with all the risks this implies.

Counselees who leave therapy with this disposition may be less clear and less certain about the concrete details of their future. But they are growing in trust that the life call will suggest to them the right solution at the right time. They have only to live in relaxed openness to all the messages the formation field may give them in the light of their transcendent formation tradition.

Before therapy, anxiety about the unknown and the untried severely hindered their faithfulness to the call. Now, however, they feel ready for whatever may happen to them. Their surrender to the formation mystery convinces them that they will be given light to take the next step at every winding of the road. They no longer feel that it is necessary for them to see the whole road clearly before they feel free to move.

Consequences of Acceptance

Consonant transcendent commitment implies the acceptance of one's life call in all its aspects, whether these give rise to joy or pain. After effective transtherapy, counselees will be better able to bear the suffering that is unavoidable in life. Before therapy their growth was impaired by their attempts to avoid painful experiences. Now, however, they dare to expose themselves to the reality of life. Doing so, they give actual form to their possibility for a fuller and deeper appraisal of their formation field and tradition. Many aspects of life are revealed only in suffering that is faced and worked through. Counselees will be increasingly able to accept without fatalism or apathy, resistance or resentment, escape or avoidance, the suffering that life brings to them.

Suffering is still present; it is still painful; but it does not disturb their inner freedom as much as before. Viewing it from a transcendent perspective, unnecessary deformative suffering within a closed-off pretranscendent life is eliminated or diminished.

The ability to face suffering paradoxically enables persons to enjoy freely the gifts of life. When one is afraid of suffering, one cannot enjoy the blessings life brings. One frantically uses what is given to escape the burden of pretranscendent existence. While attempting to forget the painful aspects of life in wild enjoyment of its pleasures, one is continually haunted by the anxiety that the burdensome side may reveal itself again when enjoyment ceases.

One who cannot suffer fully is also unable to enjoy fully. People who are haunted by anxiety about disappointment are hesitant when the possibility of deep, intense joy reveals itself at certain moments of their journey. They prefer ephemeral pleasure to transcendent joy, which touches the core of their being. They are afraid that such joy may create a possibility for an overwhelming letdown and disillusionment. Fundamentally, they are right. To be sure, the overwhelming joy of deep love always implies the risk of overwhelming pain in case one's beloved dies, disappears, or betrays one's trust. Happiness entails a threat that may evoke anxiety.

As a result, many counselees are not able to enjoy with a full and relaxed presence the gifts of life that come their way. One manifestation of their anxiety is a lack of inner freedom regarding what has been given to them. This core disposition is characterized by an anxious, possessive holding on to these gifts. Such fearful preoccupation makes it impossible for them to enjoy life fully. Authentic enjoyment is only possible if one accepts without afterthought the good gifts of life and is ready to let them go when they fade away.

In other words, transcendent commitment is just as necessary for true enjoyment as it is for true suffering. Both are possible only when one surrenders in freedom to the mystery of formation. I do not mean that after transtherapy people should throw themselves into joy or pain in blind surrender. Good therapy establishes a quiet openness to all the aspects of one's formation field and tradition. This does not mean that one can let oneself be overwhelmed passively by happiness or suffering. Life is a gift and a task. Everyone has to decide in his or her concrete life situation whether or not this joy or this pain is a gift or a demand for action. The realistic openness acquired in transtherapy will enable counselees to determine to what degree pain and joy are to be experienced without activity or resistance and to what degree they demand action.

Commitment in Self-Presence to the Mystery

Before this therapy, counselees are inclined to avoid the appeal of the present by living in the past or the future. They discover in transtherapy that surrender to the mystery of formation always means a full presence to the formation field here and now. They learn to accept every moment with the risks and possibilities it implies. They realize that life can be lived only today, not yesterday or tomorrow.

It is an aim of transtherapy to prepare counselees for gradual transcendence of their self-centeredness in commitment to reality. They should experience that commitment to life, to their duty, to the demands of the present, to others, and to their formation tradition is the condition for an enhanced unique and communal existence. The real self grows only in commitment. It realizes itself only in a transcendence of the dissonant, pretranscendent, anxious self.

This commitment is an expression of one's total readiness to make oneself available to one's life call as candidly understood in the light of one's own faith and formation tradition. This free and total commitment leads to unity and integration in one's personality. One becomes at one with oneself. This unity leads to new force and strength internally in the execution of one's daily assignments.

For example, a counselee of mine, Bill, who was also a college teacher, experienced great difficulty in preparing his lectures and in the composition of scholarly papers for presentation at conventions. One of the reasons why Bill experienced inner resistance and division during the performance of his duties was that he was not wholly and freely committed to his study. He prepared his lectures and wrote his articles because he was concerned about winning the esteem of his students, colleagues, and superiors. He was not motivated by an inner commitment to his writing and teaching. As a result, Bill's preparation was a chore that burdened and bored him. It became almost impossible for him to concentrate on the literature that he had to analyze in preparation for his classes.

As soon as he sat behind his desk with a stack of books and articles before him, he felt tired, exhausted, and disgusted. His mind wandered off in all directions except that of his study. What exhausted Bill was not the task itself but an inner conflict between what he desired to do and the demands imposed on him by his position as a teacher. He wanted and did not want to study. In fact, a considerable amount of his energy was invested in the struggle against his inner resistance to the task at hand. After therapy, however, he was a renewed man, a teacher able to prepare his lectures effectively without the overwhelming fatigue he had experienced formerly. He learned in therapy to commit himself to his task freely, to give up his inner resistance, to conquer the split in his life. All his energy was now available for the task at hand. This did not mean that his work no longer had unpleasant aspects or that it lost its own intrinsic difficulties and problems. However, his transcendent commitment made it possible for him to accept his task with all its pleasant and unpleasant angles. He became a relaxed, energetic, well-prepared teacher.

Consequences of Commitment

Transcendent commitment determines whether or not we will freely express our life call or be stunted in our growth by inhibition, fixation, and perversion. Of course, such a commitment is not an act performed once and for all. After transtherapy, we must renew our commitment many times during our lives. Often we must reaffirm the disposition of commitment and inner freedom. For the opposite, self-centered dispositions never disappear totally. Consequently, transtherapy cannot aim at a once-and-for-all commitment. It aims at a core disposition of self-commitment, which is a readiness to restore free commitment every time it is lost.

It is difficult for many counselees to understand that commitment leads to consonant self-confidence. Many counselees are successful businesspersons, scholars, scientists, or leaders who have achieved powerful political positions. They come into therapy because of symptoms that make them feel uneasy and less efficient than they would like to be. The idea of transcendent commitment and abandonment does not appeal to them. Their outlook is opposed to it. They feel they are able to gain power by looking out for themselves, by clever manipulation of their environment, by the art of forming useful friendships and relationships that foster their rise in society. They feel as if people in their environment admire them only for their apparent form, their ruthless strength, their harsh self-confidence. They do not realize that concentration on their success is what has isolated them from the fullness of life.

Manipulation of life, preoccupation with power, possessions, and status lead to impoverishment and emptiness. Material success can be accompanied by loss of humanity. This is also true of those counselees who demand love, friendship, and protection from others instead of giving to others. They do not understand that every time they demand something from life they isolate themselves from living. They should learn not to ask what they can demand from life but what life demands from them.

Sometimes during therapy a counselee may be inclined to use even commitment itself as a means of manipulation of one's own or another's life. In this case, one has not yet achieved a transcendent but only a pretranscendent commitment. It is directed toward the actualization or individuation of the pretranscendent self as an ultimate aim. People who live only by pretranscendent commitment become more and more imprisoned. All that happens to them is the expansion of their self-prison, the addition of new weapons to their arsenal of manipulating devices.

Only a commitment that is not pretranscendently self-centered but conscious and free has a liberating effect on one's life. Only such commitment makes one a full participant in the mystery of formation and offers a center from which to live an integral life, undivided by pretranscendent dispositions made ultimate.

Acceptance and Commitment

Transcendent commitment to our formation field and tradition implies that we accept ourselves with respect. We assume responsibility for the gift we are. We must acknowledge and accept our own unique communal call and defend it when necessary.

Transcendent commitment to our call sometimes means that we must learn to place ourselves in the foreground when we would prefer to stay in the background because of anxiety, defensive modesty, or pretranscendent, false humility. We must accept ourselves with our gifts and our limitations as a uniquely unfolding life assignment. Some counselees do injustice to their call by dedicating themselves to others to such a degree that they neglect to care for themselves. As a result, healthy and wholesome care for their own life is often replaced by hidden self-pity and complaint. Instead of boldly seeking their rights, they express their secret dissatisfactions in small idiosyncrasies and in stubborn insistence on insignificant privileges.

Transcendent commitment to our life call implies the will to become relatively independent in our inner life. Too strong an attachment to our parents and our milieu will render it difficult, if not impossible, for us to commit ourselves to our own calling. Moreover, if we did not receive the care and guidance we needed for our formation from our parents, we may feel a deep lack in our personality. We seek restlessly for the fulfillment of a need that was not assuaged by our parents. As a result, we become fixated on the search elsewhere for parental love, tenderness, and protection. It is true that therapists can, to some degree, fulfill this need. Nevertheless, they can never really make up for all that we missed in our childhood.

We must realize that something was really missing in our early life, a painful lack that cannot be completely filled in this later phase of our formation. Commitment here and now to reality means that we must be ready to accept with focal consciousness and freely the painful reality of our past. We must assume responsibility for our own life. We should renounce our prefocal search for fulfillment of infantile wishes, which ought to have been satisfied when we were children. Unfortunately, they cannot be fulfilled completely now that we are adults. Only when we are able to commit ourselves to our life call, even at the cost of pretranscendent fulfillment, will we be able to grow and overcome this handicap. Only when we give up our need for wish fulfillment can we discover in our deeper self the meaning we expected to receive from outside ourselves.

We cannot expect others to orient themselves toward us spontaneously as if we were small children. We must realize that we will receive the love and dedication of others only by going out toward them ourselves. The more we go out to others, the more we will receive the love we missed so much as children. Of course, it is initially impossible for counselees to understand this possibility of receiving love for love. The therapist, therefore, must ease the way by showing transcendent care and interest in the counselee as a mother treats her child, for thus we confirm them in their infantile needs.

Effective therapy aims to prepare counselees for commitment to life and others in spite of infantile needs. This commitment in turn helps people to experience increasingly the love of others whom they will meet in their many encounters during and after transtherapy.

Sometimes counselees cannot reach independence and full commitment to their own life call because of a depreciative relationship to their parents and to other figures who later replace their parents. People may try to free themselves by attacking the ideas, feelings, and life-style of parents and parent figures. They complain about their old-fashioned ideas; they try to conquer them so that they will think, feel, and act in the same way as they themselves do. This attempt leads to a new kind of dependency in the counselees, namely, their need to direct the thought and the life-style of others. They try to force others to agree with them. They are continually distressed by the different way in which older people or superiors live and act. Their emotional life is bound up by this depreciation. It makes them unhappy, tense, and frustrated. Transtherapy aims at the liberation of the person from such bindings. Only after this liberation can counselees freely grow in their relationship to parents and/or to parental substitutes whom they meet in the course of their life.

CHAPTER 17

Formation Counseling as Inspired by Transtherapy

Formation counseling is a type of counseling inspired by transtherapy. It awakens and sustains in counselees the kind of appraisal that relates directly to their life as affected by their internalized form-traditional pyramid (see volume 5 of this series). People who come to counselors with the normal problems of tradition confusion in our culture do not necessarily have to be referred to intensive transtherapeutic treatment. They may be helped by less intense and less prolonged formation counseling, which draws upon the insights and findings of the science of formation and its transcendence therapy. In turn, this science, as well as my corresponding formation anthropology, integrates the relevant contributions of the arts and sciences with the wisdom of the great formation traditions of humanity.

Transcendent Apprehension and Appraisal

I observed that one of the problems in Western European and American culture is that they are accustomed mainly to informative thinking. They lost or never acquired the art of formative transcendent apprehension and appraisal cultivated by the great wisdom traditions of humanity.

Counselees have to realize that they are always receiving or giving form in their lives in some traditional ways, be it usually in a prefocal or unfocused fashion. In the counseling sessions they learn to focus on this process in a way that is primarily formative instead of informative. They may become aware that certain experiences inspired by these traditions manifest and foster this deeper formation process. Yet I observed repeatedly in Europe as well as in America that they feel also inclined to deny these experiences. They may bypass them as insignificant or use them merely as neutral matter for informative thinking.

Formation counseling assists them in the disclosure of the unique meaning of their tradition-nourished experiences. I created my formation science and transtherapy in Europe to enable them to gain insight into dispositions that are rooted in the soil of centuries and in those that are only spawned in the wasteland of passing popular fads of a few generations. They begin to sense the consonant and dissonant directions of their character. This type of counseling creates space for an enlightened dwelling on their tradition-shaped experiences. Such abiding enables them to appraise them as helpful or harmful for their consonant human unfolding. Gradually, counselees come to see that their excessive dependence on informative-functional thought is not sufficient for the full flowering of their life. It should be balanced by my art and discipline of consonant transcendent reflection, seen as a gentle master of human existence.

Until now, transcendent experiential thinking has been represented only presystematically for the most part by masters of traditional formation in the East and the West. My science of formation integrates their insights systematically with some of the secondary relevant contributions of the arts and sciences that emerged more recently in history. Transtherapy itself and the formation counseling it fosters, either in common or in private, highlight humanity's primary tendency to give and receive form in life and world. It fosters the liberating freedom for creative dialogue with traditions shared with others. Counseling sessions bring into the open the obstacles and facilitating conditions the counselees meet on their tradition-inspired journey. They begin to unmask the ever-present threats of confusion and dissipation. They gain in the ability to cope with them effectively.

Emergence of the Need for Transtherapy and Formation Counseling

At times in our life, a congenial and compatible form of existence seems to emerge almost effortlessly. Transcendent wisdom arises spontaneously in our heart and mind. We sense that we are growing consonantly and graciously. We feel in harmony with the world. Life flows easily. The unfolding of our character in the light of wisdom traditions is not problematic.

At other moments, however, we may feel compelled to think about what happens to us in our journey. Often we are brought to reflection by some crisis that interrupts the unruffled flow of our days. Or confusing conflicts upset our daily routines. These problems may continue. We may not know how to solve the tension between the spontaneous unfolding of our life and the transcendent reflection that should guide this unfolding at moments of decisive redirection. We may have lost contact with the great traditions of humanity, which could awaken us to true wisdom. Neither is this wisdom made available to us in a living way by informational theological propositions or psychological theories, if these are not illumined by the age-old treasure of human formation experience. Hence, we may have to turn to transtherapeutic formation counseling. There we may receive the light needed for the solution of such normal problems of growth in contemporary humanity.

Our counseling sessions should help us to question the sense of the situations we are facing. What do our crisis events really mean for us? We begin to ask ourselves how we may foster consonant-character unfolding. Can we do something about it by means of meditative reflection or recourse to formation wisdom and tradition; to formative reading; to the exercise of formative apprehension, appraisal, affirmation, and other means of disclosing consonant directives? Counselees begin to feel increasingly the need to appraise who they are and where they are going. The moment they begin to reflect on their tradition-nourished experience, they initiate the possibility of critically appraising their life direction.

Field of Traditions in Transtherapy and Counseling

Human life is always unfolding within a field of traditions. This field is the totality of all the factors and traditions that impact on a person's life. The life of counselees is interwoven with this tradition-permeated field. They live in it as an oyster in its shell, a fish in its pond, a fetus in the womb. Human life is always in process, but only in and through its traditional formation fields. Each human life form, as well as each community of human forms, develops its own traditional field through unique-communal dialogue.

For example, the field in which our American counselees give form traditionally to their life differs from that of the Indians, Bantus, or Eskimos. Things have a different formative meaning for them. Even if the information about these things is the same, their *formative meaning,* the real difference they make in one's spiritual, functional, vital, and sociohistorical life may be quite different. The fact that all people over the globe are increasingly participating in the same information about things makes us assume too easily that they have the same formative impact on them. This is not necessarily the case. For instance, African converts to Islam or Christianity may be informed about the tenets of their new religion. Yet its formative impact will be modulated, subtly and usually prefocally, by the interiorized formative meanings of their traditional field of life. Briefly, formation fields are not the same for people of different periods and traditions.

The animal form of life, on the other hand, seems to maintain the same type of life field. Hence, we do not see much change in patterns of building shelter, mating behavior, or ways of rearing the young. We humans, however, are always changing the ways in which we receive and give form in our field. We dress in new fashions, cultivate the earth with new machines, differentiate our sciences into ever more specialized ones, create new forms of aesthetic expression, soar off into space. The human life form does not seem as bound to a naturally inherited formation field as that of animals. Our own human field of life is not only natural but also and foremost traditional. We cannot realize our own form potencies without using the tradition potencies that abound in the field in which we are embedded since birth. In short, we form ourselves by forming our field of traditions. We are people in constant traditional reformation.

For example, we formed ourselves as city dwellers by building cities, as industrialists by developing mills and plants. We became readers by printing books; travelers by giving form to trains, cars, and planes; astronauts by producing space crafts and satellites. These new forms generate in turn their own corresponding cognitive, aesthetic, and practical pretranscendent and transcendent formation traditions. These then enrich and expand human formation fields as a whole.

Our traditional field of formation is the domain of our form potencies. They are ours in and through this field. Without our formation field, we would be nothing potentially. We experiment with our formation field in innumerable ways because this is our only road to ongoing formation. Each time we are in touch with our field in a new manner, we receive or give form to a new mode of our humanity. When we probe our field, we actualize our form potency for empirical investigation; when we care for people we meet in this field we grow in love; when we admire the beauty of nature, our aesthetic sense is formed in depth. When we dig a hole, chop down a tree, fly a kite, or prepare a new dish, we are formed in practical insight, aptitude, and agility. In short, we are formed continually by the manifold engagements that occupy us in our traditional fields of action and contemplation. Correspondingly, our field of life itself is formed, reformed, and transformed by the formation traditions we introduce into it by these same engagements whether by design or accident. Transtherapy helps people to be more attentive to this ongoing story of traditional formation.

Form Potencies

A human form potency thus represents in my formation theory a dynamic tendency to give or receive form. I observed and noted how definite form potencies permeate the life of counselees, their apprehensions, appraisals, and affirmations of their field of life, their actions and apparent behavior. Counselees may be oblivious to the pressure of their denied potencies. Such awareness is owing to a repudiation or a refusal of the call inherent in their form potencies. This lack of awareness leads inevitably to disturbance. The relief of such disturbance presupposes that one face the denied potency and its urgent call. It does not necessarily mean that a person will realize this invitation. A free and insightful decision to forgo a certain formation possibility in favor of another can be healthy and invigorating on the condition that this option ties in with an overall consonant project of life. One sign of this consonance is that this project makes sense to the counselee and the transtherapeutic counselor here and now at this juncture of his or her formation history.

Counselees cannot find consonance of life as long as they refuse to face and appraise their emergent form potencies. They must come to terms with them realistically in accordance with their formation field as apprehended and appraised in the light of their unique-communal life call and their freely chosen or affirmed formation traditions.

Power of Emergent Formation Potencies

The emergence of a form potency implies a powerful motive to give or receive form accordingly. For example, at a certain age, children experience a challenge to give new form to their movements in the playpen. Their formation field becomes structured momentarily around this awakening of their form potency. Their field becomes different in the light of this potency, which presses for a new modulation of their bodily form. In their field, the open arms of inviting and encouraging parents appear as a harbor to which they can safely travel; chairs become instruments to lean upon in their first awkward attempts to new form donation; belts with which they are bound are resented as obstacles to formation.

Later on in life, one may apprehend and appraise similar reformations of one's field when challenged by other emergent potencies. Consider the field of the adolescent who experiences the first stirrings of love; of executives who sense that they could reach the top; of scholars or artists who feel they may achieve something great in their field. At such moments, other form potencies seem to recede in the background, at least temporarily. The human form involved in such an emergency is mainly aware of what may lead to the desired form of life and achievement.

In later life, it is our transcendent personal choice that should freely decide what kinds of form donation and reception should receive priority. We should not allow ourselves to be overcome by the pressure of emergent form potencies. Prefocally, mutually incompatible kinds of potencies may dominate our actions; we become confused and erratic, irrational and tense. Our formation journey is no longer smooth and even. A great deal of transtherapy and counseling is taken up with making these prefocal pressures of emergent form potencies focal. We assist counselees to decide on their priorities in the light of the ideological or religious traditions to which they have freely committed themselves. The latter imply necessarily that, formatively speaking, they become aware of what these implicit humane or religious traditions mean for them.

We conclude that a human form potency is a focal or prefocal (in some instances, an infra- or transfocal) dynamic tendency toward a specific form reception or donation in one's field of life. As a motivating force, it colors one's apprehension, appreciation, and affirmation. Which particular form potencies gain priority in our life depends to a large extent on our prefocal hierarchy of form potencies. This hierarchy is formed under the influence of one's formation history, one's formation phase, innate affinities, form traditions, and personal affirmations. Many, if not all, of these forming influences may enter into the dialogue of transtherapy and counseling.

Formation Counseling

Formation counseling done in the light of transtherapy is generally a short-term process, the aim of which is to set people free. Their lives need to be liberated from the pressures of crowd and collectivity. Once this happens, they can begin to appraise in relative freedom the traditions that make up their field traditions and their own form-tradition pyramid. Depending on the seriousness of their problems, they choose either formation counselors or transtherapists. Their inner freedom has been paralyzed by the pressure of a variety of unintegrated traditions. They can no longer transcend the directives imposed on them by sociohistorical pulsations. They did not allow emergent form potencies to rise into the light of their appraisal. Either that, or when these potencies knocked on the door of their appraising mind, they repudiated them. This repudiation is embodied in dissonant reactions and responses. This rejection impulse may be extinguished gradually after they gain insight in such self-defeating dynamics during the counseling sessions. They may be replaced by the conditioning of other responses. These may be generated by new directives found during counseling in dialogue with consonant formation traditions.

We come to know counselees by the way their character is focused by all spheres of their traditional field of formation. We cannot restrict ourselves to what they tell us about their isolated intrasphere only. Therefore, from the very beginning, the transtherapist or counselor orients the attention of the counselees toward themselves as concretely receiving and giving form in their life to self, to people, events, and things, in the light of the formation mystery. They are encouraged not to escape their ongoing ascent by a flight into the past, where there are no decisions to make, where one's life form seems explained and justified by inescapable determinants. We do not compel the counselees to revise the fixed history of their past. They are invited to face the present. They should not excuse themselves but confront their here-and-now situation, accepting its challenges. The past should only be referred to in service of a clarification of the challenges of the present.

Transcending the barriers to the relatively free unfolding of their personality, the counselees learn how to move with a new harmony and consonance in their daily existence. Only people who can call the here and now their dwelling place can cope with transcendence anxiety. They accept and affirm their whole situation, not only its bright but its dark side as well.

Consonant Dispositions and Expressions

Formation counselors and transtherapists translate this approach into appropriate dispositions. These are, in turn, embodied in word, posture, facial expression, and bodily movement. Such dispositions and expressions are meant to serve the counselees. *Their* life has to be explored and expressed by means of the counseling relationship. To sense which dispositions and expressions of ours may give effective form to our directives for specific counselees, we should gradually gain an appreciation of where they really are. This will enable us to grow during the sessions into the right appraisal of the appropriate kinds of relationships. These may induce our counselees to explore and express their lives and their projects in the light of the form traditions to which they have committed themselves. Such crucial commitment itself will often be the focus of shared exploration.

Life Projects

As I mentioned earlier, the main characteristic of the human life is its ongoing unfolding by means of a succession of current projects. These projects are tentative answers to successive life situations. The character dispositions, feelings, desires, hopes, and ideas, the imaginations, memories, and anticipations of counselees are embedded in such projects, usually prefocally. They form together a loose or tight system of life directives. Every directive can become the focus of our shared exploration during our counseling sessions. Each appraised directive sheds light on all other directives. They begin to see the links of such directives with traditions, with their life call, with their character dispositions, as well as with their temperament.

The structure of a project as a differentiated whole explains the relative influence of every single directive that participates in it. Each directive, in turn, colors all directives that make up the current project of the counselees. They will be gradually able to apprehend, appraise, and express the main lines of their current project. As transcendence anxiety diminishes, they may finally dare to see and appraise the impact of dissonant directives within this system. On the basis of this appraisal, they may be ready to develop a new current project. This project should be more congenial with who they are as a unique constellation of form potencies and character dispositions. It should be more compatible with their actual life situation here and now, including the traditions to which they are committed.

Interformative Relationship

The interformative relationship between counselor and counselee is the principal means for bringing to expression the current project of life. The quality of the relationship influences to what degree one's project as well as one's personal field of life and character will find adequate expression. The transtherapist or counselor establishes a relationship that leads to diminishment of transcendence anxiety and to optimal communication.

People learn to hide their projects of life and their character dispositions. By means of a shield of security directives, they protect themselves from being misunderstood, humiliated, ridiculed, condemned, or abused. To disclose their personal project and related character dispositions is in a sense to surrender their life form. They fear to expose their sensitivity, to unveil their vulnerability. This is especially the case when directives they cherish are at odds with those popular in their environment. Fear of disapproval and depreciation limits the free admission not only of base inclinations but also of sublime aspirations. It is difficult for many to verbalize their finer sentiments. They fear that the communication of refined feelings would sound odd or ridiculous in a functionalistic world.

Refusal of higher aspirations under the pressure of functionalism may be terribly effective. Counselees themselves may not be aware of their deepest personal aspirations at the root of their preformed life. These repressed inspirations cry out for expression in their unfolding character and personality. Transtherapists and counselors may make themselves mistakenly the allies of functionalistic wit and arrogance. They may joke lightly about "noble sentiments" in order to reassure *apparently* functionalistic counselees that they, the counselors, are "regular people" like the rest of the population. As a result, the hidden aspirations of their counselees may remain a closed book. Some transtherapists or counselors may cherish the illusion that such "openmindedness" breaks down barriers. They forget that an exclusive openness to the contemporary scene may mean closure to the denied unique aspirations of counselees.

Imposition of One's Own Lifestyle

Every one of us has our own current project of life in tune with our character, temperament, and form-traditional pyramid. Such form traditions have been absorbed via the dispositions and expressions of the culture in which we are inserted by birth and initial formation. Our form traditions permeate our interformative relationships with others. This connection is particularly pervasive in the encounter between us as transtherapists or counselors and the counselees who come to us for the facilitation of their spiritual journey. The subtle influence of our own form traditions could be confusing for them. Our personal embodiment of life directives is not the only possible or desirable one for others. The identification of our own project as "the" project for all may limit our relevance to mainly a segment of the population that is spontaneously in touch with our own traditions and our personal version of them. At the same time, we risk repelling others not similarly disposed.

Therefore, transtherapeutic counselors should grow increasingly in the appraisal of their own character dispositions. Of course, they cannot do away with a personal style of life. They must embody their presence in some apparent expression, which is, of necessity, limited in time and space. But they can increasingly free themselves from the identification of consonant character unfolding as such with their own preferred form traditions. This inner freedom will enable them to sense the unique character dispositions, potencies, directives, and traditions of those who differ from them.

Transtherapeutic counselors should grow constantly in relaxed awareness of the impact of their character dispositions and temperament, of their own traditions, their cultural and subcultural stereotypes, their antipathies and sympathies, their affinities. Emotional blocks will become manifest to them in this maturity. They may disclose, for instance, that they feel uneasy with people who have aesthetic inclinations because the folks at home confused artistry with frivolity. Such confusion may be traced to a historical overreactive rejection of all art and beauty. Such rejection may have been fueled by the threat of an "unmanly aestheticism" during a certain perverse cultural period. It may have added an undesirable accretion to their tradition. Such dissonant accretions, if not worked through, render counselors less effective and unnecessarily inhibitive in their presence to the counselees.

Other counselors may realize that they one-sidedly prefer what they call "regular people." As high school or college students they disliked some companions who were delighted more by books than by baseballs. Some, on the contrary, may find that they are enamored with scholarly types because they themselves, being "bookish," are fed up with more pragmatic colleagues who made fun of them.

Certain counselors again may discover that they lean toward compulsiveness. They have identified the compulsive style of life with sound discipline and firmness. Hence, they distrust spontaneity in themselves and in their counselees.

CHAPTER 18

Formation Traditions, Interformation in Light of Transtherapy

Formation happens from infancy on. It may start already in the fetal stage of life. It is influenced by our interaction with our parents or guardians. They communicate to us in words, gestures, and actions what people in their humane and/or religious traditions appraise as advantageous in the shaping of character dispositions. Our initial character orientation is not fashioned in isolation. Character unfolds in dialogue with the life-style of representatives of one or more traditions.

It is thus not so that children develop their prefocal projects of life with a wary eye on their real potencies. Children are not faced yet with their own ideal directives but with their parents' appraisal of desirable character dispositions. The parents' appraisal may be coformed in turn by the views that prevail in their internalized jumble of popular traditions. No human life is an island in the great sea of formation. Directives are deeply interwoven with the current interests of humanity.

To be sure, our counselees ought to assimilate the directives of traditions in a unique and congenial way. They should be consonant, and they should really become theirs in the course of their therapy or counseling sessions. The basic directives of the great classical traditions are not ordinarily contrary to the givenness of human life. They are the fruit of wisdom, revelation, and the experiences of generations. The sober core of such age-old wisdom is usually consonant with at least the main foundations of human existence. This wisdom, however, is incorporated in directives, dispositions, and customs which change with historical situations. Its adaptive embodiment in concrete styles of life may be at odds with what each counselee may be called to be by the all-embracing mystery. These concrete expressions of traditions are dictated not only by the vision of generations. They are influenced also by the demands of the changing situations in which this vision has to be realized.

Counselees often confuse the core of the accumulated wisdom of their traditions with its historical accretions, some of which may be dissonant. They may represent safeguards or secondary security directives. Counselees may have made such security blankets ends in themselves. Safeguards have perhaps taken the place of the directives they were designed to protect. They take on a life of their own. Their growth is no longer rooted in the fundamental directives of their traditions; rather, they loom up as isolated powers. Thus, the myriad safeguards developed over the centuries may have become for some counselees a stern police force hemming in their human aspirations. Safety directives may have become excessive in extent and intensity.

Transtherapists and counselors should carefully watch their own prefocal dispositions. They should not depreciate the consonant foundations of the tradition to which their counselees have committed themselves in their style of life. They should help people to clarify the formation potential of the tradition they have chosen. They should encourage the unique-communal way in which persons try to implement such foundations.

Transtherapists and counselors ought to distinguish in their appraisal between the truly fundamental and the merely personal. They may discover that certain people live the directives of their tradition in an unwholesome, overanxious fashion. Inexperienced or uninformed counselors may identify this unhealthy expression with the directives themselves. They may be appalled by the adverse consequences. Implicitly or explicitly, counselors may then communicate that they do not appreciate the fundamental directives themselves of the traditions of their counselees. By doing so, they may drain away the motivating and integrating power of the traditional infrastructure of a person's life. However, it is in the light of this traditional internalized structure that counselees may eventually be able to integrate their character unfolding more consonantly with the personality they are called to be. Outside their tradition they may lose their possibility for consonant integration. It may be replaced by a syncretism that is intrinsically schizoid and confusing—the opposite of integration.

Syncretism is the attempt to force selected life directives from intrinsically different traditions into an artificial unity—artificial because it may be only an arbitrary collection of incompatible elements. Syncretic character structure is a source of a dissipated and scattered life-style. It kills joy and peace in many people. They vegetate without wise, well-informed appraisals of the pulsations flowing through their pluritraditional society.

Underlying Subcultural Traditions of Transtherapist
and Formation Counselor

Formation counselors as well as transtherapists are rooted in subcultures of their own. They are influenced implicitly by one or various traditions. These subcultures and their underlying traditions may differ from those of their counselees. They may implicitly impose on their counselees their own subcultural view of life. An unguarded reaction, a certain look, a smile, a slight impatience or surprise may communicate more than words what they really feel. They may unwittingly suggest that their counselees should develop their projects of life on the basis of the subcultural structure that nourishes the counselor's own directives and dispositions. If counselees attempt to follow this suggestion, they may fail. The counselor's own life directives may flow from traditions counselees do not share.

The project that the counselor personally cultivates will be for such counselees an abstract ideal. They cannot enflesh it in the ongoing history of their own life. Such an imposition of alien directives may compound the confusion about desirable character dispositions. Their own project may at least in part be rooted in their own tradition as embodied in their own culture or subculture. Now they may try to develop an alien project suggested to them by a tactless counselor. Their project of character unfolding will then be directed from two conflicting centers: the directives of their own traditions and those of their counselor. What I have just said does not exclude, of course, the possibility that counselees may freely, reasonably, and volitionally decide to change to another subculture, population segment, or tradition.

Counselors can prevent such confusion if they remain aware of the implicit impact of their own form traditions on their communications. Simultaneously, they should try to apprehend and appraise the background of the counselee's character dispositions. This appraisal should be guided by the distinction made between the traditions of their counselees, its current cultural embodiment, and the personally consonant or dissonant manner in which counselees try to implement it.

Structure of the Interformative Relationship

The interformative relationship of counseling, done in the light of transtherapy, differs in structure from other relationships. First, it is different because of its focus, and, second, because of the dispositions the counselor brings to the relationship.

The sessions are meant to facilitate the expression and appraisal of the traditional field of life of the counselee. The basic disposition is one of genuine acceptance of counselees, regardless of what feature of their life they may disclose to us. Any sign of depreciation of such candor awakens transcendence anxiety. Bringing to focal apprehension and appraisal one's tradition-nourished field of life can also be impeded by a too emphatic involvement of the counselor in one or another of its spheres. Such preferential focusing on one facet may impede the spontaneous communication of others. These may be as or more significant for full apprehension and appraisal. The counselor prompts counselees, by his or her accepting disposition, to lift candidly into the light of shared focal attention vague and confused apprehensions, appraisals, affirmations, memories, imaginations, anticipations, and accompanying feelings. All of these play a role in their current life project.

The counselor should be affectively present to the extent necessary to keep the counselees motivated in the exploration of their project. Yet, his or her affective presence should be modulated by the necessary strategic distance. Distance in the midst of affective presence makes the interformative relationship of counseling different from other affective relationships that are interformative in their own fashion. Strategic distance facilitates the relaxed acceptance of all facets of the field and project of the counselees without reacting to them emotionally in a favorable or unfavorable fashion. Either reaction may evoke an appreciative or depreciative fixation on some particular facet of one's life or project at the expense of the disclosure of other significant aspects. The counselor must be an observing participant in the story and present project of the counselee; he or she must also be its respectful appraiser.

The description of the ideal relationship elicits the question of dispositions that may facilitate this kind of encounter. In this light, there are two main dispositions a counselor should develop in service of this relationship: one is the formative; the other is the interformative.

Formative Disposition

The center of our presence is not our own life. It is the emergent life of our counselee, its congenial, compatible, and compassionate unfolding within its own everyday surroundings.

Counseling or transtherapy becomes formative when we refuse to consider our counselees as mere compilations of symptoms, problems, diagnostic indicators, constellations of personality theories, or exponents of philosophical or informational theological propositions. This kind of information should remain available in the background of our attention. It should not dominate our relationship exclusively.

We must continually transcend such functional evaluations, no matter how significant they are in their own right. We should be disposed to hear primarily the distinctively human appeal of counselees to be wholly with and for them as struggling human beings called forth uniquely by a transcendent mystery. What motivates our transtherapeutic counseling is the unfolding of the counselees in consonance with the traditional core of their life. We are the humble yet critical-creative observers of the gift and the struggle of their unfolding.

It would be impossible to appraise fully a unique life story by means of the methods of the exact sciences alone. Such approaches accept as significant only what is reducible to measurement. The unique life call of a person cannot be disclosed in this way. Only a loving, respectful presence to each life in its gifted uniqueness and painful defeats can disclose this call, insofar as it is knowable at this moment.

Every meaningful description presupposes our loving apprehension, appreciation, and confirmation of the present limited disclosure of the counselee's calling. The disposition of loving respect fosters our shared reflection on this disclosure. Together, we ponder the facilitating conditions for fidelity to the inner light that may enter our hearts.

A positivistic approach reduces the mystery of life to a summary of functional and vital qualities, to a list of symptoms, to an inventory of significant incidents, to a static profile of a personality type. It may freeze an unfolding human person into a filled-out questionnaire, a test, protocol, or case history.

Life as mystery and call is beyond pretranscendent categorization. Yet counseling should take into account the information thus gathered. In its light, counselors realize some of the background and the environmental conditions of their counselees, the scenery of their struggles, so to say. However, they do not merely identify such conditions and symptoms. They reach out to their deepest roots in the traditional life field and character of their counselees.

The counseling approach—in the spirit of transtherapy—enables them to apprehend holistically both the symptoms of dissipation and the repudiated or refused facets of the life call as disclosed to the counselees at this moment of their history. The disclosures of the call and the symptoms of disharmony are mutually illuminating aspects of the same life story. The counselee is not reduced to a series of functional categories or test scores. The counselor is present, first of all, to what is more than symptoms, personality profiles, and problems of adjustment without denying the relative significance of such facets. No diagnostic category by itself can do justice to the emergent disclosure of the unique-communal call of a human being in its personal and traditional life situation.

Interformative Disposition

Formative counseling can give new form to the life of counselees. To understand what this means in the context of my science of formation and transtherapy we must realize that not only counseling is interformative. Every human meeting shares in some way in this quality.

The manner in which we give form to the life of others is, first of all, influenced by the kind of meeting in which we engage. Take a simple situation. Two men meet each other in a bar. The first phase of this meeting may be one of casual informality. One man makes a pleasant remark to the other; the other responds in kind. Further talk ensues, and for each expression of interest and companionship, there is evoked a counterexpression of interest in the other. As a result of these increasingly pleasant exchanges, the two feel at ease with each other. Then, one man says something about a current political controversy that has many people stirred up. He says it in a way that leaves no doubt which side he is on. The other holds the opposite opinion. He feels threatened, offended, hurt. He answers this challenge hotly with an equally forceful argument of this own. His voice is a shade louder than that of his challenger. The other responds in kind. Before either of them realizes it, the friendly meeting has become a heated debate. Soon it turns into a shouting match.

Looking more closely at the interformative development of this encounter, what do we see? Notice how the disposition and expression of one person gave form at every moment to the disposition and expression of the other. The two started out as superficial acquaintances. This mode of peripheral interformation was succeeded by one of companionship between mutually interested people. They interformed one another in this mode of presence by friendly dispositions and expressions. Then they switched to giving form mutually to an encounter of heated discussants. Finally, they interformed each other as boisterous fighters.

The point is that they interformed their mutual presence "through" or "by" each other. They really formed each other—first as casual acquaintances, then as sympathetic friends, next as irate debaters, and finally as shouting opponents.

We are used to modulating the form of each other's life. We are rarely focally aware that we give form to another's presence and its manifestations. We may be even less conscious of the fact that the other gives form to our life similarly. And yet, we cannot think realistically about any form which our life assumed that would be merely the effect of our own form donation alone. We can apprehend ourselves only as born from others, as nourished and shaped by others, as speaking the language others developed before us; as wearing clothes designed and produced by others, and as cultivating dispositions generated and unfolded by many others preceding us in history.

Take, for example, small infants born black. They only assume inwardly the shape of an unjustly treated minority at the moment they are treated differently from children who are not black. This treatment shapes their life. It makes them feel, think, and act in a different fashion. It changes their character dispositions. Note well, it was the interformative encounter that effected this change.

Principle of Interformation Applied to Counseling

We can apply this principle to the transtherapy and counseling situation. The interformative disposition one brings to counseling affects counselees and oneself in a way no other encounter, except that of friendship or marital love, can compare.

Encounters, which are not encounters of love or of respectful counseling, are often rooted in stereotypical classifications. These unspoken categories subtly influence the way in which we give form to others and in which others receive the form we impose upon them.

Judy takes a psychological test. A psychologist communicates to her the outcome of the test, such as an IQ or a profile of aptitudes. By this communication, the psychologist gives form to Judy in a certain way. She is now a person who is more conscious of the limitations of her "intelligence" or of the range of her "skills." Similar communications by parents, friends, acquaintances, medical doctors, teachers, and moralists indicate a certain number of valid facts about her life. They certainly make Judy aware of these realities. They modulate somewhat the form of her life and of her self-appraisal in relation to concrete data she can neither deny nor ignore. For example, her life would be significantly changed were she to leave the office of a physician who told her that she had breast cancer, high blood pressure, diabetes, or an ulcer. She is somewhat different than she was before she learned these physical facts. Her response to this communication in some way affected interformatively her physician too, if they had a real encounter. The doctor may feel compassion and concern; and he or she may experience anew the effect of being medically competent.

When counseling is done in the spirit of transtherapy, the relationship gains a far deeper dimension. This disposition as cultivated by counselors makes them rise beyond mere facts. They apprehend counselees primarily as called to relatively free personality unfolding. They experience them as people endowed with hidden character dispositions, potencies, and a unique-communal life call. This endowment challenges them to give form to their life in a way not determined exclusively by disharmonious symptoms, problems, and deficits. Counseling, done in the spirit of transtherapy, helps the counselees to see their factual determinants no longer as mere hindrances to human growth. They begin to appreciate them as opportunities to orient their life in some admittedly limited yet meaningful direction. This creation of new meaning allows them to use events inventively. These signposts may point to new modulations of their existence in consonance with the present disclosure of their life call. They become increasingly able to turn obstacles into opportunities. They become ready to affirm themselves as sources of initiative in the midst of seemingly invincible determinants and failures.

Interformation as Participation
in the Core of the Personality

Interformation means that we participate in the character unfolding of our counselees. By our cordial presence as participant observers, we foster the free unfolding of their character. The consonant evolvement of their character may be hampered by irrational inhibitions, fears, stereotypes, compulsions, vital pulsions, and popular pulsations. Thanks to our participant observation, counselees no longer feel like lonely, threatened individuals. They are less overwhelmed by the responsibility to devise their life projects in isolation. Because we are wholeheartedly with them, they dare to open up to their potencies. We present them, as it were, to themselves. We enable them to let their own life call emerge, to take hold of their possibilities and limitations. Anxiety-evoking events lose their aura of insurmountability. Counselees begin to emerge as the flexible masters of their field of form reception and donation.

The interformative disposition of counselors, if shared by counselees, generates a "we" experience, a companionship that is different from the "we's" of daily situations. This interformative "we" marks the art and discipline of counseling done in the spirit of transtherapy. Before this healing encounter, our counselees may have experienced their situation as frightening or desolate. They may have felt choked and oppressed, smothered by anxiety.

In transtherapeutic interformation we become a new appearance in their situation, a sign of hope. Our sustaining presence is a source of inner freedom. They will be touched and relieved sooner or later by the unmistakable absence of any forcing, imposing or overpowering on our part. Their expanding consciousness now shows to them our confirming face. Finally, they may begin to believe in the possibility that not all people, events, and things are as untrustworthy as they tended to anticipate. Our transcendent disposition enables them to feel truly at home in a life situation that is at last opening up for them.

Before our confirmation of their uniqueness, they may have succumbed to an anxious conformity to the wishes of others. The compulsion to be indiscriminate people-pleasers made them lose the relative freedom needed for distinctively human living. They may have become parrots of popular pulsations, inviting control and enslavement by their surroundings. The repudiation of their life call may have generated an impotent rage against real or imagined oppressors. Their flow of life energy may have been halted or fixated.

Our transcendent presence helps them to restore and foster respectfully their inner freedom. We try to release their encapsulated energy into a free flow of life.

Transcendent interformation makes us vulnerable. We are exposed by our generosity. Initially, it may lead to the eruption of stored-up resentment, hostility, and aggression. These emotions are directed toward counselors as the only persons in their present situation against whom they can dare to live out these angry feelings. The transcendent mode of presence implies that we maintain our manifestation of loving respect for the transcendent call others are as human persons, even though this call may first reveal itself in a negative fashion.

Free Participation of Counselees in Interformation

Interformation in counseling and transtherapy can be effective only when counselees accept freely their counselors' loving concern. They gradually share in it by candidly focusing with them on their problems. Otherwise, it would not really be interformation. The yes of the counselees must ratify the concern of the counselor to make true transcendent interformation possible. Formation counselors and transtherapists desire the freedom and transcendence of their counselees. Hence, they can only hope that counselees will enter into interformation by freely collaborating with the loving care extended to them.

Doing counseling in the spirit of transtherapy amounts to wanting, above all, inner freedom for our counselees. When counselees simply do what they are told because of the fact that to them the counselor is an expert or "sees through them" or is "such a nice fellow," the subtle process of growth to freedom is stillborn.

Interformation is fertile only when the person who has to grow chooses to grow. Interformation in depth is an interchange between two human lives in which both are actively involved. Without this free participation by counselees, transcendent counseling cannot occur. This yes of counselees to a freely interforming relationship is their gift to counselors.

CHAPTER 19

Transcendent Encounter in Transtherapy

Transtherapy is rooted in human encounter. What makes an encounter truly human?

Everyone senses that an incidental crossing of someone's path cannot be called an encounter in the deeper sense. In a human encounter, I am fully with people. In some way I share their field of life.

Human encounter may emerge at once as an unexpected gift in daily life. For example, I meet someone at a table in a cafeteria. We speak to each other in a casual manner. We exchange the usual niceties that people are expected to exchange when they meet acquaintances. But then, all at once, the other speaks to me about an illness in his or her family, the sudden loss of a friend, or a painful experience that has occurred during the day. Something in this communication touches me, appeals to me, affects me. It moves me to answer in a way that goes beyond the casual, the formal, or the incidental. It is as if the other has dropped for a moment the apparent form, the social mask we wear, and invited me into the sanctuary of his or her inner being. I answered that appeal: I went beyond my own set of preferred form traditions. In my answer vibrates my own inner concern, my empathy. I am really with the other, and she or he becomes, therefore, more real with me. Something grows between us. True togetherness is experienced by both of us. What is this new and vital relationship all about?

Some may answer, "Nothing." Indeed, it seems to be nearly nothing. Yet something did happen. Something so real has emerged in our relationship that I shall not be able to meet this person again the same day, or even the next day, without experiencing a more than casual acquaintanceship.

Sometimes a simple meeting of the eyes, the rendering of a service in a specific way, a little word, a change of tone, a gesture of hand is enough to evoke the experience of a hidden community of mutual concern between two distinctively human lives. They discover in and through these words and gestures each other's dispositions and needs on a deeply felt level. Again we may ask ourselves, "What happens in such a meeting?"

My formation science tries, first of all, to make explicit what is implicitly experienced. But this is only the beginning. Once I know what encounter *is* in an experiential sense, I can start to reason about its position in the framework of my theory of personality which I have presented thus far. I can also fall back on my concept of the process of interformation which I described in the previous chapter. I worked hard to clarify this process. For, as long as we are not clear about the content of our experience, we may be lost in a maze of ambiguous statements.

I begin to realize that the "we-experience" which emerged has a deeper meaning; it is pervaded by much more humanness and affection than is usually the case in routine encounters that fill our lives. Many chance encounters during the day are marked by polite indifference. In the distinctively human encounter, however, we experience transcendent care for one another.

There is another remarkable difference between, for instance, a transtherapy meeting and routine meetings with people. Every person manifests a host of what can be called objective qualities. For example, I might have noticed that the other was rather tall, had a loud voice, blue eyes, and an odd complexion. When I meet someone by chance in society, I tend to categorize the person in such ways. I tend to reduce the whole person to general predicates which in one way or another could be said about everyone. In transtherapy, strangely enough, such qualities seem to fade into the background or shrink into insignificance. I am so engaged in the other's personal feelings, experiences, and attitudes that I become less aware of such accidental features as the color of the skin, the quality of the voice, or the movements of the hands of the other. I do not notice them anymore. The other person is no longer for me one of the many whose external profile I have filed away in my memory. Even if I possess information about his IQ performance on an aptitude test, his age and social status, his credit card, I seem to become less aware of these facts when I am experiencing a distinctively human encounter.

At such moments, I am unable to reduce the person to what I call in my theory of personality measurable reified characteristics. The personal seems to be so overwhelmingly present in transtherapy that it takes precedence over anything else. If I had reduced the counselee to those peripheral qualities, there would not have grown between us the reality of a distinctively human togetherness. The next day I would not experience the unique counselee for whom I really care; I might only perceive the man with the active hands, or the woman with the IQ of 120, or the girl with a classical face

Similarly, in a transtherapy session, my spontaneous interest is not, first of all, in the objectified statements of the informational theological, philosophical, or educational ideology of people. My spontaneous interest is in the "lived" form traditions of persons and their influence on their character structure, dispositions, and expressions. I cannot reduce them to only the facts and figures I look up in handbooks of informational theology, philosophy, or education. Reductions of the unique counselee to a few measurable qualities or a selection of reified quantities make a distinctively human encounter impossible. A truly transcendent meeting is at the heart of formative counseling and transtherapy. Being with and for others as they are is the basis of change and growth in any human relationship. It is also the ground of healing in the deepest sense, the measure of making whole.

In the situations I have described thus far, there is already present a beginning of true human care. Many encounters outside the transtherapy situation can also be called caring. They manifest care and empathy without being therapeutic in a strict sense. A woman who guides a blind man through traffic shows real care for this person. A stranger who takes pains to help me find my way downtown in a city unknown to me, and who goes out of her way to do this, manifests genuine concern for me. A young man who loves a girl and expresses his love in many attentions truly encounters her and unmistakably cares for her. Still, we would not say that the manifestations of care in these situations are expressions of therapeutic care. Thus the question arises, What is characteristic of a therapeutic encounter? What are the conditions that make certain encounters transtherapeutic while others are not?

Transcendent Encounter as Turning
toward a Person as Unique

Any distinctively human encounter presupposes the appeal of the other as a unique person. When I become truly involved in the life of a counselee, my commitment is an answer to some appeal. It tells me that they need me in regard to something concerning their personal life. Many people make demands on me during a given day, on my energy, time, skills, and interests. But these demands usually do not concern their personal growth and transcendent character unfolding. They may ask for money. They may want me to listen to their stories or their jokes, to give them a hand doing some work, to explain a mathematical problem or a difficult selection of literature or of biblical exegesis they cannot understand. None of these demands amounts to a real appeal to help them grow in the area of their life where they are most uniquely themselves. It is for this reason that I can answer these demands without involving the depth of my own being, without exposing the uniqueness of my own personhood, without risking to be hurt when I lay bare the deeper recesses of my soul.

I can hide myself and maintain my self-preoccupation while neatly answering daily demands which are of a more formal and passing nature. It is true that such an answer would grow in depth and richness if I were to engage more of my personality. Nevertheless, even if I do not do so, I can make a satisfactory response. This, however, is inadequate when the personal appeal comes from the other's inner core. When a person cries out to me in despair about anxiety, I cannot answer that appeal with the cool and exact information of how people can overcome such difficulties according to a self-help book or a textbook on psychology. Nor can I offer only the abstract statements of informational theologies and philosophies. If I reduce the gift of my unique presence to such intellectual, general information, I am not fully and really present as a transtherapist. I am only there as a factual intellect or an objective informant.

A catalogue of information may be a part of the presence of the full me to the person, but it can never answer deeper personal needs. This appeal of the other to me is not necessarily expressed in an explicit way. It may be implicitly present in a gesture, in a casual word or look, in a seemingly innocent question. My human sensitivity may discover an invitation to deeper sharing. This muffled outcry is hidden in the movements of the body, the tone of voice, or the story with a secret meaning. It is difficult for the other to verbalize this hidden claim on my personal presence. It is as if he or she is deeply afraid of being hurt by my refusal of a request that comes from the depth of a life in crisis. Therefore, the counselee may leave me a way out. The appeal is clothed in words, body movements, and facial expressions that may be ambiguous and hesitant. The counselee may hide behind a simple request. This plea could be interpreted by me either as a superficial question or as a desperate begging for real understanding of a turning point in their life. In transtherapy or counseling the appeal often emerges from the dissonances of an internalized patchwork of confusing popular form traditions.

No matter how tenuous and hidden the appeal may be, it always contains an invitation to come out of myself. It is as if the counselee begs me to break through my self-preoccupation, to escape fascination with my self-centered world, to transcend my apparent form of life and my own collection of internalized form traditions. The other seems to say, "Please be with me, not only as a well-informed, learned man or woman." "Make my world for once the center of your loving attention, your sympathy, your kind understanding, your benevolence." Why is it so difficult for me to hear the appeal of a counselee?

To become a counselor faithful to the spirit of transtherapy means to go beyond my everyday disposition to concentrate on myself, on the study of medicine, psychology, psychiatry, education, sociology, informational philosophy or theology. It means to go beyond my anxious involvement in persons, books, things, and events that serve my own well-being, career, learning, entertainment, and growth. The question now before me is, How can I make my own learning serve the experiential unfolding of others affectively, effectively, reasonably, and volitionally.

This prefocal preoccupation with things that are important for my own life and with the impression I make in my surroundings makes it difficult for me to be with the counselee. If I am not fully present, I cannot sense the deeper meaning of the appeals that may be hidden in the words, stories, body movements, or questions of counselees. It is not enough that I have eyes and ears to perceive what they say or look like. During the transtherapy hour, I need more than vision or hearing and far more than what I have learned in books of psychology, medicine, psychiatry, informational philosophy, theology, and education. What I need in the first place, and what is most difficult to obtain, is to break through my self-preoccupation.

The first condition and necessary basis for formation counseling and transcendence therapy is to leave my self-centered world of daily involvement as guided by my internalized tree of my own form traditions. When I am full of myself—*my* learning, *my* position, *my* style of existence—or when I am overly concerned about the things other people may think or say of me, I myself am at the center of my interest, not the counselee. When there is still in me a grain of professional pride or a hidden need for the sympathy, the admiration, or the dependency of counselees, I am unable to be purely sensitive to their appeal and to the subtle nuances of their quest for empathic comprehension.

Many counselees are anxious and vulnerable. At any moment they may be on the point of retiring into their own inner world. Therefore, the hesitant expression of needs, which counselees themselves may not fully understand, is neither violent nor brusque, nor is it crystal clear. It is not an open attempt to conquer my interest. It does not necessarily surprise, excite, or shock me. Especially in the beginning it leaves an opening for refusal. It often is too humble, too weak, too concealed, and too delicate to force my attention. Therefore, I shall not understand the subtle shades of meaning in the words and movements of counselees as long as I am occupied with my own prior conceptions about their case or obsessed by my need to impress them by my understanding, interpretations, or fast and easy solutions.

When I am occupied in this way by my own desires, professional pride, and learning, I know that I am already excused from every demand made on my warm, personal presence. Some counselees may reveal this to me in cautious expressions. Of course, I do not excuse myself inwardly in a clear, focally conscious, and reflective way. Rather, I make this decision implicitly in my very attitude of refusal to go beyond the technical use of psychological, medical, psychiatric, philosophical, or theological knowledge. It is an unspoken attitude of refusal of the transtherapeutic presence I can be. This refusal makes me insensitive, deaf, blind, and mute to the delicate concealed needs of some counselees. They bury these painful wants under the make-believe layer of their surface remarks or hesitant questions.

One special form this refusal of presence can take is to reduce myself to a professional role during the transtherapy hour. I am used to playing a role in daily life. As a counselor or transtherapist, I carry usually one or another professional identification. I am a psychiatrist, physician, surgeon, psychologist, clergyperson, social worker, educator, psychodiagnostician, or counselor. I am, of course, far more than such roles I am compelled to play in society. The core of my humanity is richer than any of these social labels. As soon as I identify the whole of my being with only my professional role in society, I close myself off from the full, human appeal of my counselees. I can understand them only when I am present to them as unique persons with untapped resources. When I reduce myself to a professional role, I am again preoccupied with myself, with my appearance in daily society, and with the rules of making a perfect impression as the player of this role. Any self-preoccupation—even this one—reduces immediately my ability to hear, see, sense, understand, and be present as a person who cares for another in need.

I warn in my transtherapy and counseling theory that any informational philosophical, theological, and educational learning that is mine may be abused by me as a shield. It prevents me from entering into the whirl and confusion of the "lived" potpourri of popular form traditions of the person under my care. He or she needs the love and light of empathic understanding by a participant observer, not a standoffish posture of informational superiority.

Appeal of Counselees

What really is the basic appeal of a person who comes to us for counseling? To answer this question, I want first to consider what it is not. First of all, the appeal of a counselee ought not to be understood as the attraction of one or the other quality or characteristic, such as a charming appearance, a beautiful voice, poised behavior, intelligent conversation, or educational background. To be sure, such attractive qualities may make it interesting or desirable for me to be with this person. However, this superficial attraction cannot be the deepest appeal the counselee is for me. Were this the case, such an appeal would no longer function if a counselee did not have engaging manners or no longer showed them in our sessions. I established in my transtherapy theory that such qualities and manners call forth only a more superficial desire to be *with* my counselee, although transcendent care is basically about one's consistent will to be *for* a counselee. In my transtherapy and counseling theory, I stress especially the "love-will" that the counselor should maintain when love feelings may dry up under the pressure of distorting form traditions assimilated in offensive ways by confused counselees.

Transtherapists who really care understand that the qualities, virtues, intelligence, and background of counselees do not matter that much in a healing relationship. These fade into the background. They make room for personal and unique qualities in which counselees are more than case histories or collections of the pretranscendent influences of past and present social situations. Transtherapeutic care is not motivated by the attractions, charms, or signs of promise in counselees. None of these can explain why transtherapists are able to commit themselves wholly to the unique journey of each counselee. Neither does it shed light on why they can persist in their love-inspired participant observation of a disharmonious maze of popular distorted form traditions in which counselees may be caught unaware.

Neither can their appeal to transtherapists be understood as identical with a concrete demand or request. It is not merely a demand for the solution of a concrete problem, for the explanation of a certain confusion, or even for the interpretation of a dream or symptom. It is always more than what it seems to be if it hides a real transcendent appeal of the person as a whole.

Life Story of the Counselee

Such a demand harbors superficially nothing more than the expression and the presentation to the counselor of a factual problem or symptom that needs explanation, advice, or interpretation. However, when I satisfy informationally and prosaically such demands, counselees may depart unsatisfied. I answer only the apparent question and not the far deeper cry which underlies the simple, factual presentation of a problem. People leave me without perhaps being able to explain a feeling of disillusionment. On the surface, everything has seemed fine. A psychological, medical, philosophical, theological, or educational problem was presented, and I gave a neat, logical, clear-cut, informational answer according to the best textbooks dealing with this matter. But the person is still as lonely, confused, and anxious as before my counseling. Why does this feeling of dissatisfaction linger when I clearly and neatly answered the manifest question or problem?

It is there because the appeal made by a counselee is more than the expressed problem or manifest question. The counselee who comes to me for counseling is not a person who has a problem or a request. He or she is one who *is* an appeal. This appeal to my presence is expressed in a limited, awkward, and deceptive way in the form of a concrete problem described to me. My deeper understanding of the appeal of counselees transcends their concrete problems, demands, and questions. It approaches respectfully the area that lies beyond all qualities, problems and questions. It touches the unique mysterious core of the personality. This core itself is an appeal to me to share as a unique person in the unfolding core form of this counselee. I could translate this appeal into the simple words, "Please be with and for me. Please share my journey." In transtherapy and counseling, this appeal points implicitly to the jumble of current form traditions of a pluritraditional society that may have been assimilated in the split character structure of the counselee.

The condition for fruitful counseling is that the counselor hear this appeal. This does not mean that it is necessary that I clearly and reflectively know that I hear it. Such reflection may even disturb my spontaneous sharing of the life story of my counselees. Their appeal is a hidden prayer, a silent begging, an unspoken outcry. I am being asked to go out of my self-centered daily preoccupation with my own world. The question is: Am I willing to sustain the unique and embattled core of a confused and painful existence? To strengthen by my presence another's free core of life? To facilitate an opening up to one's life call and to confirm a person's will to persevere? Will I help people in need to find their own consonant path of integration in a jungle of internalized, insufficiently appraised form traditions?

Spiral of Interformation

As I have shown previously, it is necessary to break through fascination with myself. Such preoccupation prevents me from catching the hidden plea of my counselee, "Please be with me and for me. Share my journey." It is precisely the appeal of counselees that enables me to free myself from myself, to escape the prison of pride and self-preoccupation, to transcend the narrow horizons of my daily life. In other words, I not only give form to the life of my counselees; the appeal of counselees gives form to my life. This is what I call in my theory the transcendent quality of counseling done in the spirit of transtherapy.

There seems to be a spiral of growth in my life as a formation counselor and transtherapist. I break through my narrow self-involvement. This enables me in turn to be sensitive to the appeal of counselees. These appeals then help me to go more and more out of myself. When I transcend myself on account of such appeals, I am more sensitive to the next invitation to be with and for my counselees. This greater openness enables me to listen more deeply to the next appeal, and this again helps me to transcend myself.

The life of a good counselor is thus like a widening spiral. Starting out humbly as a person who has a hard time breaking through my self-preoccupation, I grow increasingly to openness, sharing, and presence. In transtherapy and counseling, I myself become more aware of my own collection of popular form traditions and their lack of integration. My life is enriched, expanded, and deepened. This is the beautiful reward of the life of transcendence therapy and counseling. However, such counseling can never be practiced mainly for the sake of reward. Such search for reward itself would be a sign of self-preoccupation. It would diminish or destroy the goal I have sought, namely, full presence to the other as a participant observer animated by the "love-will" of the mystery for all who suffer.

Transcendent Appeal

The transcendent appeal of counselees thus reveals to me a totally new, perhaps unsuspected, dimension of my own life. It forces me to experience what I really am. Perhaps up to this moment I had the mistaken notion that I was the sum of my achievements. I thought I was this outstanding collection of reputation, talents, studies, degrees of informational theologies, philosophies, educational learning, and all similar professional identifications. Maybe I felt that I was nothing more than the role I was playing as a physician, surgeon, clergyperson, teacher, social worker, educator, counselor, or member of a charitable institution. Maybe I considered myself as nothing more than a professional expert who could provide a certain number of memorized informational answers. Perhaps I perceived myself only as a clever diagnostician or as a well-organized administrator. Now, when I hear the distinctively human appeal of a suffering person, I realize at once that my humanity is far richer than my professional cleverness, my administrative abilities, status, learnedness, economic success, political correctness and proficiency.

The appeal of my counselees reveals to me a whole new horizon of my life. I am called to realize myself as a full human being for my counselees. The call of my counselees announces to me that it is part of my destiny at this moment in time to accompany them along this stretch of their way, to be a companion on this leg of their journey. Through my counselees I become at once aware of the meaninglessness of my self-centeredness and glib informationalism. Without my counselees, I might be seduced by success and status; I might want to lock myself up, to imprison myself in a tight professional and informational world. If I were to become the victim of this world and of my career, I would not be able to realize myself as a full human being. Therefore, the appeal of my counselees helps me to free myself. I may be a gift to them, but they surely are a gift to me. They gift me with the courage to face what my own, often distorted, form traditions have become under the smooth surface of my display of abstract information about my faith tradition. Maybe I am affected more than I know by popular form traditions that are at odds with the faith tradition to which I am freely committed and about which I may theologize so cleverly and proudly.

Distinctively Human Response of the Counselor

The appeals of my counselees of necessity demand an answer. This answer has to emerge from the real me to their plea, "Be with me and for me. Share my journey." Psychological, medical, or theological information alone, a piece of advice, a clever interpretation, a polite show of interest—these are not the answers asked of me. They may be used by me as a means to buy off the genuine answers I should give. This plea is an appeal to the best that I am, an appeal to be present to the core, heart, and matching character of my counselees. "Be satisfied when I give you what I have, not what I am" is the meaning implied by mere logical advice, a diagnostic explanation, a sharp or surprising interpretation, a prescription for drugs, or any other plan or cure. After that, I shut myself off in my world, hoping that the other will not disturb me again. I remain alone as the expert, the doctor, the surgeon, the professor, the administrator, the clergyperson, the pastoral worker, the social worker, the educator, or the diagnostician. And the other remains far away as the diagnosed, the patient, the client, the sick or deranged person, the parishioner, or the interesting case history. Since the appeal of counselees does not come merely from factual symptoms and problems, my response should not merely aim at them either.

The meaning of my being called uniquely as a counselor for the counselee was difficult for me to define in my transtherapy theory and my underlying formation anthropology. The appeal of the counselee is not an expressed, clearly formulated demand, nor is my response a logical compliance with a clear request or desire. Sometimes my refusal to answer neatly a demand for information may be the best way to be present to the counselee in depth. The response to the appeal of the counselee is an answer given to a unique person with an inalienable dignity. The counselee as a responsible other is the origin, the source, of one's own field of life *direction*. As a free and responsible person, the counselee is called to give direction to symptoms, problems, life situations, faith and formation traditions.

My counselee, as another "I," has to find his or her way in a unique situation of presence and action. This path in the jungle of life has to be cut in the light of his or her commitment to one's own basic faith and form tradition. We all have to unveil over a lifetime our own life call. We have to disclose and overcome the obstacles to its implementation. We have to invent our own history. The appeal of others to me means that they invite me to will their own free, responsible journey. It is my task to present them with the possibility to realize the unique-communal character of their existence in their own responsible way. I am called to join in their freedom and responsibility, to accept and sustain their free discovery of life's meaning. They appeal to the genuine focus of my concern: who they are, what they are called to be. Transcendent care is to will the existence of the counselee as a responsible and free "you" who discloses and implements his or her own call of life. Transtherapy and counseling represent my commitment to the transcendent-immanent coformation of that "you" in the light of the consonant form traditions to which you freely commit yourself.

CHAPTER 20

Consonant and Dissonant Care and Sympathy in Formation Counseling and Transcendence Therapy

When I say that I as a counselor should really care for my counselees and be in sympathy with them, I must not misunderstand such terms. In daily life, care and sympathy can mean unwise indulgence, unrealistic leniency, or spineless compliance with the needs and desires of others. Such indulgence differs significantly from true transcendent care. The wishes of counselees, whether expressed or not, may be arbitrary. They may be unrealistic and out of tune with their true life call. They may hinder human character unfolding. Many of their desires may be impulses or compulsions that are isolated from the core of their free and unique personhood.

As a thoughtful counselor, I try to sense and understand such wishes. Otherwise, these counselees may repress or deny this emergent awareness. However, my idea of sympathy and care may be wrongheaded. I may feel inclined not only to empathize with such tendencies as participant observer but to encourage their execution. Yet they may be contrary to the distinctively human formation, reformation, or transformation of the person. Love for the truth and empathic compassion should always accompany each other in transcendent counseling.

In transtherapy and counseling, I may, in a show of false sympathy, encourage attachment to formation traditions that are violent, destructive, or egocentric distortions of the consonant faith traditions of my counselees. These are not necessarily the basic doctrinal faith traditions to which counselees adhere. These basic doctrines may not harm society. What may do so are a person's distorted formation traditions. They, not the faith traditions as such, may often be the sources of war and conflict.

Caring for Counselees

Transcendent counselors are participant observers of the transcendence dynamics in their counselees. They look at their free life formation in the light of the claims of their life call, of the pyramid of their internalized consonant traditions, and of their here-and-now life situation. This implies that transcendent counseling excludes everything that could inhibit, arrest, diminish, or destroy one's free formation in the light of one's life call and situation. Consonant care refuses to do this on the basis of the aim of transcendent counseling itself. Therefore, if tendencies, wishes, and inclinations make impossible the distinctively human growth of the counselee, the therapist will refuse to confirm their execution. For example, the acting out of suicidal wishes or sexual desires in regard to children cannot be condoned by the counselor. Such acting out would sever counselees from reality; it would seriously inhibit their possibility of growth in congeniality with their unique-communal life call in compatibility with their consonant faith and formation traditions as well as with their life situations.

Another form of dissonant sympathy is a show of warm affection for others under the condition that they show the same to me. In that case, my care and sympathy are not expressions of real love and concern for their unfolding but a subtle kind of self-indulgence. Prefocally, I may want to see mirrored in my counselees an image of myself. I may secretly hope that their growth will be a testimony to my view of life, my structure of formation traditions, my personal style of being. Such subtle self-centeredness uses the other as a mirror in which I can admire the beauty of my own unfulfilled ideals. In other words, I may be inclined to make others extensions of my own pretranscendent individuation or of the common character of a group of people with whom I identify myself. Every sign in their behavior of a growing identification with my style of life evokes a noticeable increase in my care and sympathy.

This false type of sympathy goads and directs counselees away from their own uniqueness, from their own initiative, from their own life call and consonant traditions. It represents a form of not involving myself in the world of my counselees but of involving them in my world, of making them a part of my situation. This type of care and affection is poisoned by self-centeredness, and it is most harmful to counselees. Consonant concern demands at least an implicit awareness of the unique-communal calling and the inalienable dignity of the other's life. Consonant care confirms counselees as independent, responsible origins and sources of direction in their own field of presence and action. The transcendent counselor is delighted when counselees find their own way, when they form themselves in accordance with their own style and disclose more and more their calling and consonant life traditions. In no other sense am I called to counsel them. I counsel them precisely to enable them to form themselves within their own life situation, and in their personal vital body, all of which are different from mine.

Their vital bodily situation and their life situation as a whole contain for counselees factual realities. These are the only possible points of departure for the free realization of the unique-individual form potencies characteristic of their life —not of mine. My presence to them should enable them to give form to their life in their unique situation. It will never be the same for anyone else. The realistic limitations of our formation potential can be discerned over time by careful appraisal of our factual environment, including both the limitations of our bodily givens and those found in the social sphere that surrounds and penetrates us. For this reason it is advantageous if different kinds of counseling are available. Each ought to address itself to one special area of this complex arena I call our field of formation. Some specialties are pretranscendent counseling, psychiatric therapy, psychological therapy, medical counseling, vocational counseling, religious counseling, rehabilitation counseling, marriage counseling, addiction counseling, and, of course, transcendence therapy and counseling, complementing respectfully all of them. Each type directs itself primarily toward one or the other concrete life situation in which counselees find it difficult to give form to their personal life call in a harmonious, well-integrated way. A full understanding of each of these life situations may require special training, experience, and study. Underlying all possible forms of counseling is the fundamental attitude of consonant care without which no specialized training or knowledge about any sector of life can help others to grow as unique, responsible persons.

When I begin a transcendent counseling relationship, I cannot be clear about the details of the life call of my counselees. I can only be aware of their call in a general way. I can see their calling as a unique, increasingly free formation of life through their appreciative participation in the goodness, truth, and beauty to be found in their life situation and consonant traditions. Serenity will be the result of both accepting and appraising wisely all such opportunities for growth in the wisdom of living. Consonant transcendent care makes me want to foster the unique participation of my counselees in their own life situation and tradition. Such forgetful counseling and sympathetic care always imply that I assist others in looking for their own way, their own style, their own consonant character dispositions and the implementation of them. Respectful obedience to the voice of their life call and of the traditions to which they freely commit themselves is essential. It is for this reason again that I depreciate life directives that would remove them from the traditions to which they freely adhere. What if counselees are suicidal? Abusive? Prone to molest little children or to torture people? They have to face and explore such inclinations so that they can strongly depreciate that part of their behavior that would prompt indulgence in such destructive activities.

Transcendent care further risks degenerating into self-indulgence when love and concern fixate on the peripheral, attractive qualities of counselees. Sentimental involvement could destroy the consonance of my presence. Consonant care is not mainly motivated by the attractive qualities in a person nor by the absence of such qualities. Care is given to those in need.

By contrast, dissonant care may become a subtle attempt to dominate counselees, to get them to see things my way; I may even enjoy my own dominating influence in their life. In that case, I reduce them to pawns or playthings in my world; I destroy their free, unique responsibility for their own life direction. The same would apply to so-called loving parents who compel their children against their own talents and inclinations to play a role they have chosen for them. Consonant care has nothing to do with attempts to dominate, control, and direct the lives of counselees according to my own project of life and its preferred form traditions. Transcendent presence means to will the counselees' freedom, to see them as the unique origin of wisdom directives coformed by their freely chosen and modulated traditions. A transcendent counselor who really cares wills counselees as free and unique subjects.

In this connection I would like to mention the "reserve quality" of transcendent concern. Loving counselors express immense respect for the unique responsibility of each counselee. They know that lack of respect and timely reserve would destroy the effectiveness of the counseling situation. Transcendent counselors allow others to be what they are called to be. They respectfully participate as wise observers in the unique ways of being in the world they witness in their counselees. They are animated by the hope of helping them to become more fully who they are meant to be. This reserve implies attitudes that prevent counselors from interfering arbitrarily in the life world of their counselees. They transcend such self-centered inclinations.

Care for Counselors

In what way is the life of counselors affected by their care for others? Transcendent care fosters within reasonable and realistic limits the freedom of the counselee; it transcends the world of the counselor for the others' sake. This presupposes a profound hope for and a deep confidence in the possibility of an "awakening" to the "more than." Such hope implies an appeal to the person to whom one is present, a silent invitation to trust the mysterious power of transcendence. What, then, is the appeal to the counselee that is implicit in transcendent care?

First of all, it is not the will, desire, or subtle attempt of the counselor to profit by or to reap benefits from the affection, sympathy, and care manifested for the other. Transcendent counselors consider it impossible to strive for the fulfillment of their own needs or the promotion of their own growth and at the same time to keep pure their detached, yet concerned, care for others. Counselees may suspect that counselors care for them mainly in order to make money or to grow in experience or to become self-actualized. In that case, they cannot have the feeling that they are really accepted for themselves, for their own sake.

The appeal of counselees in turn should not be a subtle asking to be dominated in some way. Real care wants others to grow in consonance with their own unique call of life. The transcendent counselor desires that the counselees themselves choose in freedom consonant ways of life and avoid dissonant ones. Transcendent care means that one affirms others as persons who transcend one's own life and who have the right to pursue their life call beyond their pretranscendent individuation. They transcend the therapist too in choosing the form-traditional coformant of their life. They freely choose or ratify it. Therefore, transcendent counseling implies one's being genuinely at the disposal of the other's journey. This entails being attentive to any temptation to enhance oneself by taking care of another or by dominating a counselee in indirect or suggestive ways.

Lower-"I" Motivations in Counselors

Another call for self-abandonment in the counselor is more difficult to grasp. In transcendent care, one wills the other to unfold uniquely. Yet at the same time, as a counselor, one experiences in such care that one is on the way toward the fulfillment of one's own humanity. Counselors cannot escape the probability that they enrich, expand, and deepen their own personality by caring for counselees.

Being a transtherapist is paradoxical in many ways. One exists not only for the counselee; one exists also for oneself. Even when one is fully present to a counselee, one remains both a pretranscendent "I" and a transcendent "I."

In my theory of personality, being human is a paradox of self-awareness and self-transcendence. This paradox expresses itself even more dramatically in a counseling situation. Being a transcendent counselor means being at the disposal of the awakening of the transcendent "I" of a counselee. It entails total dedication to the unique, personal life call the counselee is. In the giving of oneself to a counselee, one's own deeper transcendent "I" is manifested; it is growing and expanding. The lower "I" that is functional, practical, or social should be at the service of the counselor's higher "I" rooted in the formation mystery.

This insight leads immediately to more questions: Is one's implicit appeal to counselees perhaps a silent supplication to them to give one the possibility of fulfilling one's own life call as a counselor? Is disinterested care really possible? Can one ever want something good for counselees without wanting this good at the same time for oneself?

Transcendent care offers a striking manifestation of this dilemma. The care giver should want the disclosure of the unique life call of the care receiver. It is impossible for one to really care transcendently for counselees without growing in the disclosure of their own life call during this process. One's transcendent turning toward the counselee implies the fulfillment of one's own deepest being, understood as a being-toward-the-other as called uniquely by the mystery of transformation. However, this does not mean that the ongoing disclosure of one's own life would by itself alone be a sufficient motivation for the loving care of a counselee.

The opposite is true. Transtherapy and counseling necessarily serve one's own growth in transcendence, but this growth is certainly not the prime motivation behind one's work. Imagine for a moment that your counselee was thanking you for the care, understanding, and therapy you offered and that you waved the thanks away by saying that what you did was really a way of serving your own self-unfolding. A counselee would immediately sense that he or she had not been cared for in a transcendent way. What motivated you first of all was your own growth, and this clearly affected your capacity for full and primary attentiveness to the other.

Such pretranscendent "lower-I" motivations may permeate our best attempts to be transcendent counselors. If this is the case, our presence is bound to be less effective, less full and open. Counselees may not know why, but they feel less understood, less inclined to open up to us, less at home, and less at ease. There is an invisible curtain between us and them. This screen of a dominant "lower-I" motivation prevents full openness on both sides. Even if we give counsel only because it is the obligatory thing to do, this motivation is in some subtle way directed toward the "lower I." The feeling that one should fulfill this counseling obligation still implies a concern for one's "lower I." Another way of saying this is that one's functional conscience is isolated from one's transcendent conscience.

Pretranscendent motivations diminish the effectiveness of the transtherapy relationship. Concern for one's own pretranscendent functional righteousness may be deeply rooted in one's history, environment, or form traditions. The counselor may need therapy to become clearly aware of these obstacles and to transcend them. They spoil not only the relationship between a counselor and a counselee but also other relationships, such as that between teachers and the students who come to them with personality problems, or that between religious counselors and counselees who ask about their spiritual life. When teachers or religious counselors are influenced by the idea that they should counsel to grow in self-disclosure or in their profession, the counseling relationship deteriorates. It is somehow vitiated. There is a dissonance between the counselor and the counselee that cannot be taken away by any amount of advice or sympathetic verbalization. The only way in which this relationship can be fulfilled is by transcending such lower self-preoccupied concerns as main motivations for transtherapy and counseling.

Necessity of the Ratification of Care by Counselees

As I have stressed repeatedly, when one acts as a transcendent counselor, one wants the unique life call, the freedom, the spontaneous initiative of the counselee to emerge. One wants the other to grow as a free response to the call of life. This motivation can bear fruit only when counselees ratify it by their own consent. Transcendent care does not strive to force, push, impose, charm, or seduce. What is more, as soon as counselors try to overpower counselees, if only by subtle suggestion, the activity is no longer caring in the transcendent sense.

In this respect, transcendent counselors must become the servants of the awakening transcendent "I" of their counselees. It is essential that our interforming relationship with the counselee strive for the transcendent freedom of this unique person and that it aim at the growth and expansion of this freedom. For this reason, both formation counseling and transcendence therapy can become effective only by means of the free consent and cooperation of the counselee. If one does not consent freely, all the improvement that one shows as a result of counselors' suggestions and interpretations will not be real improvement. It may help them to adjust more smoothly to the demands of society, but none of this has anything to do with real growth in free openness to one's call of life.

External changes in this case will not be rooted in free, personal *insight,* but in the counselor's pretranscendent *sight.* One may have brainwashed another by means of cold logic, information overload, clever interpretations, seductive promises of kindness, or the overwhelming impression of one's personality. Instead of helping the other to become free, one robs him or her of freedom, steals initiative, and paralyzes personal sensitivity for reality. Counselors may ornament counselees with new external behavior techniques or with better ways of adaptation to the community. But none of this can make up for the mistake of having taken away their own basic, well-informed insight and consonant freedom.

Without this freedom, no adjustment can be truly one's own. We can see from this example that transcendent care reaches its aim only if the counselee ratifies the counselor's desire that he or she choose freely that which is disclosed as a probable manifestation of one's life call here and now.

Implicit Appeal of the Counselor to the Counselee

The implicit appeal of the counselor to the counselee is again at the forefront of the encounter: "Please accept my being at your disposal as a servant of your awakening to your deeper 'I.' Please use me for your growth. Make me a source of your well-being."

Even though counselors may have to facilitate the closure of dissonant ways of life for counselees, their hope is that counselees take it upon themselves to transcend such ways. It is not enough for transtherapeutic care to make it literally impossible for counselees to harm themselves or others. The appeal of counselors to counselees is that they develop the power to appreciate for themselves and to experience by themselves that dissonant life traditions cannot lead to the fulfillment of one's unique transcendent call of life. "See for yourself, and realize in freedom your own being, your own unique call, and your own happiness. Never do it merely because I suggest it or because I say it or like it. Never do it merely because you like me. All such reasons lie outside your own free awakening. Your advance should grow out of your own openness to reality as revealed in your unique life situation."

The only fruit for which one may hope is that counselees may find new, probable disclosures of their life direction. Help them to take their own initiative. It is their life, not yours. Help them to disclose and implement freely the wisdom of the consonant formation traditions to which they are committed.

Mutuality of Concern

Should the concern of counselors and counselees be mutual? In my thinking, if counseling is to be effective, it has to be rooted, first of all, in the counselor's readiness to be at the disposal of counselees. This does not exclude that counselees care for their counselors. Of course, they will usually not care for their counselors with the same intensity as counselors care for them. It is unrealistic for counselors to expect the demonstration of like care and love for themselves in their counselees. It requires a lifelong growth to attain the ability to make oneself fully available to another. Not everyone is ready to be used for the awakening of another, especially when the other does not feel obliged to give anything back. In the counselor it is precisely this availability to the counselee without strings attached that enables the counselee to use the counselor without fear. There is less of a risk of becoming so dependent on the counselor that one loses one's own freedom to give and receive form in life.

In the situation of transcendence therapy or counseling, the counselor has sufficiently matured to be capable of this gift of transcendent self-giving. The counselee remains the person in whom this is still a more limited possibility. Therefore, the initial counseling relationship is unilateral. This unilateral, total gift of oneself to another's life-call disclosure makes for one of the differences between the counseling relationship and the love relationship as we know it in daily life between people.

It would be difficult for any person to maintain this attitude of unilateral total availability to the growth of somebody else for long periods of time. For this reason, counselors must always limit themselves to fixed periods of counseling. Otherwise, they would not be able to maintain peacefully this inner availability. Irritation, impatience, and tension would grow and show themselves if the periods of counseling were too prolonged. The flow and effectiveness of the healing relationship would inevitably be diminished.

Awakening of the Transcendent "You"

The lines that gradually become visible in this approach to transcendence therapy and counseling converge on one point, namely, "you," the counselee in search of awakening. In a deep sense the transcendence therapy relationship is only about this self-disclosing "you." Otherwise, the relationship would lose its transcendency and could even fail. Transcendent care becomes possible only when one is sensitive to the hidden unique-communal call of a counselee. No counselee should be seen as mainly a compilation of pretranscendent symptoms, problems, or diagnostic characteristics, a textbook syndrome, or an "interesting case."

What appeals to counselors are counselees in their whole being, not in one or the other of their expressed demands. Transcendent care may be succinctly summarized by saying that the motivation for the counseling is "you." I care for you because it is you to whom I am available, because you are potentially what you are called to be. I care for you because you are lovable, and you are essentially lovable because you are you. This "you" does not have the merely neutral meaning of being the object of one's counseling. It means rather that I try to be present to you in your deepest uniqueness, that is to say, in your unique rootedness in the mystery of formation.

It is not possible to meet this unique transcendent "you" of the life call by means of the methods of the positive sciences. The positive sciences are about the pretranscendent "I." They are prone to accept as meaningful only what can be expressed by means of measurement or well orchestrated interview techniques and tests. These may indeed be helpful and necessary in pretranscendent therapies. But one cannot disclose anything one thinks of as being the transcendent "you" in the pretranscendent "you" analyzed by tests and measurements. The only way in which I can discover you in your uniqueness is in experiencing the deeper you, and this experience will only become truly mine when I really care for you as you. It cannot be fully taught, explained, measured. Such description presupposes the experience: "My care of you is the same as my transcendent love for you."

If one has never experienced transcendent love, reading heavy volumes about it will not help. One's transcendent disposition as a counselor reveals who the client, as a unique person in this world, really is. An exclusively positivist approach can only reduce the unique, transcendent "you" of a client to a summation of psychological and physical qualities, to a descriptive list of symptoms or of pretranscendent dispositions and inclinations. In that case, one looks then only for the pretranscendent "you" of a counselee as summarized in a filled-out questionnaire and in a case-history file, where the personality is catalogued, diagnosed, and categorized. The transcendent "you"-as-"you" of a counselee is essentially beyond categorization, beyond diagnosis, beyond interpretations.

This does not mean, of course, that I, the counselor, am no longer able to determine that a counselee is, for example, aggressive, immature, hostile, or overdependent. On the contrary, the counselor who really cares sees not only these symptoms but reaches out to their deepest roots in the core of the personality of a counselee. Transcendent care enables one to see both the symptom and the transcendent "you" and to interrelate them as a whole to the client's deepest life call insofar as it can be disclosed at this moment in time. It makes impossible a reduction of the counselee to a series of pretranscendent pathological categories or test scores. Yet, one still takes them wisely into account. One relates them wisely to the transcendent call of the counselee who has benefitted so much from these during pretranscendent therapy sessions.

Transcendent care keeps the therapist present to that which is *more than* symptoms, test profiles, and problems of adjustment. It enables transtherapists to go beyond diagnostic categories. Persons find themselves in the world also in a uniquely transcendent way. No pretranscendent diagnostic category can do justice to this deeper dimension of personhood, for it is a gift of the mystery not to be mastered by facts and figures, charts and statistics, however accurate they may be.

Transcendence Therapy as an Interformational Process

The counselor's active "turning toward" the counselee entails a creative movement. Every time we are open to reality in wonder, it appears to us in new and surprising ways. In a deep sense, we let reality be for us. We allow reality to disclose itself. We respect and accept the manifestations and epiphanies of reality. We are active in this "letting-be" of disclosures of the reality of our life call and of its field of implementation. We are also receptive. Openness to reality implies an active sensitivity and an active receptivity. A "letting-be" of reality in a merely passive way cannot be called creative.

Let me give an example. When a carpenter makes a table from a slab of wood, he is far more than passively sensitive and receptive. Not only is he sensitive to the meaning and possibilities of the wood; he also fashions patiently the beautiful table he images in it. He establishes a new meaning; he creates something that was not yet there in that form.

The same could be said about the work of a poet. When a poet writes a poem, it is because she receives and uses the words of her language in a new and surprising way. She creates something that was not yet present in this form. The same could be applied to a musical composition, a painting, a sculpture, or the creation of a meal.

The transcendent encounter is creative in the same way. One's active turning toward a counselee really makes him or her be in a new fashion. To understand this sort of interformation in its proper context, one must first realize that not only the therapeutic encounter but every encounter gives form to the other in some new way.

Universality of Interformation

We are so used to coforming each other in daily life that we are seldom aware of the fact that one gives form to the other and that the other gives form to oneself in specific ways. We cannot think about any formation of life that happens by ourselves *alone*. All forms of life are influenced by the forms of others. Others make us be just as we make them be. We are not an isolated reality, totally independent of others. We can only understand ourselves as born from the other, as nourished and formed by the other, as speaking the language others speak, as wearing clothing created by others, as having customs generated by many before us. A mother is a mother through her child. An asocial family is only completely asocial when they are left insulated from or rejected by society.

An outcast is not an outcast in the same way that a chair is a chair or a cabbage a cabbage. For the chair or the cabbage does not know or care about being a chair or a cabbage. But a human being who is dubbed an outcast is conscious of being that in the eyes and minds of others. What makes people distinct from chairs or cabbages is that they are always giving meaning to their forms of life, also those imposed by others. The meaning a homeless person gives to being homeless is dependent for a great part on the way in which other people treat him or her. To put it briefly, we are formed largely through others just as the forms others assume are what they are largely through us.

Interformation in Transcendence Therapy and Counseling

Let me apply my theory of interformation to the specific nature of transcendent care. In what way can we give form to the other through our attitude of care? In what way does such care coform us?

Our transcendent care makes counselees be in a way no other encounter can. By the same token, their receptivity or resistance gives form to our presence as counselors. We interform with one another. Encounters that are not encounters of creative love and of revealing care result in social classifications imposed by others as they meet and measure people with a functional, scientific, or bureaucratic eye only.

When a Native American child in her interforming encounter with white people experiences what it means to be an Indian in a white society, she becomes more or less formed by this experience. It is a fact, a social fact, that may categorize her, hem her in, limit her, and bind her.

The same sort of thing happens when a test diagnostician has a professional encounter with the person taking the test. The outcome of the test, such as an IQ or a profile of aptitudes, gives form to the tested person in a certain way, namely, as a person who is now conscious of the limitations of her "intelligence" or of the range of his "skills." Other examples of the same would include the writing of one's case history by a social worker or the careful enumeration of one's physical symptoms by a medical expert.

All such descriptions indicate a number of more or less valid pretranscendent facts about one's life and person. They make one focally aware of these facts. Therefore, they form one's focal and prefocal awareness in relation to the data assembled. I was quite a different person when I left the office of my doctor after he told me that I had a heart condition. The same is true of a counselee who "learns" about "himself" in meetings with experts at testing. In my view, however, a counselee as a unique transcendent "I" is not wholly identical with these pretranscendent facts.

Such symptoms, problems, assets, and deficits are only a starting point for the realization of the formation possibilities implied in these givens. To be sure, pretranscendent facts, when valid, indicate certain broad limits within which one can grow and develop one's capacities; they can help one to eliminate certain mistaken orientations. A counselee with an accurately measured IQ of 90 is no more likely to become a quantum physicist of great renown than a deaf person is likely to become a famous opera singer. Within the limits of one's pretranscendent orientation, however, the opportunities for transcendent formation are almost inexhaustible. How one chooses to grow within and beyond one's limits depends upon one's freedom. This transcendent choice hinges also on the unique stand one can take in one's life situation. To accept one's limits is to transcend them. A transcendent encounter is one way to grant counselees their freedom. It becomes possible for them to be not only within but also over and beyond their pretranscendent limitations. It makes them experience such determinations no longer as thinglike, unchangeable objects. They become celebrated as dynamic points of departure, as harbors from which to set sail for the exciting sea of a transcendent-immanent existence.

Transcendent Potential or Actual Freedom of the Counselee

The counselee is basically a free person, not a thing, even when this freedom is stifled or crushed under the weight of neurotic anxiety, guilt feelings, destructive predispositions, overdependency, compulsions, depressions, and paranoid attitudes. One is never like a stone or any other thing. One is always fundamentally and potentially free, at least in one's inmost transcendence.

It is precisely the radical nature of this transcendent freedom which makes transcendence therapy possible. Freedom has roots (*radices*) in one's nature as human. It cannot be totally eradicated by circumstances, no matter how severely it is stifled under the stiff iron mesh of neurotic patterns. We may also use the expression "free, unique-communal personality" to characterize a person who has realized a high degree of freedom from pretranscendent individualism. This freedom enables one to bestow a transcendent-immanent meaning on each of the facts that go toward making up one's pretranscendent personality. It may grow into a freedom that stretches widely into all corners of one's life. It enables one to turn each obstacle, adversity, and resistance into an opportunity for formation, reformation, or transformation.

In freedom gained by effective transtherapy or counseling, one becomes able to appreciate one's illnesses and frailties in such a way that they help one to grow. Counselees, limited at first by neurotic or coercive controls, may, after a period of transcendence therapy, attain more freedom. They become able to affirm themselves as sources of initiative within the life situation in which they find themselves. As I have stressed earlier, this does not exclude the necessity in severe cases of the use of one of the many pretranscendent therapies that address the specific type of pretranscendent obstacle in question. Transcendence therapy or counseling is only possible after this pretranscendent healing has happened to a sufficient degree.

Freedom is not the same as mere physical mobility. Even a restrained prisoner can still be free deep down. The meaning of the life call of prison counselors is to set prisoners free. Prison counselors are called to liberate them not in a physical sense but in a far more fundamental fashion. Their highest mission is to nurture in them the birth of a transforming meaning to the restraints of incarceration. This enables the prisoner to soar beyond confining walls, to give form to an imprisoned life in a way unknown to one who faces the bars as only bars.

By our transcendent presence we participate in the free, unique core form of a counselee. We sustain, strengthen, and promote this unique heart and its corresponding character, hampered for too long by one's inhibitions, stereotypes, and compulsions. Therefore, in the core form of one's life one is no longer alone. One is no longer a lonely, threatened individual faced with the responsibility of devising a project of life against the tremendous odds stacked up in one's present pretranscendent personality. One may open up to one's potential and face one's limitations because I am with and for this suffering person. I am present to that transcendent call where one is more than one's confusions, indecisions, and fears. I give the other, as it were, to herself. I enable her deeper "I" to emerge and to take hold of her potentialities and limitations.

The transcendent-immanent relationship is fructifying and creative. Transcendent presence creates a new "you." Its aim is not to fashion a person only in accordance with a pretranscendent psychological or social approach to personality. These approaches ought to be respected as most useful for pretranscendent healing. They prepare the way, albeit unwittingly, for transcendence therapy and counseling.

Transcendence therapy crowns the marvelous accomplishments of pretranscendent therapies. It sets free the transcendent-immanent integrating "I" of the person healed already pretranscendently. This liberated "I" will give form to life in and through one's own unique-communal call. It then becomes possible to begin to feel, perceive, think, and act as a transcendent "I." One is then released from any school of psychology or psychiatry as an end in itself or as an exclusive, final psychological faith and form tradition.

Transcendent love and concern lead to the moment in which anxiety-evoking situations lose their insurmountability for counselees. Genuine empathy enables them to emerge as the relaxed and flexible masters of their life situation. Transcendence therapy challenges people to actualize themselves on a level and to a degree they never would have reached if they had been left alone in their pretranscendent encapsulation.

The awareness of being no longer alone in the depth of one's being is perhaps the clearest manifestation of the creativity of the transtherapeutic counseling relationship. Transcendent love and concern create the "we" of transcendent interformation. This companionship is experienced as different from the "we's" of daily social situations. It is nearly impossible to describe to another this "we" experience, which is characteristic of the best hours of trans-therapeutic counseling. When we try to express it, we fall back on such terms as "fullness," "fulfillment," "full presence," and "joy of being."

Re-creation of the Field of Life of the Counselee

Transcendence therapy or counseling makes people experience the joy and the vigor of being a new "I." Not only the counselees but also their fields of presence and action undergo a re-creation through the transtherapeutic encounter. The life situation of counselees is a correlate of their unique, free personality. The meaning of reality for them is re-created by their free, transcendent character dispositions.

Before the transtherapeutic encounter their deepest personal dispositions were not awakened. They were smothered by anxieties. These conjured up for them a desolate, frightening life situation that choked and oppressed them. However, as we participate lovingly in the probable disclosures of their deepest, unique-communal life call, we participate also in the new world of meaning which any disclosure of the call creates. Therefore, they experience in our concern for their uniqueness that we want their field of presence and action to assume a personal meaning as a formation opportunity for them.

In the light of our love, the world shows counselees its mildest face. When they *experience* the world as benign, it will enable them to believe in the possibility that not all people and situations are dangerous or oppressive. Our transtherapeutic care and love will make the world for them "home" once again. Not only in the transtherapy situation will they see aspects of reality that are lovable and enjoyable; also other encounters will be seen in a different light.

Transcendent care creates this new field of life for counselees. This field is congruent with the new "I" disclosed in transcendence therapy. Many counselees have had to meet the world always at its most crude and hateful. Parents withheld from them respectful love. Fathers and mothers might have been preoccupied with the pretranscendent assets and deficits of their children, with their correct or incorrect behavior, with their success or failure in school, and with their comportment in the eyes of their neighbors. They did not permit themselves to be present to the unique core of their children in freedom. They did not show the kind of concern that lies far beyond all mere lists of pretranscendent determinations. As a result, such children have never found themselves. They are only able to experience themselves as collections of assets and deficiencies, of successes and failures. They perceive their field of presence and action as a place in which one is acceptable only as a public failure or success. They perceive people as approving or condemning one according to one's bland conformity or rebellious originality.

The world for these loveless children becomes a living hell, tortured as they are by the constant need to be accepted. They hope desperately to escape destruction by being seen as beyond reproach in the eyes of others. Their anxious conformity to the wishes of others, the compulsion to please them at any price, makes them lose the freedom they need for wholeness. They become the parrots of society or of one of its dissonant form traditions, the slaves of group opinion. The absence of a unique, free stand invites sadistic control and enslavement by the people around them. The denied unique "I" leads, in turn, to a dominance of the suppressed pretranscendent individualistic "I," which is filled with a deep hate, a limitless rage, against the oppressors. Anger of this intensity paralyzes growth and movement.

Many of these wounds have first to be healed by outstanding pretranscendent therapies. Then they may be ready for a respectful fostering of the transcendent unique life. Transcendence therapy may break the monotonous circle of the last lingering remnants of doubt and lack of full inner peace.

One's presence to the veiled transcendent uniqueness of counselees may lead first to the eruption of the last residues of stored-up hate, hostility, anger, and aggression. These will be directed toward me as counselor. For I am perceived as the only person against whom one can dare to live out these last lingering traces of depreciative feelings. Be this as it may, one should maintain one's disposition and attitude of unshakable respect and love for the unique, independent source of initiative the person is transcendently, even though it reveals itself first in this depreciative, aggressive fashion.

Effectiveness of Transtherapy

From what I have said, it should be clear that we cannot describe transcendence therapy or counseling as a literal cause-effect relationship. The effectiveness of transtherapeutic counseling differs from that of pretranscendent counseling. The latter directs itself primarily and necessarily to pretranscendent psychological and educational aspects of the counselee.

My transcendent treatment, however, does the opposite: it aims at the transcendent freedom of the counselee. It approaches the heart and its matching character as the core of human life, as a transcending whole. It does not attempt, as do effective pretranscendent therapies, to cure this or that biological, psychological, or educational symptom. It fosters dispositions of respectful presence to the classic treasures of transcendent-immanent wisdom.

Pretranscendent therapies, combined with this approach to transcendence therapy, when offered to the same person, may complement each other, much to the benefit of counselees. This is especially true when these complementary types of treatment are offered by experts in each field who do not confound them.

The different dispositions and attitudes the two approaches focus on should be kept distinct while practitioners work together to benefit the life of a counselee as a whole.

The pretranscendent practitioner should show transcendent concern for the patient. However, it is not the primary task of the pretranscendent healer to foster the growth in transcendent freedom of the counselee's unique core of life in the light of his or her transcendent-immanent formation tradition. The primary concentration of the pretranscendent therapist is on certain factual, psychological symptoms, their dynamics and causes. This is not to deny that the inner pretranscendent dispositions of the counselee may already spontaneously show some beginning transcendent freedom toward his or her disabilities. This may facilitate in turn the process of healing on the lower-"I" level.

The transcendence therapist wants the ultimate freedom and transcendence of counselees to shine in the light of freely chosen wisdom traditions. He or she can only want a counselee's free consent to the loving care and wisdom offered to them. Transcendent care amounts to wanting an ultimate *freedom* that transcends the limited freedoms of the already healed pretranscendent life. When counselees do simply what they are told because of the fact that to them the transcendence counselor is an expert or "sees through them" or is "such a nice person," the refined process of growth in transcendent freedom is not likely to occur.

Transtherapy is fertile only when people come to their own personal options in the light of the consonant wisdom traditions to which the are committed. For this reason the approach of transcendence therapy differs from that of pretranscendent therapy. Transcendent interformation is an interchange between persons as transcendent-immanent beings potentially responsive to classical wisdom traditions. Both parties must be active and both must participate in this ascent. Without this free, dynamic participation by the counselee, transtherapy cannot be done. Their yes to their counselors is the starting point of the transtherapeutic process. It is a gift that must be freely offered, not a demand counselors can coerce.

Of course, the transtherapist or counselor has to make a living. Therefore, he or she has to charge a fee for services. That is one of the aspects in which transtherapy and counseling differ from denominational spiritual direction. Transtherapy and counseling as such do not represent one specific religion or denomination. The shift from transtherapy to denominational spiritual direction occurs when the counselor is guided in his or her counseling by the informational and formational doctrines of a church or community to which he or she as well as the directees are committed.

Denominational spiritual direction, therefore, as well as pastoral counseling presuppose a solid training in formation theology of the church concerned as well as in related informational theological perspectives to which the formation theology refers implicitly or explicitly. Obviously, the study of transtherapy and counseling can deepen the insights of the denominational spiritual director.

Another difference of denominational spiritual direction is that it focuses more on the denominationally supported prayer life of the directee than on the other aspects of transcendent character and personality formation. In volume 8 of this series I will deal more extensively with denominational spiritual direction and the basic differences between it and pretheological transtherapy and counseling.

CHAPTER 21

Transtherapy and Transcendent Parenting

In previous chapters I mentioned the central role child formation plays in all phases of transtherapy. I want now to focus specifically on the influence of transcendent parenting. In my thinking, it is one of the more decisive powers in child formation. It is for that reason that we offer through the Epiphany Association formation sessions-in-common that can be attended by present and future parents. These sessions embody my principles of transcendence therapy and counseling.

Transcendent traditions can teach parents how to form and guide their children in a wise and lasting way. Their example ought to make children ready to open themselves to the mystery of transcendent transformation later in life in a way that is trusting and touched by awe. Transcendent presence will facilitate affective togetherness with others in everyday life. The boundaries of pretranscendent life will be less rigid. As adults, children will be more outgoing and sensitive, more open to the needs and feelings of others.

Small children are not yet aware of the transcendent dimension of their life. Many pretranscendent needs overshadow the giving side of their love. Theirs is a needy love dependent on vital closeness to their parents. They look to them for care, security, confirmation, and gratification. A child's outlook on life is marked by vital sensitivity, a parent's by vital affectivity and the commitment to provide loving care for their children. If parental care becomes too vitalistic, it may block transcendent wisdom and functional reasoning. The latter cognitive element should temper the vital affective component of parental love. Otherwise, children may become overly dependent on pleasing their father or mother. In that case, the "Alma Mater" disposition says in effect, "I am nothing; my all-powerful, overly protective parent is everything."

Transcendent Parenting and Individuation
Transcendent parenting instills in the hearts of children the seeds of appreciative living, of faith, hope, and love, of inner joy and security. These seeds

will flower in children later in life when they awaken to their transcendent dimension. Such parenting also prevents an "I-other separation" on the pretranscendent level. Insofar as this is fostered by pretranscendent traditions, it forecasts a lifelong individualism. Contacts with others may be polite, charming, or entertaining, but they will miss out on transcendent depth, spontaneity, warmth, and flow. Certain parents subscribe only to some externals of a transcendent tradition to which they adhere by sheer inheritance. What really matters to them are popular traditions and/or depleted versions of transcendent traditions. Both condone a certain self-centeredness. Swayed by what they preach and practice, I fear that they may equate their own tradition only with a "what's-in-it-for-me" disposition. Children will catch on prefocally that such parents live by a mentality of salvation by external performance and appearance, self-indulgence with minimal social care and concern for others.

Affection, Confirmation, Reverence

Transcendent parenting does not neglect the individual development of children. It cherishes their individuality without making it the ultimate norm of human existence. Parents see pretranscendent individuality as granted by the mystery. This gift helps their children to put their unique-communal call into practice. Once they reach the point in life when this call begins to be disclosed to them, one source of disclosure may be their individual aptitudes. Individual gifts and limits point to certain aspects of their call. For example, superb body coordination in a child may point to the possibility that part of her call may be to excel in athletics.

Transcendent parents look with appreciation on the individual talents of their children. They confirm their performance whenever this is wise and reasonable. Confirmation works best for children when it backs up any performance that is consonant with the wisdom of their religious or ideological traditions. This link with transcendent traditions lifts their individual human growth potentially beyond sheer pretranscendent development. It turns mere development into also a preparation for transcendent formation itself. Skillfulness is revered by transcendent parents against the horizon of the transcendent-immanent meaning of life. By the same token, parents must honor and foster the aptitudes particular to each child. Their effective individuation, in service of their unique-communal life call, demands parental support. If one is to gain access to advanced education and training in service of the same transcendent call, one needs to excel in individual technological and professional skills.

Transcendent parents and teachers thus attend especially to any probable manifestation of the unique-communal call of the children entrusted to their care. They ask themselves how might this or that individual development serve or harm their unique calling. Children may sense, while not yet focally understanding, this kind of respect. When it is absent, they feel it acutely. When it is present, it touches the prefocal region of their consciousness. The more this level of consciousness absorbs such genuine reverence for their unique-communal call, the more ready they will be for the later awakening of the transcendent dimension of their heart and corresponding character.

What happens if parents are lacking in transcendent awe? A child may be used or abused for the gratification of their pretranscendent needs. For example, if parents become too vitalistic, they may set too few limits so as not to be disturbed by their children's need for discipline. The sad fact is that lack of discipline in early life leads to lack of self-discipline in later life.

The weaker the transcendent, the stronger the vitalistic bond may be between parents and children. One can expect that the separation anxiety the child feels when leaving home will be greater. Later separations from familiar people and situations rekindle the anxiety of childhood and infancy. Relationships with one's children may then demand fulfillment by the same vitalistic bonds one once had with one's own parents. When these bonds do not last, the next generation goes through the same anxiety of separation, and thus the cycle of deformation continues.

When pretranscendent dynamics prevail in parenting, children are often the victims of unreasonable expectations. The more sensitive they are, the more they may carry these expectations with them for a lifetime. They cannot shake off the sense of failure that gnaws away at their self-appreciation. Sometimes special kinds of effective pretranscendent therapies may be necessary to heal their pretranscendent traumas. The healing may be less than it could be if not followed up by transtherapy or counseling that makes up for the lack of transcendent formation in the family.

Tradition Directives for Child Formation

Directives of the same form tradition do not have the same effect on all children. Each child has within him- or herself powers of formation or what I call "form potencies." John, for example, is outgoing; Mary, withdrawn. Both pick up from the tradition of their parents the directive to care for people in need. John's way of helping is more gregarious, demonstrative, and outspoken. When he grows up, he loves to take part in boisterous demonstrations and movements for social justice. Mary, the more reserved child, feels ill at ease with any conspicuous venture, even one promoting the rights of the oppressed. Her more subdued way of caring will be to seek out and befriend lonely sufferers in need of a quiet attentive person.

One way of living the same form tradition may be no better and no worse than another. The question is: Am I choosing a way that is congenial with my faith and formation tradition? Is it in touch with my life call? Is this lifestyle in tune with all facets of my here-and-now situation? All these questions are dealt with in transtherapy or counseling sessions.

Tradition Directives for Adolescent Formation

What happens to adolescents in a culture that is predominantly pretranscendent? From early in life, teenagers have been shown the directives of individualism, competition, and mainly pretranscendent self-esteem. They do not really learn how to complement these by awe-filled fidelity to the probable manifestations of their life call. Neither do they know how to engage in joyful and peaceful emulation inspired by transcendent motives. These motives may peak when adolescents separate themselves from their families. Reasonable separation is essential for growth in transcendent-immanent adulthood.

This time of parting is generally less intense and conflict laden in transcendent cultures. In finding their own way, adolescents in these cultures do not totally forsake the basics of their transcendent family traditions. They move at the proper pace from childhood to adult life, directed toward their own form of responsible living while drawing on the foundations of sound and solid traditions. Most are ready to discover personally the higher dimension of their life. They speak of finding themselves, of becoming better persons, of making their traditions more meaningful.

As I have said earlier, people in individualizing traditions set up stronger lines of partition between themselves and others. Any threat to their "space" arouses anxiety. They weave around themselves webs of safety directives to quell any symptoms of dread or despair and to safeguard their pretranscendent boundaries. For example, a dominating show of motherly affection can so threaten the boundaries of an adolescent girl that she retreats with the help of such safety directives as rejection, avoidance, or withdrawal.

Adolescents formed in transcendent traditions often feel less in need of setting themselves apart from others pretranscendently. They seek togetherness in a deeper sense. Their own ease of communication poses a threat to the pretranscendent boundaries of people who have grown up in individualistic traditions. It surprises open and outgoing adolescents of a "lived" transcendent tradition when their sympathy and childlike (not childish) enthusiasm is rejected by their anxious, defensive peers. They may be seen as wimpy or as lacking in self-assertion; their cheerful openness and trust of life strikes the fear-dominated individualistic adolescent as childish.

I want to stress again that a transcendent form tradition helps adolescents to discover their deeper, unique call of life. This is always a source of fearless self-appreciation. It helps adolescents to unfold and transform their individuality in ways that serve their life call. Their call appreciation sustains them even when anxious, defensive individualists do not understand their joy and freedom from what others may think. Converts from anxiety-laden individualism to the joy and freedom of transcendent unique-communal life may go through a period of transition that can be facilitated by transtherapy.

Concentration on Individual Development

Mere developmental traditions are basically self-centered and prone to separation. The same holds for many social, clinical, educational, and managerial disciplines in pretranscendent cultures. Their main concern is with the processes of autonomy, self-esteem, separation, and individuation. They aim at the development of firm boundaries to seal off and protect their individualistic life of anxious self-actualization, not enlightened by the great wisdom traditions of humanity. Functional-cognitive development in service of individual autonomy seems to them the most important guide to wholesome living. They posit a sharp differentiation between self and other. They are less intent on fostering openness to a transcendent horizon. They seem interested mainly in what I designate in my personality theory as "functional reality testing." My complementary concept of "transcendent reality testing" is usually unknown to such fear-ridden, individualistic adolescents.

Unfamiliar as they are with the directives of transcendent conscience, functional individualists stress the formation of directives that build what many call the superego. To strengthen the autonomy of their vulnerable pretranscendent ego, they try to develop in people an optimal tolerance for ego-frustration. By the same token, they tend to misunderstand transcendent traditions as inferior, free-floating, or unrealistic.

The truth is, these transcendent traditions give form to other kinds of structures and other ways of appraisal. Transcendent life formation is concerned not only with *developmental* phases but with the far deeper *formation* phases. Character development that stays pretranscendent develops a strong lower "I." Without it the followers of merely pretranscendent popular traditions would not gain sufficient strength, independence, and lower self-esteem to survive their dread of not being liked by their peers or of not succeeding in life as self-actualizing money makers.

For example, in pretranscendent child development, parents show a dual disposition of presence to their children. They are disposed to encourage the toddler's distancing from themselves in explorations of the environment. Yet they attach to this encouragement the string of a hidden demand that their children return to them for reassurance. If not, they will diminish their expressions of affection. Children are unsure of their own attempts at some desirable separation. They fear the threat of dissonance between themselves and parents who are hungry for confirmation of their shaky pretranscendent self-esteem by their children. They seek to please. The dispositions of supportive parental closeness and confirmation of their own attempts to separation become internalized already in the intradevelopmental sphere of the toddler.

Parents who form their children in an affective transcendent tradition promote a different set of dispositions. It, too, fosters the necessary distancing of their children from themselves. The difference is that this is done through affective communication of awe for their child's still-hidden, unique higher "I," founding life form, or true nature. Respect for their transcendent life call prevents parents from seeing their children as vital-functional extensions of themselves. Mere imitation of parents can create the climate for serious psychopathology later in life. The differentiation of a child from a parent happens more gradually in this transcendent climate. In the end it is more rooted in the still-dormant, deepest life call of the child. Children reared in awe for their unique dignity can later withstand more easily sufferings and failures in their individual life. Their separation from their parents is likely to be less loaded with crises and conflicts. Temptations to individualistic separation from cosmos, humanity, history, and their mysterious source are likely to be overcome. Growth in universal love is often a mark of such children when they mature into adulthood.

Uniqueness and Individuation

Some take it for granted that transcendent traditions keep people immature; that they disincline them to show initiative; that anyone so formed will turn out to be a low achiever, who does not wholeheartedly pursue worthwhile social and practical endeavors.

To answer such assumptions I had to invent my distinction between transcendent uniqueness and pretranscendent individuality. What were the differences between individuation guided by developmental pretranscendent and functional-transcendent directives or guided also by transcendent-functional formation directives?

Development of only pretranscendent individuality turns people toward anxious competitive self-concern instead of inspiring, joy-filled emulation. Excessive competition makes them vulnerable; they feel easily threatened. For them the way to advance their own worth over others is to push for individualistic success, achievement, and perfection. Unlike emulation, these self-directed dispositions arouse strain, anxiety, despondency, envy, jealousy, gossip, condemnation, and exhaustion of vital energy. Attractive appearances and clever maneuverings become the measure of "maturity."

Transcendent uniqueness, by contrast, is open in awe to a life call that inspires people to much more than mere individual success and a striking demeanor. It inspires invigorating, mutually appreciative emulation. One tries to do the best one can in service of transcendent goals through their vital-functional expression in society.

The transcendent dimension is present, at least in some nascent way, even in those who are directed mostly by pretranscendent traditions. All of us are always also transcendent. This is an essential coformant of our humanity. We can never lose that dimension. Likewise, we are always also pretranscendent. That, too, belongs equally to our very being. Transtherapy and counseling appeal to that hidden dimension that was perhaps not sufficiently appealed to by the parents or later lost by the children.

Main Difference between the Two Kinds of Traditions

Transcendent traditions awaken us to the truth that the leading dimension of our life is the transcendent. It is the carrier of our call and dignity, our true unique-communal nature. Such traditions help us to appreciate our call by their symbols and directives. Parents offer these to children more through dispositions and attitudes than words. They show an unconditional, loving reverence for the dignity and uniqueness of each other and of each child.

A transcendent tradition thus fosters affective responsiveness on the part of parents to children. It makes them believe that their worth does not reside only in their gifts or skills, their successes in the classroom, their appearance, temperament, strength, or health. What counts is doing the best they can within limits that will influence all they do to put their life call into practice. The frantic striving for a selfish kind of esteem, a pretranscendent self-adulation, is replaced by an unconditional appreciation-in-praise of the call by a mystery of loving formation that sets their spirit free.

Abandonment to this forming mystery dispels the anxiety called forth by the need to prove oneself by standing out in a self-preoccupied way. It opens one up to the fulfilling experience of universal love, consonance, and interformation. This takes us beyond feelings of separation and excessive competition and proves that inner divisiveness can be bridged by love and wisdom. It diminishes the depression that may set in if such pretranscendent dreams are not fulfilled. I distinguish what I call "individuation depression" from clinical depression. The latter is dealt with in appropriate types of pretranscendent therapy. Individuation depression, if not excessive, can be helped in transtherapies.

Liberating Power of Transcendent Hierarchies

The inspirations of our unique-communal life call—as coformed by the foundationals of our tradition—help us to give form in freedom to our individuality. We may be called, for example, to assume a leadership role, to be the captain of a ship. We are then part of the hierarchy of a group, club, or social institution, tasked by the call to live our hierarchical responsibility in a transcendent-communal way.

A transcendent hierarchy as distinguished from one based solely on social power places fewer restraints on people because it is based on love and bounded by a tradition freely accepted by fellow adherents. It is also less constraining and more flexible and adaptive than other hierarchies. It can allow for variations to accommodate the style of each person within reasonable communal limits.

Transcendent traditions—provided they are not functionalized—set people free. They help them to be more liberated inwardly from the pressures of social, political, professional, or other hierarchies in their formation fields. Inner freedom from functionalistic pretranscendent hierarchies enables people to give form to an unusually rich intraformational sphere. They grow to be rich in feelings, thoughts, symbols, and images. Those who hold higher positions, even in the hierarchy of a transcendent tradition, are always in danger of becoming functionalized. They may be plagued by childhood deformations that led to coercive dispositions. Among the most common are insecurity, resentment, fanaticism, vitalistic devotionalism, rigorism, paralysis of creative thought and imagination. Leaders may retreat to the past or escape the here and now by striking out wildly into the future. In such cases, it is not necessarily the transcendent hierarchical tradition that is at fault. One should not confuse a tradition with any one of its imperfect representatives.

By now it should be clear that the sources and the norms of effective, subordinated individuality in transcendent traditions are different from those found in pretranscendent traditions. Representatives of social, political, and managerial disciplines often confine themselves to the lower level of pretranscendence. They tend to depreciate the higher levels of transcendence. These functional disciplines may be by-products of merely developmental theories. They start out from pretranscendent and implicit prescientific assumptions. They conclude that self-actualization and self-esteem on this level can embrace all the traditions of life in all cultures and populations.

Transcendent traditions, as well as the formation science I initiated to explore them, assign a different place to pretranscendent development. It is situated within a far wider transcendent frame of reference. Parents may let a pretranscendent frame direct the formation of their children in its lower developmental aspects. But implicitly they subordinate these from the start to the transcendent dimension. The outcome is not mere human development but its implicit subordination to transcendent formation. Parents who find it difficult to make this crucial shift in parental dispositions often show up for transtherapy and counseling sessions.

Consonance of the Transcendent and the Pretranscendent "I"

The mystery of formation integrates both our higher and lower modes of presence. They interform with one another and together move on to consonance. Our transcendent life is linked in three ways with our pretranscendent life: by means of consonance, dissonance, and partial dissonance.

Consonance refers to the harmony between our higher and lower dimensions of life. They are meant to sound harmoniously together. For example, a woman volunteers to help pregnant teenagers who want to have their babies in supportive surroundings. Her transcendent love and respect for these young mothers inspire her to put her lower functional skills at their service. Her every act of functional assistance and vital sympathy reveals the depth of her transcendent love, respect, and wise sensitivity.

Another volunteer does not have the same kind of motivation. She comes to do something for the girls because she wants to be in with the social circle that pushes this work among their well-to-do friends. She has not personally grown in transcendent respect and love for these teenagers. She dons the garb of vital affection and functional performance. This works well, but what is missing is transcendent esteem. Some of the girls sense the difference between the consonant care offered by the first volunteer and the dissonant care of the second.

A third person shows neither full consonance nor total dissonance. She stands in the place most of us often find ourselves—between these two dispositions. She is partially consonant, partially dissonant. At some moments she lets her higher motivations shine through in her work for the girls; at others she senses that she is losing "it." She regresses to her earlier lack of unconditional awe for their dignity. She still does what she has pledged to do but in a routine fashion. She flashes the right smile, says the right thing at the right time, but her heart is not in the work.

We can sympathize with her plight. We, too, are only on the road to transcendence. We, too, find that we do not always make room for our higher aspirations. However, the transcendence dynamic prods us toward consonance between our higher and our lower "I's." It aims at the step-by-step transformation of our life as a whole. The longer we walk the path of consonance, the more the mystery makes us uncover and release the finer and subtler powers of our own transcendence dynamic. These powers propel us forward with an ever-renewed force. If we are parents, the dynamic of transcendence inspires us to unconditional, transcendent parenting that sets free the spirit of our children. There is no greater gift we can give them than this. If we feel unsure in this regard, we may attend transcendent formation sessions-in-common that embody the principles of transcendence therapy for parents.

How do transcendent traditions help parents to tune into their own and their children's deepest "I"? What are the bridges they hold out to them to link their lower and higher dimensions of life? In seeking the main ways to align the higher "I" and the lower "I," I want to point out some of the basic means the classical formation traditions have in common. These common ways, I might add, are not enough. They must be deepened by the teachings, symbols, and rituals of a particular, fully intact classical formation tradition—one in which we freely invest our life.

Spiritual Guidance and the Journey to Consonance

Almost all transcendent traditions put forward masters, directors, mentors, and guides of formation. A hierarchy of administrative authorities, supported by professional informational and formational theologians or ideological philosophers, protect and unfold the faith tradition. Their work is complemented by an informed hierarchy of directors, guides, and teachers of formation. Foremost among them in initial formation power are the parents. All make themselves available to people who want to put their faith tradition into practice. Through writings, talks, formation-in-common, and sometimes private spiritual or parental guidance, they help people stay in touch with the classical formation traditions of their own faith.

Some who come to them for help may not share their faith tradition. They may only be made ready by the mystery to receive some of the wisdom common to all spiritual formation. It may happen that a bond of transcendent love grows between the guide and the person guided. Personal transcendent affection gives a special glow to this tie between masters, teachers, and disciples, or parents and children. In the end it is always the mystery of formation that has to turn the dry wood of human wisdom and affection into the awe-filled wisdom and the soaring fire that warms the heart.

Psychological and educational writers, if they are not enlightened by the wisdom of higher formation, may reduce this relationship of consonance to a mere repetition of the fusion of the infant with the mother. To be sure, the master–disciple relationship can carry some traces of past ways of fusion with the mother. This should not make one overlook that over and above such traces the experience of transcendence puts us in touch with our own unique-communal life call. This call by its very nature pulls us beyond our earliest experiences of fusion. Traces of early fusion with our parents may stay with us for a lifetime. Yet these outer remnants of earlier bindings are hollowed out, as it were, bit by bit. The outer appearance of vital fusion with the mother lingers on, though not necessarily in its original meaning.

Transcendent consonance little by little takes the place of the vital fusion that once gave shape to the mother–child relationship. It then becomes a healthier human relationship, as opposed to a neurotic and controlling one. We should remember by now that symbols lend themselves to meanings and interpretations that go beyond the original meaning of childhood fusion and ought not to be reduced to it alone. By far, the greatest gift in the phase of child formation is transcendent parenting. Without this awe-filled love, it can be both difficult and painful for children to gain later the freedom of spirit. That freedom is the source of their peace and joy as well as their personal and social effectiveness.

CHAPTER 22

Intimacy and Transtherapy

In my formation anthropology and transtherapy, I make a distinction between childhood intimacy, manifested in the child's intimacy with its parents, and advanced personal intimacy. Childhood intimacy is one-sided. It is dependent on the loving presence of the parent to the child; hence, it is chiefly receptive. Children are at the receiving end of the relationship; they cannot share their yet insufficiently formed interiority; they cannot give in the same way as they receive. They do not yet possess themselves sufficiently in self-disclosing love to be able to communicate that self to others. The one-sidedness of childhood intimacy may be maintained in later life, usually unwittingly. Transtherapy and counseling sessions aim at disclosing and overcoming this "my way" mentality.

Unique Life Form Disclosure:
A Preparation for Personal Intimacy

Advanced intimacy that goes beyond one-sided childhood intimacy becomes possible in adolescence provided one lives in propitious circumstances. Adolescence is the phase in which self-disclosure is heightened. It enables adolescents either to share or to withhold what they feel about their life. They may fear losing to parents or others what vaguely announces itself as their own vulnerable uniqueness. Therefore, adolescents engage as much and often more in the dynamics of withholding as in attempts to intimate communing. The formation mystery involves them in a sometimes painful process of transition. Advanced intimacy can, therefore, be called "advancing" intimacy.

Maturing of intimacy accompanies the deepening and widening of the heart. Because the amplification of the heart should never cease, the maturing of intimacy is by no means finished with the end of adolescence. On the contrary, adolescence signifies the transition from restricted childhood intimacy to successive phases of advancing intimacy. The mystery allows these phases of intimacy in our life as periods of new communications of its wisdom, power, and energy. Each of these phases generates a current form of life that lasts until the next phase of intimacy. Here I shall restrict myself to certain remarks pertinent to the transition from initial parental intimacy to increasingly personal or advancing intimacy. This begins when initial parent–child intimacy has sufficiently opened up the life of the child or if its inadequacy has been remedied by others.

Transtherapy and counseling can help persons go through the phases of intimacy they somehow missed. Severe psychological and other disturbances on the pretranscendent level must be solved before transtherapy can be effective. Certain pretranscendent therapies specialize in such healing. One ought to enlist these therapies in the healing process. Only after such pretranscendent healing occurs can one start post-therapeutic integration. What I mean by this is the integration of the pretranscendent changes that have taken place within one's character as a whole. This character has been formed earlier in the light of one's transcendent formation tradition. The pretranscendent change must be integrated in one's traditional transcendent character. Otherwise, one's character will be less well structured and whole than it could have been.

Transcendent Formation of the Heart
in Uniqueness and Intimacy

Young adults are called to affirm their own uniqueness and its corresponding subordinated individuality. They often have to affirm themselves in the face of emergent anxiety. Such affirmations of new challenges imply a leaving behind of the security of sharing intimately in the life of a confirming family. Trusting in life's mystery, one has to find one's own path. Loss of family security evokes anxiety. There is no clarity and certainty about where the journey may lead us.

We have to grow in the patient hope that we shall find other intimacies that complement parental intimacy. We have outgrown its exclusiveness. We can cope with this anxiety in the measure that our intimacy with our parents has formed us sufficiently in the foundational triad of faith, hope, and consonance.

The adolescent phase of formation is one of a first disclosure of uniqueness. Adolescents should not get stuck in the process of their pretranscendent "I" development or individuation. They should open up also to the unique disclosures of their transcendent-functional "I" instead of only to their functional-transcendent "I" and its individuation. Intimacy dynamics were operative in them during the initial parental-intimacy phase. After being latent during certain periods of the pre-adolescent and adolescent phase, these intimacy strivings become operative again. They complement more definitely parental intimacy with personal intimacy with others. Later, in due time, they may resume intimacy with the parents again, albeit in a more critical fashion. The task of this postadolescent phase is to initiate a free intimacy with others. It ought not to diminish but to enhance fidelity to one's own transcendent uniqueness. The effectiveness of these dynamics of free intimacy depends on adolescents' overcoming the counterdynamics of vitalistic fusionism. Transtherapy and counseling can be a mighty companion on the journey beyond the latter aberration.

Fusion Dynamics and Individuation Dynamics

Fusion dynamics threaten initially our advance to distinctively human intimacy. Well-integrated human intimacy implies vital-fusional facets, but it should not be ruled one-sidedly by them. These fusion dynamics are nourished by a nonfocal longing for childhood intimacy.

The other threat to effective personal intimacy with others comes from our individuation dynamics. Unlike fusion dynamics, the latter operate mainly in the functional or functional-transcendent dimension of our life. They enable us to develop ambitions, skills, and aptitudes as well as other assets peculiar to our individuality and pretranscendent individuation. These should be illumined by our transcendent uniqueness. Otherwise, they can insulate us within a skill-oriented individualism. This can seriously curtail our growth in transcendent intimacy.

To put it briefly the dynamics of vital fusion and functional individualization are meaningful. They should be especially developed in earlier phases of our pretranscendent development. When maintained too long as dominant, however, they can become an obstacle to the advance of intimacy dynamics in this later phase of our journey. By contrast, the greatest help in this phase is courageous and candid openness to any disclosures of our call to transcendence. The transcendence dynamic aligns us in intimacy with the mystery. It saves us from the destructive dominance of mere fusion or of individuation. It is one of the aims of transtherapy and counseling to awaken this transcendence dynamic in people who are not too severely handicapped by psychological problems.

Congeniality Dynamics; Fusion Dynamics; Pseudo-Intimacy Dynamics

Dynamics of congeniality sustain fidelity to one's unique-communal call by the mystery. These dynamics of congeniality may still be weak. In that case they are not sufficiently resistant to the seduction of one-sided fusionism. Diffused, insecure life forms are ruled by anxiety. Its victims may shy away from any attempt to personal intimacy. Others let fusion dynamics submerge them in a fusion with the life call of others. They ignore in the process their own unique-communal destiny and responsibility.

They replace their own fragile self-image with the stronger image of others. They admire them as bearers of a strongly self-defined image of unicity and/or individuality. They adorn their own diffuse self-image with other persons' clear and self-assured self-definition.

Some—because of their fear of any immediate intimacy—may practice the dynamics of what I define as *distant pseudo-intimacy*. An example can be found in many followers of Adolph Hitler. They were people with weakly defined images of their own identity. Transposing their image within the contours of the loudly proclaimed, strong delineations of the Hitler image, they began to identify their image, their life call, their strength with his. They even imitated some of his swaggering ways. When Hitler collapsed, so did they. They had no unique self-image to fall back upon. Similar dynamics of distant pseudo-intimacy can emerge in relation to any secular or religious leader as well as to superiors, saints, heroes, stars, and other celebrities. Sexual intimacy dynamics may be abused in a similar fashion for the sake of finding in the partner the unique transcendent meaningfulness one is missing in one's own life.

Clever or powerful people often play on the need for intimacy to serve their own ambitions. For example, intimate care and concern is portrayed in commercials and by salespersons to move insecure listeners to buy certain products, or by politicians to gain followers. The more pseudo-intimacy dominates, the more it arouses the fear of true intimacy. Many are terrified by the threat that their intimacy longing may be abused. They flee when intimacy is offered by anyone. They may have suffered too many disappointments in pretended or true intimacies. One aim of transtherapy and counseling is to create a space and time where those desperate for genuine intimacy can taste the beauty of distinctively human togetherness. Before being able to profit from participation in the transtherapy process, they may have to be healed of their more deeply rooted psychological problems by practitioners who specialize in pre-transcendent therapies.

Transcendent Intimacy and Dynamics of Individuation

A main obstacle to intimacy of heart is individualism. With animals, plants, and minerals, we humans share the quality of individuality. Like them we have individual marks that set us apart from others. No two snowflakes are alike; neither are two people in their vital and functional make-up. They share in the individuation of all material forms in the universe. For instance, human fingerprints, voices, cells, and organs are marked by individuality as rooted in the individual materialization of forms. Human forms differ from other cosmic forms because they feel driven to develop intelligently and volitionally some of their individual assets. These human assets are the basis of their own insightful aptitudes, skills, appearances, and strategies. These in turn are meant to serve the effectiveness of their consonant ambitions.

Early in life, dynamics of individuation move people to focus on developing individual ambitions. These dynamics stimulate our functional dimension to disclose and actualize our individual potencies. This focus sets us temporarily more apart from others. It makes us less inclined to merge with them in intimacy of heart and its matching character dispositions. While this current form is important during the early phase of life, to become stuck in it would be counterproductive. Lasting exalted dynamics of individuation lead to individualism. Individualism spells paralysis, or at least underformation, of the potency of our heart and character for transcendent intimacy. Our social life situation may be functionalistic. It may foster individualism not intimacy; competition not consonance; envy not love; depreciation not appreciation; condemnation not confirmation. Post-therapeutic care in transtherapy sessions can help in the disclosure and appraisal of remnants of individualism that may still linger on after solution of problems by pretranscendent therapies has occurred.

Dynamics of Collision or Collusion

Individualism leads to a collision with others with whom we are in competition. We will see later that some collision is unavoidable; it can serve our consonant character unfolding. What is harmful is a life dominated by collisions.

Another opposite threat to intimacy is collusion. We may collide with the intrasphere of others to such a degree that we betray our fidelity to our own destiny. Collusion makes intimacy impossible because our blind blending with others diminishes what is personal in our self-expression. As a result, there is not enough unique personality left to which people can relate with wonder and intimate appreciation.

The hunger for fusion and collusion is sometimes an overreaction against the crass individualism of our society. It explains also the attraction some feel for certain pantheistic tendencies that suggest we fuse with cosmos and humanity.

True intimacy avoids the extremes of either collision or collusion; it sinks its roots into the shared basics of our unique-communal life calls. Transtherapy and counseling assist us in disclosing such foundations.

Call Congeniality and Intimacy

Congeniality with our call makes us dethrone individuation strivings as the supreme power in our life. Instead, individuality becomes the servant of our uniqueness. We begin to realize that certain individual talents cannot be fully developed because of our unique higher calling, which includes intimacy with others. For example, people who find out that one fundamental facet of their call is intimate family care and responsibility may have to forgo certain attractive possibilities for individual success and prominence.

When we are most detached from our individuality, we are most capable of attentiveness to others. We can share with them wholeheartedly. The extent and intensity of such sharing should be modulated by the unique-communal type of intimacy to which we are called in different situations. Sharing is different between parents and children, married couples and friends, neighbors and colleagues, comrades and buddies. There are as many gradations of styles of intimacy as there are human relationships. Moreover, some people are called to a relatively solitary life with fewer intimate relationships; others to a relatively gregarious life, implying more intimate connections. The degree of relativity in both callings depends on the gradual disclosure of one's unique-communal life call. It may also differ in the same persons at different phases of their life. Moreover, the segments of society in which they participate influence the style of expression of either the relative solitude or gregariousness of their life of intimacy. Southern Italians, for instance, foster more lively expressions of gregariousness than Scottish farmers and fishermen do. Transtherapy and counseling enable people to examine such dynamics. They are encouraged to do so in the light of the disclosure of their life call in both its unique and communal aspects. This exploration entails a dialogue with their own form-tradition pyramid.

Intimacy and Its Metalanguage

Human life forms are always in interformation. Its degree and intensity can vary from most peripheral to most profound. If interformation is intimate, it is marked by reciprocal communication in depth. Such personal communication entails a risk. Yet it is only in taking the risk that intimacy becomes possible.

Intimate communication implies the disclosure of those unique facets of each other's life story that are relevant to the type of intimacy in which we are involved. For example, the range of self-revelation is different between married people and neighbors who have established a certain kind of neighborly intimacy with one another.

Intimate communication can be expressed by means of the dynamics of verbal or body language. In their own way, intimates may create a kind of nonscientific metalanguage of intimacy. It consists of common words of preference filled for them with connotations of memories of shared experiences. Like the metalanguage of a science, the cordial metalanguage of intimacy often develops shorthand words and sentences over years of intimate togetherness on a journey of interformation in which people grow old together.

Body language expresses itself in various modes and modalities that are in great measure culturally determined. They consist of communications by eye contact, embracing, kissing, physical nearness, touch, handshake, facial mimicking. They extend to bodily postures, meaningful gestures, sexual expressions. All of these can become vehicles of disclosure of certain facets of one's formation story. Many participants in transtherapy and counseling begin to appraise the aptness, the consonance or dissonance, of their unique-communal metalanguage of bodily expressions and movements.

Limits of Intimate Self-Disclosure

People cannot disclose their ongoing journey in its totality. First of all, the disclosure of their own life to themselves is always partial. What is not yet sufficiently available to their focal consciousness cannot be disclosed to others. Second, even what is disclosed to them inwardly can be so subtle and unclear from the viewpoint of focal consciousness that it is not yet within their power of communication. Moreover, people differ in communication skills. Third, their life story is still unfolding. At no moment can this movement itself be frozen and packaged for final, detailed communication. Fourth, intimacy is true to itself and hence appealing, at times enchanting, only when it retains a rhythm of detachment and attachment, of closure and disclosure, of concealment and unconcealment, of nearness and distance, of stillness and speaking.

Unmitigated disclosure with the pretense to be able to tell it all "as it was, is, and shall be" is deceptive and destructive of true intimacy. It pretends to attain the unattainable. One cannot render a full account of a story that is still unfolding. It can only be fully understood when the ending is known. Only then can we disclose in fuller perspective what preceded the finale. The human heart cannot fully know or communicate the mystery of its ongoing formation. It can only tell what certain fragments of the story mean to one's sensibility and responsibility here and now. We should not pretend to ourselves or others that we can spell the story out in detail in all its possible meanings. If we try too hard the human heart loses its wisdom and its mystery. Therewith its fascination for self and others evaporates in empty chatter. When the heart is no longer fascinated and fascinating, intimacy dies.

It is clear from this that transtherapy and counseling, in private or in common, intend to cultivate a climate of wise and congenial intimacy. One communicates only what can be communicated here and now in a relaxed way, in wise consonance with one's life situation and one's unique-communal life call.

Dynamics of Marital Love and Intimacy

Marital love enables people to express in genital-bodily language the intimacy they concelebrate. Marital love is for many a main way to intimacy. Certain people may never reach the phase of interformation, which would make them transcend their individualism, if it were not for the moment of marital ecstasy.

Sexual desire does not necessarily express itself in the language of intimacy. The vital facet of sexuality may dominate the marital relationship to the exclusion of the transcendent facet of intimacy. Individualism may be too pronounced in one or both of the marriage partners. As a result, mutual abandonment in intimacy of heart is unattainable. Anxiety may be evoked by the awareness of one's vulnerability. One does not dare to expose one's uniqueness. The ensuing withholding of the heart diminishes the full humanness of the marital sexual expression.

In spite of such obstacles, we still surmise that for many married people sexual love is a preferred path and for some it is the main path to intimacy. This seems to be true especially in functionalistic societies. Lost or neglected are precious nonerogenous zones of intimacy. Even the art of intimate conversation may have died. Romance may not find time and space. Leisurely togetherness around the fire may be replaced by an indifferent grouping of lonely spectators around the television. All seem absorbed in their own inner conversation with actors, announcers, speakers, dancers. The teaching of art, literature, and spiritual formation may be replaced by the teaching of positive science, techniques, and practical skills. Parents may not find ample time to be intimate with their children. High school children may reach out in despair for a premature expression of sexual love. Unknown to themselves, they try to grasp the intimacy their deserted hearts long for but do not find in the everyday life of family, school, and social gathering. Even religiously based presentations may be almost exclusively informational instead of also formational.

Marital sexual love as intimacy is not the origin or the prototype of all intimacy. Nor is sexual intimacy sufficient for enduring intimacy in the everyday life of a married couple. The beauty and burden of the intimacy of married life cannot be carried by the dynamics of vital-sexual or functional team spirit only. It must be sustained by the intimacy of everydayness, of sharing, in the light of the mystery, the tenuousness and tediousness of each other's daily journey. The transcendent intimacy of married everydayness will enhance in turn the intimacy of sexual encounter.

Especially, transtherapy and counseling sessions-in-common create an atmosphere in which the lost art of intimate communication is restored in dialogue with the classical wisdom traditions of loving togetherness.

Intimacy and Empathy

Dynamics of empathy move us to enter into the intrasphere of others. Empathy is our affective-imaginative participation in the unfolding sensibility of people. It enables them to feel really understood by us. The dynamics of intimacy are effective in the measure that the dynamics of transcendent empathy flow freely between those who are intimate. This flow is vulnerable. Any distortion of the communication, any slight attempt to manipulation, any minute manifestation of possible rejection, any inappropriate teasing may interrupt the flow. An anxious flight in caution and reticence may follow, especially in oversensitive people. The dynamics of empathy, when they are well received, foster growth in intimacy. Empathy with others allows us to become aware of our own heart and its feelings. It enables us to risk opening the door to our own repudiated or refused sensibilities. Our frozen transcendent sensibilities may be defrosted by the warmth of empathy. As I already argued in earlier chapters, the art and discipline of wise empathy plays a central role in transtherapy and counseling. Transtherapy-in-common forms all participants in this lost art by their compassionate presence to each other's communications.

Intimacy and Anxiety

The dynamics of anxiety play an important part in our transcendent formation. One facet of transcendent anxiety is the vague, floating dread that somehow, somewhere, something could paralyze our life. Could our life become dissonant with the mystery at the core of our being? Could we come to feel like nothing in an indifferent universe? Fear, rooted in transcendent anxiety, is also evoked by the danger of being misunderstood, misinterpreted, misquoted, ridiculed, and depreciated. People have a certain image of each other, sustained by their selective observation, imagination, and memory. The dynamics of conservation make us reluctant to let go of the familiar slots into which we have put people once and for all. To admit that we may have been mistaken offends our pride. It diminishes our sense of security. The dynamics of conservation made us impose predictable stereotypes on people with whom we may have to interact in daily life.

Another fear, rooted in transcendent anxiety, is generated by the directives that regulate appropriate distance and nearness in our contacts with others. We fear that we might invade the privacy of others by untimely or inappropriate intimacy. If we would meet with a cool reception or pointed rejection, we would have to withdraw in embarrassment. We fear the possibility of such humiliation.

To withdraw once and for all in a disposition of polite reservation and cool distance from everyone will paralyze the heart's sensibility. Reserve has its suitable place in our life in respect to certain situations. Deadly for the life of consonance would be a reserve that extends itself indiscriminately to any possible person entering our ambience. Transtherapy and counseling may help overly reserved people to prepare themselves, within a trustworthy relationship of transcendent intimacy, for intimacy in daily life.

Fear, rooted in transcendent anxiety, can also be triggered by the awareness of the possible rupture of the intimate relationship. This fear of rupture, when not worked through, falsifies intimacy. It hinders frank communication. Lack of forthrightness will terminate the intimacy sooner or later. Hence, the sessions-in-common of transtherapy and counseling are marked by mutual respect and concern. These gradually shared dispositions begin slowly to melt the withdrawal and withholding patterns of overly reserved hearts and characters.

Intimacy and Willfulness

If we do not overcome our fear, we dare only to enter into make-believe intimacies. We refuse to expose ourselves to a real communion of deeper insights and feelings. We mistake our actual form of life for our founding form itself with its unique-communal life call.

The dread that we may lose all that we are makes us cling desperately to our overreserved actual form of life. We may fear that real intimacy could destroy us. At the root of this anxiety is our self-exalting pride form, the source of our basic dissonance. This dissonance hardens our will into an autarkic, unreasonable force of resistance. We hold out against any intimate communion with others that would threaten our actual way of life. Recent biographies of such historical figures as Adolph Hitler, Benito Mussolini, and Joseph Stalin are striking illustrations of this cementing of their dominant functionalistic will against humanness. They resist any transcendent intimacy. It threatens to undermine the false complacency and merciless ambitions of their fixated lives. A similar steeling of the heart marks our own smaller resistances to intimacy. In short, willfulness is the enemy of intimacy.

My approach to transtherapy and counseling aims to expose these common resistances. Of course, as I have argued repeatedly, pretranscendent therapies are needed if the underlying causes of such resistances stem from serious pretranscendent disturbances.

Insufficiently Appraised Self-Disclosure to Others

The sensibility facet of the heart must always be permeated by its responsibility facet. The responsible heart engages in wise appraisal. When we feel an impulse to intimate self-disclosures, we must ask ourselves where this desire is coming from. Is this impulse congenial with who we most deeply are? Can it be an expression of obedience to the call of the mystery in regard to this companion or circle of acquaintants? Or are we only overcome by an inner void, an emptiness of heart, a lack of at-homeness in our own life? Does it compel us to bare our souls prematurely or unwisely to people who cannot understand, respect, or cope with our intimate disclosures? Are we so lacking in appreciation of our unique dignity that we want to make ourselves interesting, pitied, or admired through indiscriminate self-revelation? Is it perhaps a trick to allow us in turn to ask intimate questions that give us a key to another's interiority? Or worse still, do we prefocally want that information so that we can manipulate the other by emotional control? Do we collect material for a hidden threat of blackmail? Do we frighten the person who confided in us with the thought that we might divulge to others what we found out?

Are such self-disclosures compatible with the people with whom we choose to be intimate? Is there between us the consonance of affinity regarding the facets of inner life that are communicated? Is there love or sympathy between us? Are they trustworthy? Without such proven compatibility, we should not risk disclosures of our inner life. Even in the choice of a formation director, guide, counselor, or transtherapist we should appraise such compatibility.

Responsible compassion makes us appraise if people can tolerate our self-disclosures without too much loss of their own basic equanimity. We should ponder their vulnerability. Sometimes parents, teachers, or counselors may disclose their own weaknesses, doubts, and worries to insecure children, students, and counselees. They may not be able to bear with such exposures of the foibles of people on whom they have to depend.

The same applies to whole segments or communities who need to believe in their leaders. They need a certain distance from the inner crises that may disturb those who guide them.

The compassionate heart and character also appraise their own vulnerability. Would intimate disclosure be too much for us to tolerate at this moment of our life? Is our insecurity still too deep? Can we cope with the fear and suspicion that may begin to bother us after our self-disclosure? Can we bear with the fear that others might abuse our vulnerability to enlist us in their projects or to overwhelm us with their style of life?

The responsible heart asks itself if there is sufficient competence in one's own verbal and body language? What about the capacities for understanding us in those we have chosen for our intimate self-disclosure? Can we communicate with them effectively? If not, the responsible heart will delay disclosure until it is assured of its effectiveness.

To put it briefly, the responsible heart and character neither hides from self-disclosure nor squanders its secrets heedlessly. An excited pouring out of thought and feeling before the time is ripe can destroy an emerging intimacy as effectively as rigid retrenchment. The responsible heart cultivates gentle appraisal during the slow emergence of an intimate relationship. It watches against precipitous abandonment to others. It appraises the danger of losing one's uniqueness in fusion. On the other hand, it also guards against the dynamics of withdrawal in anxious insulation from all others.

Consonant intimacy leads to appreciation-in-depth of each other's unique-communal call by the mystery, of relaxed mutuality in spontaneous self-disclosure. Transcendent intimates do not try to outdo each other. They trust one another. Neither affectation nor anxious constraint mars their relationship. There is an ease of mutual form reception and donation. This communion between responsible-sensible hearts enhances the uniqueness and privacy of the participants. They share their transcendent formation. Yet their mutual dependence does not compromise their unique-communal life call. Transtherapy and counseling sessions-in-common image and model this ideal of well-appraised, wise intimacy between all participants concerned.

Vicarious Intimacy

The striving for intimacy can be consonant or dissonant. One source of dissonance is vicarious formation. The heart that lives vicariously betrays itself. It shares the life of others with such anxious intensity that it loses its in-touchness with its own inspiration. The alienated heart replaces congeniality with fusion. The story of other lives is substituted for that of one's own. The germ of such overdependency can be found in the depreciation of one's own founding form of life. Faith, hope, and love in the founding mystery at the root of one's being have somehow been paralyzed. To live with an all-pervasive sense of depreciation of one's own story becomes intolerable. To escape despair, one may flee into absorption in the tale or myth of others. One can, of course, appreciate the saga of others as admirable in itself without losing sight of one's own story. We may detect in their narrative certain aspects that mirror affinities we also experience, albeit in a unique way, in our own unfolding drama of life. We recognize the difference between affinity and clinging to the script of others as if it were the only one that could fill the empty pages of our own depreciated existence. A blind plagiarism of alien formation replaces congenial self-formation. The dynamics of vicarious formation are compelling. They demand a constant quasi intimacy with others. An insatiable hunger for continual confirmation dominates our heart. Confirmation takes the place of our own self-affirmation. Indeed, the starved heart cultivates a delusional quasi intimacy.

The vicarious formation disposition concretizes itself in many dependency attitudes and their directives. One may behave as a "clinging vine" type of person, showing helplessness, overcompliance, and blind obedience. Added to this is often the bribery of excessive service, bestowal of praise, overloading others with gifts or with sensual or sexual favors. Depreciation of our calling makes us feel as if no one else can appreciate it. We may then try to find intimacy with others not because of who we are but because of what we have and can give to them without measure. Our latent anxiety may become linked with our vicarious life form. Any threat of loss of this substitute call kindles real dread.

Anxiety dynamics in collusion with vicarious formation strivings result in possessive, grasping, devouring relationships. Their object may be a spouse, friend, colleague, or child. Ours may be an imagined intimacy with a public figure, such as a royal person, a teacher, a member of the clergy, an author, a pop musician, a newscaster, a movie star, a charismatic leader, a general, a sports hero. In that case the thirst for information about the intimate details of that person's life story seems unquenchable. Information may lead to an obsessive imitation of the apparent form these idolized models give to one's life. Imitations of dress, hairdo, smoking and drinking habits, intonation of voice, gestures, movements may be symptomatic of this aggressive, imaginary, and distant intimacy. The symbiotic identification may reach such an intensity that one's imagination, memory, and anticipation are totally ruled by the story of the star. When the hero dies, it may seem as if one's own journey has ended with hers or his. One may mourn forever and keep collecting memorabilia. Transtherapy and counseling help the counselee to disclose the social and related personal plague of vicarious intimacy.

Vicarious Intimacy in Adolescence

Adolescence is often marked by insecurity about one's own capacities. Many adolescents may resort to vicarious intimacy. If life teaches them to listen to their own call, they will grow beyond this phase. Some less fortunate people may be stuck in vicarious intimacy for a lifetime.

The intensity and duration of vicarious living is linked with people's absence from or presence to the mystery at the root of their being. Intimacy with the mystery diminishes the hunger for a surrogate existence. Alienation from this mystery increases the need for it. In that case life by proxy fills the gnawing sense of emptiness at the center of one's being. Fusion is often mistaken for intimacy. The spiritual adage that we should see the mystery in others is misappraised. For the victims, it often means that we can find the mystery only in idolized others and not first of all in our own center. The counsel that we should love others as we love ourselves no longer works for those who live in self-estrangement, for they have no self that they truly love and appreciate.

So far I have considered the problems of people whose lives are almost exclusively dominated by the delusion of fusion. Try to realize, however, that we, too, can be touched by similar problems at certain moments of our life. We should be vigilant in regard to this ever-present possibility, alert for its appearance, and ready to correct it. Such vigilance is especially called for when we feel attracted to a new relationship of intimacy.

Marital partners as well may replace intimacy with fusion only. Every time this happens, it diminishes the richness of their marriage. It has to be nourished by the unique endowment of each partner. The naïve outsider may be unduly impressed by the seemingly close and mutually absorbing unity of such fused marriages. If one of the partners begins to realize her or his unique calling, the consequences may be devastating for the relationship. This factor explains certain unexpected divorces between people who seemed to be crazy about each other. Of course they were! They suffered together the delusion of total fusion.

CHAPTER 23

Transtherapy and Dilemmas of Intimacy

Among the dilemmas brought to my attention in the Dutch Hunger Winter were those of intimate interformation between stressed hungry people hiding with one another. Intimacy was often in peril under the pressures of threats of deportation, loss of friends and family members by execution or imprisonment, fights about the division of the little parcels of food, like a few tulip bulbs or one potato, available to a family or a team of friends. Crises of intimacy were unavoidable. Often they were brought to my doorstep in The Hague. Such crises brought out the best and the worst in people. Dealing with them deepened my unfolding creation of transtherapy and counseling.

Each human life is an ineffable mystery in and through the all-forming mystery in which it uniquely shares. Transcendent intimacy with others is possible only when we appreciate in reverence that other people resemble us in their call to transcendent humanness. At the same time they differ from us in their potential transcendent uniqueness. Intimacy loses its consonance the moment we try to manipulate the personal-communal life call of others instead of confirming it.

Our founding form is our solitary mystery. People emerge out of the solitude of their uniqueness to meet each other. The more intimate this meeting, the more it will deepen the awareness of the solitary mystery they are. Paradoxically, our search for intimacy with others discloses to us our solitude. While it extends our awareness of what we can share, it also brings into focus what we cannot share. Transtherapy sessions-in-common confirm this experience for all those engaged in them.

Twofold growth in transcendent intimacy enables growth in solitude. Each intimate meeting carries the pain of loneliness simultaneously or shortly thereafter. My transtherapy helped me to transpose the pain of loneliness suffered by many of the people hiding with me into fruitful solitude. Solitude opened them to intimacy with the mystery both in their own life and in the lives of others with whom they shared the same misery of persecution, hunger, and threats of capture and deportation.

People are unique epiphanies of the ineffable mystery and, hence, mysterious themselves. In some measure we may know people at a certain moment of their journey, yet the moment after, the next page of their story may already have changed what we thought we had come to know. To see others as already-finished forms is to deny their ongoing story of life. Transtherapy shows us how to revere the mystery silently at work in them. Only when we appreciate the differences between us and encourage each other's unfolding do we grow in the generosity of healing intimacy.

The human heart is sacred. Abuse of intimacy, such as pretending intimacy merely to pry something out of people they would not otherwise divulge, is a desecration.

Transtherapy and counseling make us experience that we never know fully the unfolding of this sacred domain of interiority. The people we meet are unchartered courses of life. Neither they nor we can fathom their journey. Even the most profound intimacy in the best hours of transtherapy cannot pierce the ultimate impenetrability that we remain for each other. Our uniqueness is an occasion for the celebration of the miracle of the mystery in each of us. It also draws a veil of concealment between us, no matter the depth of intimacy with which we have been gifted.

Phases of Intimacy

The first affective intimacy we experience is that of the consonance between mother and child. This primitive consonance is vital-symbiotic. It may in some way affect all our dynamics and feelings in future relationships. The mother–child consonance satisfies the heart of the mother. She expresses her need for consonance in caring for her child. The infant finds satisfaction, too. Children's needs are fulfilled through the caring presence of their mothers. Both experience a kind of vital intimacy. This vital-symbiotic relationship changes when the inherent powers of human unfolding raise the child beyond the vital to the functional dimension of personhood. The awakening potency for mastery makes children aware that they can function in some independence from the mother. This awareness breaks the original bonding of vital-symbiotic consonance and intimacy.

Before this breakthrough, the seeming magic of total consonance and intimacy extended itself not only to the mother but to all facets of her field of life. This maternal field is not yet experienced by infants as differentiated from a field of life of their own. First there was only an experiential sense of primitive blind consonance without differentiation. Now the still-anonymous transcendence dynamic gives birth to an embryonic awareness of differentiation of the child's field of life. Forms begin now to appear to children in their distinctness, including their own form of life. First there was the spontaneous dominance of the experience of undifferentiated consonance of vital-symbiotic intimacy. Now it is replaced by the dominance of the differentiating consonance of functionality.

A functional awakening to the differentiation of its field of presence makes the child aware of the dissonance dynamics that operate in this field. The possibility of dissonance—implied in differentiation—is the most striking change the child experiences from a former field of undifferentiated consonance. Children in the phase of formation transition do not yet know that consonance in a differentiated field can only be approximated by much struggle; it will never be perfectly achieved; it has ultimately to be grounded in consonance with the all-pervading formation mystery.

Transtherapists and counselors are often faced with false modes of spirituality. Such modes inhibit true transcendent-functional unfolding. One of these modes is rooted in the secret wish to return to the lost paradise of undifferentiated consonance. It can give rise to attempts to live in a mainly symbiotic consonance with the mystery, not bothered by familial, professional, and social concerns.

Transcendence Anxiety

In this phase, children experience for the first time their own life as thrown back on itself. In contrast with the symbiotic consonance of the past phase, they now experience relative isolation from other forms in an increasingly differentiating field. The threat of aloneness evokes at least slight manifestations of transcendence anxiety. What evokes it are primitive nonfocal stirrings of what will develop later into the sensibility or responsibility dimension of the human heart. Having to respond in some way to the demand of the unfolding of one's life creates the vague, floating anxiety of being unable to respond effectively. The thought of losing one's still-anonymous basic life direction and meaning can evoke fear and trembling in the best of us.

Transcendence anxiety implies a certain amount of dissonance anxiety, too. The initial experience of dissonance stems from differentiation. It makes one feel compelled to respond to the challenges of a differentiating field of life. One seeks for new harmony in some form of consonance. Empirical dissonance is related in turn to our empirical inclination toward dissonance in regard to the mystery. This inclination points to the primordial dissonance of refusal of the mystery. It is a hidden basic refusal tendency rooted in the human condition. To put it succinctly, the awakening of the infant to the differentiation of its field of life signals the awakening of a vague, anonymous transcendence anxiety. From now on, it may have at least some influence on all of one's relationships.

The experience of dissonance fills us with restless dissatisfaction. Yet this basic experience also enables us to express in our individual vital-functional life who we are uniquely. The experience of dissonance makes it possible for us to disclose relationships of differentiating consonance. Without the disclosure of dissonance and differentiation, it would have been impossible for us to form any other relationship than a vital-symbiotic one. The loss of undifferentiated consonance with its pleasant embodiment in total maternal care leaves lasting traces in our heart. It fills us with a primitive longing to regain the infant's Eden of at oneness with doting parents. This longing enters in some disguised way into our attempts to intimacy, especially in its primitive beginnings. They may infect our striving for wise compatibility and lead to its distortion through desires for fusion and collusion.

Despite this fundamental anxiety, mature dispositions of compatibility and intimacy can temper the primitive anticipation that someone may restore for us the bliss of early infancy. Transtherapy alerts us to the threats of regression to infancy, of fusion and collusion, of both transcendence and dissonance anxiety. Transtherapy warns us of their deforming influence on our openness to true intimacy. The same applies not only to our relationships with individuals but also to our belonging to communities.

Many totalitarian regimes, for instance, play on these primitive stirrings. They offer adherents the promise of a carefree life, social security from cradle to grave with no responsible decisions to be made. All of this is promised in exchange for the surrender of one's personal freedom to the state, collectivity, or cult concerned.

During our whole life, the secret longing for some restoration of the utopia of infancy remains potentially active in our relationships. Crude attempts to root it out would be in vain. They would only serve to drive our infantile desires deeper into the infrafocal region of our consciousness. Unavailable to our focal control, they would wield more influence in our relationships. Transtherapy lets these desires come to the surface of our consciousness. It enables us to feel them and to appraise their actual influence on our life without surrendering to them. Transtherapy helps us to relate them to our transcendent longing for ultimate consonance with the mystery and its manifold epiphanous forms.

Transtherapy makes us grow in awareness and affirmation of our unique-communal life call. It sets us free to express this call in our pretranscendent individuality. It prepares us for the tolerance of collisions between our call and the world. Such therapy can liberate us from our infantile longings. It thereby advances our quest for transcendent intimacy. Transtherapy prepares us to be ready at all times to elucidate the infantile desires that estrange us from our transcendent-functional life call. It teaches us how to surmount them in a ceaseless struggle of affective and effective reformation and transformation. It shows us through the transtherapy relationship how the best of our initial childhood can be restored and elevated in our second transcendent childhood, deleting traces of childishness.

Disengagement of Friendship Intimacy

Intimacy can take many forms; friendship is one of them. A necessary condition for the intimacy between friends is the special affinity and trust they feel for one another. Unlike general human intimacy, which can be extended to all, soul friendship can be celebrated only among those who share a unique bonding. There is no guarantee that a friendship will last.

For all kinds of reasons, the bonding between friends may come to an end. Affinity may diminish under the pressure of divergent current formations. Mutual trust may have been violated to such a degree that temporal or lasting disengagement becomes an option. Withdrawal from the special intimacy of friendship should not end the general human intimacy we can extend to others, also to former friends. Often people who have suffered the breakup of a friendship or marriage come to transtherapy or counseling. They ask what this crisis means for their further life. In the light of the great wisdom traditions of humanity, they ponder possible answers.

Intimacy with the Mystery

Intimacy is ultimately intimacy with the mystery and its epiphanies. In the order of phasic unfolding, what usually comes first is intimacy with the epiphanies of the mystery in other caring people. In the beginning, and often later on, we do not experience these epiphanies explicitly. We may be only dimly aware of an intimacy with the epiphanies of a mystery that pervades us all. Children, as I have shown, may directly enjoy intimacy with their loving, caring mothers. Mothers may evoke in them the first stirrings of human faith, hope, and consonance. Good mothers show these transcendent virtues in their loving care for their children. The same holds for the intimacy of friendship later in life.

There is, however, a crucial difference between the intimacy between friends and that between infants or children and their parents. Children have not yet found the uniqueness of their own life call. Uncertainty about who they themselves most intimately are makes it impossible for them to be fully engaged in intimacy with others. They can and should receive the gifts of intimacy from their parents and significant others. They cannot yet respond with the full gift of themselves. Hence the child–parent intimacy is somewhat one-sided. Yet childhood intimacy is a necessary preparation for deeper intimacy later in life. Therefore in my formation science, I call childhood intimacy *pre-intimacy,* which means that it prepares for the fuller intimacy of the future. Transtherapy clarifies experientially the features of both pre-intimacy and mature intimacy.

Intimacy as Transcendent

Intimacy comes from the Latin word *intimus,* which means "innermost." As such, it refers to that which is most deeply within the people with whom we are intimate. I have identified this deepest *within* as our founding life form or life call. This unique ground is not directly available to awareness and communication. We do not at once experience our intimacy with other people as an intimacy with their innermost center. Neither do they feel immediate intimacy with our own founding form of life. Our inmost nobility can be mirrored, usually through the spirit, in our core form as heart and character. If this mirroring happens, our inmost unique life call becomes available to our awareness and communication potencies. This availability enables us in turn to become intimate with our own unique-communal form of life insofar as it has been disclosed in our heart. We are then able to communicate something of our unique life form to others, who can respond with communications in kind. In this way, we can give form to transcendent relationships of intimacy that are both transient and enduring.

Transtherapy and counseling aim at facilitating this unconcealing of what points to the presence of a founding life form in self and others.

Passing Intimacy

I make a distinction between passing and lasting intimacy. I will look first at passing and then at lasting intimacy. Passing intimacy with others implies that we are, at least for some moments, cordially present to them as companions on life's way. We engage in more than a merely functional-vital interaction; we interform in a deeper sense.

The dynamics of intimacy may function unexpectedly. For example, I sit beside an unknown middle-aged woman during a plane ride. We exchange remarks about the flight, the weather, our destination. But then, all at once, she begins to speak to me about the concerns she has for her children. The goodness of her heart shines through. It touches me. It appeals to me. I am moved to respond in a way that is more than formal or indifferent. She drops for a moment the outward facet of her apparent form, and I drop mine. A certain intimacy emerges between us.

I define this everyday moment of intimacy as a "passing compatibility-indepth." I distinguish this concept from my concept of "mere sociability."

Sociability can masquerade as compatibility. The dynamics of sociability refer mainly to the outward facet of the apparent compatible life form—the manifestation of pleasant camaraderie, polite behavior, or clever wit. These are often used as protections against deeper intimacy or transcendent cordiality.

Sometimes a meeting of the eyes, a kind word, a little service, a change of tone, a gesture of nearness may be sufficient to evoke dynamics of intimacy. They affect some facet of what I call our love-will toward others.

Intimacy is pervaded by cordiality, by commencing consonance and care, by transcendent human warmth. Such moments are unlike routine meetings marked by mere functionality. These may go by and not leave a trace of our love-will.

The tight control of our relationships by functionalism is based on our disposition to be attentive mainly to the functional-vital qualities we notice in others. Meeting people functionally, we tag them as useless or usable, as tall, small, smooth, clumsy, boring, interesting, clever, dumb, well-informed, superficial, fast, slow, well-to-do, poor, black, white, and so on. We cut their unique personality down to general labels, which could be said about anyone. There ought to be instead some minimal, distinctively human respect and care in all relations, even those that are functional. To be degraded to mere generalities is to be dehumanized.

Passing intimacy makes us somewhat aware of each other's sensitivities and dispositions. All people, as distinctively human, are constantly faced with the option to give or to withhold themselves. A passing, at least minimal, intimacy embodies a simple everyday movement of cordial attention to others as fellow human beings. Such passing intimacy is crucial in a humane society. The balm of cordial kindness humanizes our everydayness.

Usually, however, the term "intimacy" is applied to a more lasting togetherness, such as that of marriage, friendship, family, or community; of counseling, teaching, direction, and transtherapy.

More Lasting Intimacy

The passing intimacy I detailed above goes beyond mere functionality. It teaches us about intimacy, but it is too brief and too little to show us its inner richness. The transcendent bounty of true intimacy can become evident in ongoing intimate relationships.

Lasting intimacy enables us to tune in to ever new facets of each other's life call. We experience each other as unique persons. In mutual intimacy, we share each other's uniqueness in some of its facets. We may participate also in the personal ranges of life situations we happen to have in common with our intimates. For example, two mothers who are intimate friends may share their concern for their children. They communicate how they personally feel about them and the shared conditions that affect their lives as mothers in a particular neighborhood. By placing the personal range of their shared formation field at the center of their mutual attention they interform with one another. They develop an intimate interconsciousness.

The dynamics of lasting intimacy are such that intimate interformation in regard to one facet of a person's unique formation story tends to extend itself gradually to others. Instead of growing old alone, we grow old together. The dynamics of cordial intimacy generate a vivid presence-in-common to similar facets of our life situation. Tuning in to shared demands of life causes self-disclosure to be enriched by the disclosures that flow from attentive, appreciative togetherness. We are present together to those facets of our field that are equally accessible to us. These reverberate in our hearts. We feel in tune with one another; we sense our affinity in the light of the mystery.

The sessions-in-common of transtherapy and counseling facilitate for all concerned the experience of a vivid presence-in-common to shared aspects of their life situations. This sense of sharing and caring carries over in their everyday life with others.

Intimate Presence and Absence

Consonant intimacy implies the possibility and necessity of pauses of absence within the life of presence. To be always exclusively present to others would be pathological. In that case, consonance with others would interfere with consonance with our own inner demands, with our work, our obligations, and our functional responsibilities. Intimate presence to others is limited in time and space. Permanent presence without pause would be impossible and unbearable. It would destroy us. Hence, consonant intimacy implies a wise rhythm of intimate presence and absence. Pauses of absence should be a source of renewed presence. They belong as much to the dynamics of intimacy as presence does. Absence would only destroy presence if it were abused constantly to exclude intimate presence at the appropriate time and occasion.

Presence cannot be forced. Intimate presence implies only that we develop a willingness and readiness to be intimately there at the appropriate time when it seems congenial, compatible, and compassionate for both of us, and when we feel competent to be that way.

The dynamics of intimacy with others are effective when we have grown in sufficient intimacy with our own uniqueness and have reached a certain attunement to who we are called to be. This at homeness with who-we-are-most-deeply diminishes the anxiety and insecurity that inhibit our spontaneous outgoingness to others. We become less dependent on such dynamics as subtle arrogance, one-upmanship, faked pleasantness, fawning affectivity, or anxious compliance.

Even if we have attained this basic at homeness, moments of absence will always be necessary to restore, deepen, and expand intimacy with our own intrasphere and with the mystery's manifestations within it. Such renewed rooting of our life in our interiority will enable us to be more outgoing to others in a transcendent, cordial intimacy when the occasion presents itself.

Transtherapy and counseling sessions-in-common can restore this at homeness with our unique-communal life call. They also provide a "pause of absence" that becomes a "source of renewed presence."

Preforming Intimacy

We are often present to others in ways that touch deeply our awareness. Somehow our heart senses and fosters intimacy before our focal (clearly focused) consciousness does. Affective dynamics may express themselves first in certain pervasive moods. Our moods tell us how we feel about our relations with others. They express what I have called our "preformative intimacy" (our pre-intimacy) with people.

Preformative intimacy is made up not only of such moods but also of appreciative apprehensions. Some of these may not yet be focally conscious; they represent a sensitivity of the heart secretly guiding us in our exchange with others. For example, people who fall in love often sense long before they become focally aware of their mutual love that they are meant for each other.

Something like that may happen in relations of transtherapy and counseling. Before counselees or directees open up, they may go through a phase in which their sense of being safe in this kind of intimacy increases. Finally, they reach the point where intimate communications become possible.

Unfortunately, functionality may prevail in our life. This diminishes our attunement to the subtle messages of the preforming dynamics of intimacy. Therefore, one aim of transtherapy is to create a special space and time filled with experiences of true relationships. These attune us to what is coming to life in our deeper sensitivity.

As we become increasingly open to the transfocal region of consciousness, we grow also in sensitivity to the communications of the mystery. The mystery calls us to transcendent intimacies with itself and with others. We experience a deepening of consonance with our unique-communal life call and with our faith and formation traditions.

Presence to Our Preforming Sensitivity

Our founding form of life is predisposed to distinctively human presence. These come to life in the preformative stirrings of our heart. However, this is not enough for intimacy to happen. We need to be present focally to these stirrings. Otherwise, they are not open to our wise appraisal nor may they find expression in interformation with others. They perish before they blossom.

We become attuned to our preforming sensitivity by means of moments of transcendent self-presence in quiet reflection. We question, in the light of the mystery, our moods, feelings, sensitivities, thoughts, bodily responses and reactions. We become transcendently present to the sensitivity and the sensibility or affective responsibility of our heart. We must find time to dwell gently on what is happening there without becoming overly introspective. We must ask ourselves if the sensitive presence of our heart is sensible and reasonable? What does it tell us about the wise acceptance or rejection of certain preforming feelings? Do we secretly refuse or affirm them? And why? Are they consonant with what the mystery wants for our life?

Attentiveness to any of the sensitivities that vaguely begin to announce themselves may disclose to us our heart's sensitivity and its responding sensibility. They enable us to appraise the desirability of such feelings in view of the overall direction of our calling. We cannot blindly affirm all emergent emotions of intimate longing. Here the responsible sensibility dimension of our heart must come into play. A timely awareness of such inner movements enables us to deal with them more easily. We must catch them before they have grown too strong for quiet, candid appraisal and relaxed decision. Timely acknowledgment of these inner movements will enable us to give form to our life of intimacy in accordance with our providential life orientation. Such attentiveness will help us to make sure that ours remains a responsive and responsible heart.

Without this awareness, potentially beneficial friendships, to say nothing of precious moments of passing intimacy, may be stillborn. Relationships that prove to be counterproductive may suddenly overwhelm us. We must appraise in time the true nature of intimacy dynamics arising in our heart. We do so in the light of its dynamics of responsible sensibility for the protection, ongoing disclosure, and implementation of our unique-communal life call. Transtherapy and counseling offer us a forum for such appraisal.

Preformative intimacy manifested in moods and sensitivities of the heart may be sensibly disclosed, appraised, and affirmed by us. We may then be moved to the expression of intimacy. Such expression animates and empowers our fundamental potency to give and receive form. I found out, after much observation and reflection on my transtherapy experiences, that the expression facet of our life of intimacy moves us to articulate it in three ways: the way of form-receptive attentiveness, of form-receptive abiding, and of form-giving communication.

Form-Receptive Attentiveness

Lasting intimacy means increasing consonance in depth. It presupposes our tuning in to the uniqueness of others. Such refined attunement is only possible when we listen respectfully to the mystery of uniqueness insofar as it is disclosed in them. Listening respectfully is a distinctively human way of being present to others. It is rooted in our potency for awe and in our related potency to see others as rooted uniquely in the awesome mystery of life's transcendent-functional unfolding.

In the act of respectful listening, our potency for enlightened intimacy with others finds its first articulation. We appraise the verbal and body language of others, theirs and our own unique-communal form potencies and their obstacles. We become more in touch with what we and others *are* like and with what we and others *can* be.

True love is not blind but seeing; it is not deaf but attentive. It refines the hearing of the heart. It says, in effect, "into-me-see," a nice play on the word "intimacy." It makes us hear what sheer functional or vital involvement cannot fathom. Obviously, this gift of listening with the heart is an indispensable basis also of effective transtherapy and counseling.

By the same token, listening in awe enables us to attend to the best form potencies of ourselves as gifts of the mystery.

Form-Receptive Abiding

Initially, participants in transtherapy sessions may feel somewhat surprised or uneasy when their talking together alternates with moments of silent abiding. To abide in silent presence is another way to receive and give form to intimacy. Abiding is the opposite of maintaining a silence that is empty, forgetful, or distracted. Abiding with others in quiet togetherness can be a most intensive mode of mutual presence. It signifies that we have reached a moment of togetherness that cannot be fully expressed in verbal language. We sense that we can only abide in a silence that resounds softly in the sensitivity of our hearts, touching the unspeakable mystery of our life, our joy, our suffering, our pain. Abiding springs from a rich disclosure of our inner life. It creates a pause between listening and languaging. This pause becomes a source of new hearing, of a deeper speaking in verbal and body language. Abiding in stillness precedes or accompanies a new transparency of people in their mutual celebration of consonant transcendent intimacy. It plays a significant role in transtherapy and counseling.

Transcendent Modes of Communication

Intimacy gives rise to modes of communication in which people share the fruits of respectful listening and abiding. The language of words as well as body language spring spontaneously from the need to give form to what is experienced. There are many modes of intimacy. Correspondingly, the role of communication is diversified. Communication in intimacy takes another form between parents and children, friends and lovers, marriage partners, comrades and neighbors, formative teachers, guides, counselors, directors, and transtherapists, and those who open their heart to them.

The body language of intimacy differs greatly in this vast array of intimate relationships. We should not overstep the limits inherent in each appropriate mode of body language. For this can destroy the correct patterns of intimacy. What constitutes transgressions in one mode of intimacy can be appropriate in another mode. For instance, the body language of marital intimacy cannot be extended to parent–child intimacy without destroying the consonance of this relationship, which demands its own type of body language.

The three coformants of expressed intimacy—respectful attention, abiding, and communication—do not in and by themselves create intimacy. Rather, they unfold and express an intimacy already being born in our heart. This intimacy now becomes explicitly shared. It was already there, but it was not yet focally acknowledged, affirmed, and appropriated; it did not yet give form to an embodied relationship of explicit intimacy. Once it has been given expressive form, it can sink again into our prefocal region of consciousness. From there it will radiate its influence on our intimacy and give rise to timely expressions that are candid, congenial, compatible, and compassionate.

Transtherapy and counseling sessions-in-common provide an occasion for growth in intimate, respectful attention, in abiding and communication.

CHAPTER 24

Transtherapy and Obstacles to Intimacy

Our functionalistic civilization makes it difficult for us to attune our hearts to the hearts of others. It is not easy for us to listen attentively, to abide and commune respectfully. Many pulsations in our field tend to discount the subtle dynamics of intimacy. They favor exclusively functional reason, analysis, logic, experimentation, and quantification. All of these are indispensable in the fully integrated life. But they should not exclude higher transcendent reason and the logic of the sensitive and sensible heart, which transtherapy fosters in its group gatherings. Both intimacy and functional practicality must complement and correct, not exclude, each other.

Other obstacles to intimacy spring from a faulty family preformation, from the haunting memory of disappointment and deception in tentative relationships of intimacy, from anxiety, fear, and conflicting dynamics, from refusal or repudiation of the feminine or masculine coformants of our heart. All of these block the path to intimacy. To ready us for intimacy, transtherapy and counseling help us to overcome such emotional blocks. Becoming attuned to the sensitivity of our own heart will make us grow in sensitivity to other people. This art and discipline takes a lifetime of maturation. For many people it may be helpful to enter into transtherapy for the sake of disclosing and removing the main barriers to intimacy in their life. When these obstructions are weakened, the dynamics of intimacy begin to guide the human heart. At the same time, a well-informed sensibility dimension of the heart must keep watch against unwise and premature communications of intimacy that may prove destructive.

Another impediment is our expectation of "instancy." Our society is replete with the remarkable results of technology. We enjoy instant coffee, instant tea, instant data provided by robots and computers. We are inclined to transpose this exciting instancy to the area of nontechnical life. We want instant intimacy. But instant intimacy, especially as the basis of an enduring relationship, is dubious, if not impossible. Intimacy unfolds and is modified over time.

Intimacy can be deepened by the living memory of a history of growing up together. Parent–child intimacy, marriage or community intimacy, friendship, neighbor, or comrade intimacy, transtherapy intimacy—all have a unique history. Each phase of that history coforms in some fashion the unique quality and direction of our intimacy together. This shared history is in turn coformed by the everyday dynamics of intimacy, its recurrent barriers, and our coping with constant threats to our growing older together in consonance.

A false substitute for true intimacy is anxious fusion with unduly exalted others. Lacking in secure appreciation of our own life call, we live in anxious self-depreciation, transposing all our worth to others. We want to lose our depreciated self and to fuse our life with theirs.

Our need for blind and total fusion may take over to such a degree that the pressure on others to live up to our exalted image of them, combined with our overdependency on them, becomes unbearable. At any time we may be blessedly compelled by reality to discover that others are not as exalted as we imagined. The security we invested in them crumbles. Love turns into hate, appreciation into depreciation, intimacy into alienation. We need to find ourselves before we can let others be free. My transtherapy impresses on participants that freedom from fusion is an indispensable condition for true, relaxed intimacy between the members of the group.

Right appreciation of our life call grants us security. As long as we have not found our own unique dignity as persons we are poor prospects for true intimacy. Intimacy implies reverence for the core of potential or actual goodness in others without exalting them to a pinnacle of perfection only to be found in the mystery itself. Such idealization can be the delusional work of our fantastic phantom "I" rooted in our exalting pride form.

Wise intimacy entails the dynamics of divestment from unreal idealizations. Only then can we form relationships of intimacy with various people as they really are. Exaltation leads to disappointment or hurt anticipations. We feel let down by the limited reality of exalted others. They in turn may feel oppressed by our unrealistic expectations.

"Vitalistic sentiment" is another hindrance on the path to true intimacy. Vital feeling should be integrated in the higher responsible affects of the enlightened heart. Vitalistic sentiment, on the contrary, refers to the insulation, exaltation, and totalization of the vital facet of intimacy. When vital feeling is absolutized, it leads to an anxious hunt for only the vitalistic feelings that can be aroused in an intimate relationship. Because such feelings by themselves cannot give the transcendent fulfillment we crave, they have to be exalted in fantasy. This fantasy takes over. It diminishes the possibility of a concrete here-and-now relationship to others as real persons. It vitiates the ground of distinctively human intimacy.

Transcendent intimacy is rooted in presence to the unique founding form of people as mirrored in their heart and as somehow disclosed in the ongoing evolvement of their life. They should be appreciated as unique human beings, not merely as sources of fulfillment of only our vitalistic needs. Such a disposition destroys human intimacy. At times the vitalistic feelings that cannot be fulfilled in the present thrive on past intimacy experiences. They are exalted out of proportion by the vitalistic fantasy playing upon our memory. In reality, they may never have been experienced as such in the past.

Often vicarious fulfillment of the fantasy is sought in sentimental or arousing literature, movies, plays, and pictures. The vitalistic fantasy may also dream about fulfillment in the future. All these diversions from transcendent intimacy tend to destroy the possibility of real intimacy here and now.

One refuses to let one's life be permeated by transcendence. It becomes difficult, if not impossible, to lift any relationship to the height of distinctively human intimacy. Instead of personal exchange, only idle talk fills every meeting with others, fomented by a cheap curiosity. Exchange between excited chatterboxes replaces transcendent encounter. Restlessness, excitement, empty streams of superficial information, pragmatic issue orientations are used anxiously to fill the emptiness of life with a forced liveliness. Reams of little facts are transferred from one individual's information box to another. Respectful listening, abiding, and communication in depth are avoided anxiously; they threaten to disclose the ignored emptiness of the desperate heart. The dynamics of covering up our despair, even for ourselves, are powerful in contemporary society. They paralyze the dynamics of transcendent intimacy. The false complacency of the heart that is secretly desperate may be pierced only by the shock of calamity. This shock may bring people into transtherapy and counseling. They meet there the great wisdom traditions of humanity and feel embraced by an atmosphere of lived transcendent intimacy.

Collision in Intimacy

Collision, as I indicated previously, can be a sign of truthfulness in intimacy. Weak, insecure, or pretended intimacy is often maintained at the cost of refusing to acknowledge the possibility of collision. Solid intimacy assures the intimates of the secure, cordial foundation of their shared journey. This prevents them from denying collisions. Instead of avoiding them, they face them. In facing them, they redefine the demands of their own congeniality and therewith the wise and reasonable boundaries of their intimacy. Solving their collisions, they become more themselves. In being more themselves, they know in a more nuanced way how they can be more intimate with real, rather than the wished for, others.

The deeper the intimacy, the more painful the collision. Collisions with those with whom we are not intimate are not too hurtful. In relation to strangers, we keep our inner life in reserve. Intimates do the opposite. They share some of their inner life with one another. Because of this intertwining, any expression of those who are intimate with us penetrates our heart, arousing pleasant or painful vibrations. The covenant of intimacy can save the relationship in the midst of collisions. Remember, my concept of *collision* is the opposite of my concept of *collusion*. Collusion would paralyze true feelings of intimacy under the suffocating weight of anxious fusion. By contrast, collision would lead to alienation and separation. The perils of both collision and collusion for transcendent intimacy are often considered in transtherapy sessions.

Formative and Deformative Jealousy

Collision dynamics find their strongest expression in jealousy. Jealousy is evoked by any true or imagined threat to the foundations of one's intimacy. Deep intimacy involves a covenant of hearts to be with and for each other in intimate interformation. Jealousy may be evoked the moment one's formation history brings an intimate into a new, more or less intimate relationship with others. This situation can pose a threat to the relationship. It is a factor to cope with unexpectedly. Such a collision may unleash fierce forces of doubt, anger, anxiety, and distrust. Any one of these can destroy intimacy if it is not brought into the open and resolved in a timely way in dialogue.

I want to emphasize here the distinction between formative and deformative jealousy. Formative jealousy fosters intimate interformation by bringing into the open in what way newly emerging, intimate relationships with others could be a real threat to the intimacy one has formed so carefully over a long period of time. A true dialogue of the heart enables intimates to find ways in which their relationship can deepen and continue in spite of this threat.

Deformative jealousy, on the contrary, is perverted by the dominance of fusion, collusion, possessiveness, and excessive security directives. The formation fantasy magnifies out of proportion the threat to intimacy. Effective dialogue is impossible as long as this distortion is not corrected. For only then can we deal realistically with the real facets of the threat to our relationship.

Compassion is especially important if the heart of our partner is wounded by jealousy. The wound may be caused by intimate indiscretions with others and cover-ups of them. Indiscretions may be owing to the vulnerability we all share, cover-ups to our insecurity regarding the response of our intimate mate or friend, or our fear to hurt this person. The deeper the intimacy, the less the chance that such concealments succeed. Our intraspheres are too intertwined not to sense that something is amiss in the flow of communication. Hence, in profound and secure intimate relationships it seems better, as a general rule, to be open about indiscretions. If the relationship is insecure, however, it may not be wise to divulge them without due concern for the ramifications of telling now or waiting for the right moment. The same applies to marital relationships, the intimacy of which varies among different couples. Few marriages attain the depths of the intertwining of intraspheres to which I have been alluding. It may be doubtful how much jealousy a couple can tolerate and work through in subsequent collisions. Formative family or marriage counseling by expert practitioners may be necessary if too much tension prevails.

Successive collisions and their solutions are a necessary factor in the formation of intimate affective relationships. Threats to intimacy are always possible. None of us can fully apprehend and appraise the unknown affective dynamics operative in ourselves and others. Collisions and their solutions represent a necessary reformative stage in any affective relationship. Fidelity to our own unique-communal life call may demand timely distance, detachment, and occasional collision. All of these coform the story of affective intimacy.

Intimates must develop a disposition of appreciatively apprehending collision dynamics. They should appreciate them as an integral part of their journey, not necessarily as a symptom of the dissolution of their intimacy. To grow in intimacy means to respect, confirm, and encourage the unfolding of the life call of those with whom we are intimate.

Growth in awareness and affirmation of our unique-communal life call and its increasing expression in our individuality will enable us to tolerate unavoidable collisions. The latter will actually inspire us to find solutions. Such a task sets us free from our infantile longings and thereby advances our quest for transcendent intimacy. We must thus be ready at all times to elucidate the infantile desires that estrange us from our transcendent life call. We must surmount them in a ceaseless struggle of affective and effective reformation and transformation.

Friendship Intimacy

Intimacy can take many forms, friendship being one of the most precious. A necessary condition for intimacy between friends is no doubt the special affinity and trust they feel for one another. Unlike general human intimacy, which can be extended to all, soul friendship can be celebrated only among those who share a particular bonding. There is no guarantee that this will last.

It is almost a miracle if it does. For all kinds of reasons the bonding between friends may come to an end. Affinity may diminish under the pressure of divergent current formations. Mutual trust may have been violated to such a degree that temporal or lasting disengagement becomes an option. Withdrawal from the special intimacy of friendship should not end the general human intimacy we can extend to others, even to former friends.

Disengagement from Intimacy

Disengagement can be formative or deformative. It all depends on the motives that lead up to it. Disengagement is deformative when it is wrongly motivated. Examples would be irrational fear and anxious self-assertion, stubbornness and arrogance, envy, jealousy, refusal to appraise honestly one's unwholesome need for collusion and fusion, passing irritation, lack of respect for each other's privacy and solitude. Disengagement can be deformative also when its motivation is expressed in a way that is crude, disruptive, or insulting. Ideally, disengagement should progress gradually. It should be a gentle yet firm unstitching over time of intimate meetings and confidences. In certain situations, however, there may be no time for such gradual dissolution. For example, an extramarital intimacy discovered by a spouse may in many cases destroy the marriage bond if this indiscretion is not ended at once.

Formative Disengagement

The dynamics of disengagement can be formative, provided that the motives directing them are consonant with the reality of the situation and of the relationship concerned. People can decide to part in a way that is least painful to both of them. For example, it may be impossible for people to live in congeniality with their unique-communal call by the mystery and at the same time to respond to the demands of a special friendship. It may be equally impossible to keep communicating trustfully with friends who betray that trust by indiscretion. Other friendships may fail because the partners are unable to rise above fusion dynamics to the mature intimacy of true friendship.

Yet another motive for justifiable disengagement may be that the demands of a specific intimacy have become irreconcilable with the traditional facet of one's personal formation conscience.

Disengagement may at first be operative nonfocally. It takes time before friends become conscious of what is happening so that they are able to express it vocally. The earlier they pay attention to this process, the better are their chances for either re-engagement or disengagement. Instead of repudiating or refusing to acknowledge the beginning of a process of disengagement, friends should lift it into the region of focal consciousness and discuss it openly. A shared attentiveness to manifestations of tension early in a relationship can prevent unnecessary misunderstanding and disruption.

Even if a decision to end the relationship is worked through maturely, it will still leave a scar. Friends become in some way part of one another. They have shared the same journey. Loss of friendship is experienced as the loss of something irreplaceable and precious. Former friends may be plagued by questions concerning their own responsibility for the disengagement. They may feel a vague sense of guilt. They may wonder if the wound will ever heal.

Sometimes disengagement may be replaced by re-engagement later in life. Notwithstanding this possibility, one should not be seduced to engage in deceptive sentimental re-engagements. One should maintain a gentle readiness for future re-engagement in true dialogue if and when the right opportunity offers itself to our freedom.

From all of this it may be evident that an unnecessary disengagement can be prevented by timely communication. When one of the friends closes up and refuses the struggle of dialogue, the disengagement process may take over and lead to a painful break which perhaps could have been prevented.

Intimate friendships will be punctured from time to time by misunderstandings and irritations. Without collisions friendships may become forced exercises in mutual deception. Both of us remain always persons-in-formation. Therefore, new differences are bound to arise between us owing to the impact of the current formation processes we have to go through as long as we are alive and open to transcendence. Unnecessary disengagement attitudes can be prevented in the measure that friends are willing to apprehend, appreciate, affirm, and even desire the differences that the ongoing unfolding of their life generates between them.

There is no escape from the inevitable distance and collision that emerge in friendships at certain moments. The uniqueness and solitude of each person obliges them to maintain the right distance at the right time. We have to be cautious about the primitive urges in our nonfocal regions of consciousness to restore the dreamland of fusion we experienced in our first infantile relationships. The more we grow in a healthy sense of transcendent identity rooted in intimacy with the mystery, the more we are able to bear with the otherness of the other in the midst of the intimacy of friendship. Then the necessary collision of opinions and feelings between honest, outspoken friends will not detract from their mutual intimacy. The obstacles to transcendent intimacy gain in experiential clarity when they are spontaneously communicated by participants in our transtherapy sessions.

My research in the transcendent meaning and depth of intimacy enabled me to disclose dynamics of aversion, controversion, conversion, inversion, reversion, and transversion. Any of these can affect in a unique way our history of intimacy formation. I shall discuss my findings in the following final pages of this chapter.

Aversion from Intimacy

Institutions, churches, events, countries, formation segments, or individuals may appeal, explicitly or implicitly, to our longing for human intimacy. They may invite the human heart to share their needs, dreams, hopes, and sufferings. Our answer may be to avert our eyes and ears, to close our hearts. We stay indifferent and untouchable in spite of increasing invitations to share more intimately in others' predicament. This closure necessitates the development of subtle strategies of aversion, of nonattentiveness, of blindness and deafness. These are supported by our proliferating security directives. They protect us against appeals that may disturb our vital-functional complacency. The beginnings of a new transtherapy group may be colored by aversion tactics of some anxious participants.

Controversion in Relation
to the Invitation to Intimacy

Controversion makes human intimacy even more impossible. In this case, our heart is not merely indifferent and without sympathy; it goes against anyone who threatens to evoke feelings of intimate human concern. The best defense is offense. Often the fear of intimacy and its consequent responsibility lead to harsh treatment and condemnation of those who represent for us this threat. Some participants in a transtherapy group may grow beyond their controversion. Others may have to drop out because the threat is still too overwhelming for them. In that case, appropriate pretranscendent therapies may prepare them better for the post-therapy intimacy process.

Conversion to Intimacy

At any moment, the human heart can open itself to the intimate human meanings of the great wisdom traditions and to the intimate presence of the epiphanic mystery in any of its forms. At that blessed moment, a conversion of heart, moved by human concern, begins to replace aversion or controversion. It marks the crucial turning point in transtherapy.

A similar process is initiated when the mystery itself converts the heart of people to intimate interest in spiritual deepening. This is an inspired movement beyond vital-functional religiosity or humanism to a truly transformative spirituality.

Once the heart is converted to intimate interest and concern, this conversion may expand. Such expansion enables us to share in the intimate human concerns, ideals, and needs of a person or population in need. Conversion, in this case, means that one is enabled to accompany cordially an individual, community, church, or association toward growth in human and transcendent intimacy.

Inversion of Intimacy

In certain lives, the apparent dynamics of intimacy with others may in reality be focused on oneself. Often unwittingly, we transpose imaginatively to others qualities we ourselves feel in need to possess or to admire. What we are intimate with is not people, communities, or things as they really are but our own exalted imagination of certain qualities. In other words, we invert or become intimate with some imaginings within ourselves. We falsely believe that we are turning in intimate sympathy to people and things outside ourselves when in fact we are only projecting on them our own hidden wishes and phantasies.

Reversion of Intimacy

A special type of inversion which I observed is that of reversion. It compels us to revert back to intimacy experiences we cherished in the past. We try to repeat them. Our apparent intimacy with others is in reality an intimacy with something or someone in our past. We try to fit a person, situation, or institution into the mold of past intimacies. Many people, for instance, may hunger for the restoration of the symbiotic fusion intimacy with their mothers during early infancy.

Transversion of Intimacy

Transversion intimacy goes beyond the other types of intimacy I have named thus far. True transversion welcomes and transforms lower aspects of intimacy. It brings each autonomous, consonant dynamic of intimacy, however it happens, into deeper oneness with the supreme transcendent dimension of our personality and the mystery of formation from which it emerges ongoingly. It can be said of spiritually mature persons that they are always on the road toward transversion of their intimacy dynamics. They know that they have not yet arrived, that they are always arriving, at true transformation.

CHAPTER 25

Transtherapy as Rooted
in Formation Science

Everyday experience teaches caregivers that their life and the lives of those entrusted to them are in many ways alienated, segregated, broken. It has been my contention in this book that transcendence therapy offers a way to integrate what is disintegrated. This healing or integrating process proceeds along the channels of what I call in my formation theory of personality "integrating structures." These pull together the dimensions and dynamics I articulated thus far. They operate dynamically in dialogue with all the spheres of our formation field.

Central to my theory of personality is the fact that humans cannot create their own personhood or basic personal form of life by their own power or by virtue of environmental conditions. On the contrary, my formation science assumes the opposite. Our unique essence or basic life form was in the mind or knowledge of a formation mystery before it gave this form concrete existence in time and space. It is my contention that we have to disclose, approximate, and implement during our lifetime the basic form of life meant for us.

Understandably, when we are infants or young children, at the onset of our concrete existence in time and space, we do not know what we may be called to become. This founding life form is pre-empirical. This unique essence orders and expresses itself in our empirical existence. I call the founding form as dynamically expressive in time the unique-communal life call. It is natural for us to long for a more profound integration between our essence and our existence in time.

Empirical existence signifies that empirically-experientially, over a lifetime of trial and error, we begin to disclose what our life call is to be. The same presence to empirical experience teaches us how we are to implement it in a succession of changing situations from birth to death. As we strive to disclose the basic form of our life, our hearts and matching character will begin to move in that direction. We will start to develop some continuous, enduring "dispositions of the heart" and of its corresponding character that are more and more in tune with the basic form that is ours.

The symbol of the heart, which I name the core form, is related to the French *le coeur* and the English *courage*. The core form, heart, including its compatible character, is an integrating structure. As such it brings together the various dispositions of heart and character and the promptings of our founding call as these become known to us. Blocking or obscuring this knowledge is the pride form or the fallen reality of human life. This counterfeit or false self is the source of division between the heart's longing for transcendence and one's choice of substitutes for the transcendent like drugs, alcohol, or frantic careerism. Transtherapists and counselors trained in formation science can often trace the unhappiness and disharmony in people's lives to the pride form.

We do not know at once who we are called to be. Life is a collection of ups and downs. We proceed by trial and error, over a range of successive life situations, to discover ever-new aspects of our destiny. In the midst of ambiguity and occasional clarity, our life takes on a certain shape or form in dialogue with the here-and-now situation. These passing situational and phasic dispositions constitute what I designate as our "current life form." Caregivers, transtherapists, and counselors strive to help people make sense out of the hand that has been dealt to them at any given moment. What works and why? With what positions and relationships is one compatible or incompatible? Amidst the changes of life, what is lasting?

The answers to these questions do not come easily. Light may only dawn through a series of counseling sessions, especially when a person finds him- or herself faced with a significant crisis that may call for a lasting change of life. Consonant appraisal tells us also which facets of each current form to drop and which to integrate in the enduring core form of our life insofar as the latter is in consonance with our founding life form or life call.

Both caregivers and recipients of care cannot, nor should they, show everyone around them all that they are feeling in intimate moments of disclosure. Protecting the core and current life forms from too much revelation too soon is the work of the apparent form—the way in which we appear in any given situation. At times, especially when we are most vulnerable, as in the presence of a transtherapist, we may, so to speak, wear our hearts on our sleeves. At other times, we may appear to have our life in order, although we are weeping within or trembling with anxiety or rage.

Caregivers have to be attentive to the way others appear. The apparent form gives us a first clue to what is the matter with a person, why it may be time for him or her to drop the mask and acknowledge the problem. The reverse is also true. When everything seems to come together, when joy bubbles over from within, the gift of consonance can shine through one's whole being, lighting up one's eyes, placing a spontaneous smile on one's lips, and in general leaving others with the impression of having been in the presence of a truly radiant human being.

All of these forms, taken together—core, current, and apparent—constitute in my theory of personality the actual form. This phrase designates the way we behave at any given period and indicates, in effect, the practical integration of the other structures in response to the demands of the moment. The actual life form is the present-moment integration of our inner life with the demands of our entire outer situation, seen in the light of the formation mystery that directs our unfolding.

Caregivers are aware from their work that life receives shape and form as people respond appreciatively or depreciatively to the stream of events that comprise life's journey from birth to death. As we move from one current form to another, we change inwardly and outwardly. The bragging eighteen-year-old whose parents were "out of it" begins as a thirty-eight-year-old parent to see that the "old folks were not so dense after all." Each transition, be it emotional, spiritual, neurological, or chronological, poses an opportunity for us to discover something new about our hidden direction, our unique call of life.

Whenever we come to the crossroads of life, we can choose to regress to routine responses. Often these may be motivated by strivings for security and for maintaining the status quo. We can also progress to a higher stage of self-understanding and responsible care. When the latter happens, it is as if we are writing a new chapter in the story of our adventure of discovery.

Caregiving in Crisis

Transtherapists and counselors meet people during transition periods in their lives when they are in some kind of crisis. They know they have to give up something to which they have clung for a long time (a relationship, a home, a position), yet they are not ready to let go. This break in their life's continuity causes them to feel insecure, hesitant, uneasy. Immediate concerns arise. How will I survive without him/her? Where will I/we live? Am I too old/young to handle this assignment? Deeper questions press to the surface of consciousness as well. What does this event have to do with my unique calling in life? How can I be sure that my life is worthwhile? Am I on the right track? Am I still a lovable person? Caregivers or transtherapists never offer pat answers to these life-wrenching questions. They listen and let the person tune in to his or her own inner voice. There is, however, one major disposition caregivers have to be mindful of, and that is "abandonment."

What exhausts caregivers is any attempt by human reasoning alone, or by means of clever psychological techniques or tests, to second guess the mystery of life, about which none of us has absolute certainty. Events can be so traumatic, so puzzling, that one's only option is to make a leap of faith. Despite our best efforts, we cannot posit with certitude that things will work out well for a particular person, family, or community. We can offer encouragement and counsel. We can suggest ways to rise above anxiety, depression, guilt, and feelings of worthlessness. But in the end, we, as well as those to whom we offer care, have to abandon ourselves to the mystery of formation in our life. Only spiritually abandoned transtherapists and counselors can inspire abandonment in those who come to them for care during a transcendence crisis.

The disposition of abandonment has two faces: one is appreciative, the other depreciative. Appreciative abandonment, the positive option, means that at all times, under all circumstances, one chooses to live in praise of the embracing, never-failing care of the mystery. This attitude instills in one's heart a disposition of awe-filled appreciation for anything praiseworthy, despite the darkness of the hour. It encourages a joyous outlook without denying the pain one is going through. Appreciative abandonment sheds light on situations that might at first glance appear unredeemably bleak.

By contrast, depreciation inclines one not to be abandoned to the mystery but to feel abandoned by the mystery. To cultivate such a disposition can spell disaster for caregivers. It inclines them and those around them to give up living in praise of the mystery. It severely limits one's inner radar, which is set to detect only what is dark or dreary in a crisis situation. This negative posture invades our heart and poisons any glimmer of hope. An aura of despondency hangs over facial expressions. Words, styles of reading and listening, other modes of communication serve to reinforce one's depressive mood. The atmosphere dampens accordingly. No longer are we shepherds of the spirit of encouragement; fulfillment of duty becomes a tedious chore lacking joy. We feel inclined to throw in the towel in the face of trouble. All we want is to retreat to our narrow chambers, to feed on self-pity, and to flirt with the demon of doubt.

The Appraisal Process

In the spiritual context, given the fact that one is trying to restore a sense of appreciative abandonment to the mystery, it is important to maintain a disposition of praise. Crisis situations invite people to appraise the possible direction they may be called to pursue. Such appraisal is not a sudden act but a process that includes a number of successive steps.

Preliminary Appraisal Dispositions

The first preliminary appraisal disposition is *awe*. Awe enables us, if only for a moment, to stand back from the intensity of a crisis and to wonder what is really happening. We feel humble in the light of the mystery that infinitely surpasses our little slice of life. Awe fosters the proper climate for transcendent reflection to occur.

Second, the appraisal process requires a willingness on our part to *abide* with anyone who comes to us for care, transtherapy, or counseling, to be with them where they are at the present moment, not to press too quickly for solutions to their situation.

To abide with another encourages a listening stance and leads to the third preliminary disposition, *attention.* We must remain attentive to how a person looks, feels, and behaves. What is the meaning of the images or symbols they verbalize, of the intuitive insights they offer into what is going on? We should pay attention to a person's whole field of life. We should look at the dimensions and dynamics filtering through their core, current, and apparent forms. Caregivers such as transtherapists are able to guide the appraisal process to a wise and reasonable resolution.

These preliminary dispositions, taken together, make possible an immediate or intuitive apprehension of where a person is and of what his or her future may hold. These insights must be trusted, though they are clearly distinguishable from only logically reasoned comprehensions. The word *apprehension* in English also connotes a certain fear. A child, for instance, wants to go to sleep with her nightlight on because she is apprehensive of the dark. This connotation complements the cognitive, insightful facet of the word. There is no doubt at such junctures of life that caregivers, and those who come to them for help, walk together in holy fear on sacred ground. Together they must remain attuned to any apprehension of what the mystery might be asking of them. There is reason to fear the risks that may be involved, especially in the midst of a crisis which, by definition, shakes one's certitude.

Assuming that one's counselees have made, at least prefocally, an appreciative abandonment option, the appraisal process continues. Now it is necessary to begin to make focal in one's consciousness whatever feelings diminish awe, abiding, or attention. What temptations linger that might cause one to lean in the direction of depreciative abandonment? It is necessary at all times to direct one's thoughts cognitively and affectively toward opportunity rather than obstacle. Intuitive insights flowing from abiding in awe and attention may at first be obscure in detail, and perhaps even defective. It is necessary for caregivers to clarify these insights, to remove from them shades of superficiality, and to enhance their transcendent meaning. I dub this the stage of *assessment* and *argumentation.* As much concrete information as possible must be gathered. One must sort through the "shoulds" and "what-ifs" to the truth of what actually occurred and its pain and potential for growth.

Assessment in transtherapy and counseling implies looking back from the preliminary intuitive apprehension to the exact occurrence in which the crisis first cut into the ordinary flow of life. The purpose of sober assessment is to gather solid information for ourselves and those with whom we are in dialogue. On the basis of what is, we may begin to understand what has to be. As we bring this initial intuitive grasp into rational dialogue with concrete facts, we move into *argumentation* or critical reasoning about the pros and cons in the situation. For what is one responsible? Over what has one no control? Rational cognition sharpens at this point and acts as a corrective to thoughts that may sound true but, in effect, have distorted reality. They sparked feelings of discouragement and despondency. Or they evoked premature excitement with subsequent mistaken affirmations and commitments.

Out of these two steps in the appraisal process further intuitive apprehensions requiring assessment and argumentation may emerge. Once as much information as possible is on the table, caregivers or transtherapists and counselors may begin to move people toward the next step of provisional *affirmation*. Various life directives may be suggested for a person's consideration. No coercion whatsoever is involved, no seduction, no manipulation. At this juncture a person is free to choose among various options held out. Transtherapists have to trust in this regard that if appreciative abandonment has pervaded their sessions, the choices to be made will approximate as much as possible one's free and joyful response to new insight in the midst of a life crisis. Provisional affirmation, even though it is not final, is a good gauge to the decision likely to be implemented.

This directive has to be submitted to the next step in the appraisal process, that of *application*. One tentatively applies in everyday life and practice the decision that draws one out of dissonance or disintegration toward consonance or integration. Application must meet the test of reality. New information has to be taken into account and with it new appraisal. By now a person has at least moved off dead center to the threshold of a new beginning, of a new current life form. Following this period of testing, one may be able, with a counselor's or caregiver's encouragement, to move toward the stage of definite affirmation. This is a *yes* to a new facet of life, to a true disclosure of one's life call. This *yes* implies a commitment to implementation here and now. It makes sense out of what at the onset of the transcendence crisis seemed to be only a no or *maybe*.

Caregiving Dispositions

We can ask ourselves at this point if there are some criteria by which to appraise the quality of one's capacity to offer care, especially the care of transtherapy. In other words, are there certain essential dispositions common to all kinds of caregiving? Again, formation science aids us by presenting what I analyze as the "dispositions of consonance." I detail these by using as a memory device the letter "C." Each of these conditions must somehow be present if one's transtherapy or counseling or spiritual direction is to maintain excellence amidst the pressure of time and inevitable stress.

Underlying the "C's" of consonant caregiving is *congeniality.* In this context the word means more than being a happy-go-lucky sort of person, one with whom others feel at home. Its etymology suggests a deeper meaning. The word comes from *con,* a prefix translatable as "with" or "through," and the same root word from which we derive the word "genesis," which suggests source or origin. Hence, "congeniality" has to do with being at home with the selves we most deeply are. It is a condition for caregiving because it calls for respect for the original, unrepeatable uniqueness of self and others. Respect for the congeniality factor can prevent one person's spiritual enthusiasms or awakening experiences from being imposed arbitrarily on others.

The "C" of *compatibility* is best understood by tracing the origin of the word to *cum* and *pati,* Latin roots suggesting "to undergo with others the limits of a situation" or "to endure patiently the circumstances in which one finds oneself by virtue of one's calling." To be compatible means more than getting along with others in a perfunctory fashion. It requires that we be patient and peaceful in the face of always-demanding, here-and-now situations, while being congenial to our integral calling in and with the mystery. In a social care situation, compatibility might mean seeking ways to make others comfortable and open to one's message. It would be grossly incompatible for social workers in the inner city to impose their style of care on persons in affluent neighborhoods who require another kind of care.

It would be difficult, if not impossible, to remain congenial and compatible without being compassionate. The "C" of *compassion* comes from the Latin roots *cum* and *passio,* which means "to suffer or bear empathically with our own and others' vulnerability." Caregivers, like transtherapists and counselors, by virtue of their calling are sensitive to how broken and wounded we humans are. We are called to manifest compassion for rich and poor, sheltered and homeless, believers and nonbelievers. All persons, whatever their race, creed, color, religion, or education, may have physical and spiritual needs. These may require not only special provisions. They may call for profound compassion. While providing expert help for persons suffering from substance abuse, a good counselor will manifest compassion for this person's vulnerability, revealing by eye contact and gesture that "tough love" does not exclude empathy for anyone who suffers from addictive diseases. Compassion is perhaps the central aspiration of caregiving.

Competence, the next "C" of consonance implies that caregivers strive to use to the full their gifts and talents. This disposition goes together with the pursuit of excellence. Competence concentrates on effective, practical outreach programs uplifted by transcendent inspirations and aspirations. Dedicated, competent caregivers prove that the height of spirituality enhances effective functionality and in no way detracts from productivity.

Connecting these four central dispositions of consonance, are the "C's" of *courage* and *confidence*. Courage is a disposition of the heart that enables us to persevere in situations that, humanly speaking, might tempt one to discouragement, if not despair. It takes a lot of courage to keep on caring when we do not see instant results. Without this disposition, caregivers would not be able to continue their service in a determined way despite opposition, fear of failure, or lack of respect. It takes courage not to swing with the trends and fashions of the times but to stay faithful to one's original vision. Caregivers must remain confident of the worthwhileness of their work in the face of opposition. They must trust that even in the worst of situations the forming mystery sustains their efforts. Confidence in the mystery enables caregivers to relax and do what they can without developing a "savior complex."

Transtherapists, like all persons in the helping professions, need a support system as they work to foster the common good. An essential shared dispositions is that of *concern*. Caregivers have to express interest in the problems people bring to them, but at some point they have to show concern also for one another. This can happen in casual conversation or in such significant exchanges as a "case consultation" session where counselors or social workers discuss progress with an individual or a family. Such occasions offer caregivers a chance to express their trust and confidence in one another.

The same rationale stands behind the need to foster the disposition of *confirmation*. This is the capacity to offer to others verbally or nonverbally expressions of assurance and encouragement as they attempt to affirm themselves before the mystery and their family members, friends, and coworkers. Leading people to affirm their own value and dignity is an important aspect of receiving care; confirming others in their progress is an essential aspect of giving care.

No counseling situation could continue to excel were it not for the disposition of *cooperation*. Everyone in such a setting needs to work together in teams or as partners to serve the common good. Through this cooperation programs and courses of benefit to care recipients may begin to develop.

The atmosphere of cooperation would be poisoned by petty envy or a putdown style of competition were it not for the protective coating supplied by the disposition of *collegiality*. Here caregivers rely on their readiness to listen to one another in an atmosphere of dialogue without usurping a position of authoritarian dominance. Colleagues know that at some point a discussion or plan has to be brought to appropriate and creative closure. Due to the sensitive areas in which caregivers have to work, decision making must be preceded by respectful dialogue and genuine listening.

With these interformative dispositions in place, caregivers can enjoy what I call *concelebration.* To celebrate together each person's unique gifts, talents, and achievements can have a replenishing effect when pressures of work become too much to bear. The ability to have fun together, to play and recreate, relieves stress and reminds people that, despite their responsibilities, they are, after all, only human.

Such occasions of repletion will affect in turn the capacity of caregivers to reaffirm their commitment to pursue social and professional excellence to the best of their ability. Promises made will be kept. People's expectations of them will not be disappointed. The disposition of *commitment* binds us to the relationships, organizations, and tasks to which we have pledged fidelity in service of effective caregiving.

In the deepest sense, quality transtherapy can only be sustained by the transtherapist's own abandonment to the beneficial meaning of the mystery of formation in faith, hope, and love. No matter what happens to people in any given sociohistorical situation, it is important not to lose confidence in the undergirding, embracing love of the mystery for persons, events, and things. This attitude of abandonment enables us to recommit ourselves to the service of others, despite periods when little or no progress can be perceived. Though we may not always be able to see the light at the end of the tunnel, we wager that something good is happening and that in due time its meaning may be understood.

Afterword

Volume 7 marks the last book in this series on formation science. It is a transitional text, for in the next volume, the eighth in this series, I will move from my pretheological formation science to my systematic theology of Christian character and personality formation, a work begun by me over fifty years ago in the Netherlands.

The center of my interformation paradigm in the seven volumes on formation science has been the Mystery of formation as generally understood in a significant number of classical wisdom traditions. In the upcoming volume on Christian formation I will speak of this mystery in terms of my Christian formation theology. I shall present the radical mystery of formation as the mystery of the Holy Trinity. For me this mystery shines forth epiphanically in Christ, who is God and man, the Word made flesh, the second person of the Blessed Trinity. Through him, the splendor of the Trinity radiates into our Christian character and personality and transforms them in the process.

Human nature is formed by the Father from the beginning in the image of Christ's human character. I described our distinctively human character in detail both in volume 6 and in this volume 7 in terms of my pre-Christian formation science. My intention is to show in volume 8 that the graced formation of Christian character unites us with Christ's divine and human character. In no way do I mean to say that our character is changed into the divine character or the divine personhood as such. Rather, our character is Christ-like. It is united with God's inmost core through grace and through Christian character dispositions or virtues. Our character *likeness* to God is real, but it does not change our proper human nature. I have described the human character and its corresponding heart in my pre-Christian formation science, notably in volume 3, *Formation of the Human Heart.*

Having described in terms of formation science human nature and character with its created formation potencies, I shall indicate in volume 8 among these form potencies the divinely infused capacity to disclose the image and revelation of God. The divine actualization of this potency implies for the Christian the possibility of receiving the gift of a character likeness with Christ. Human persons can actualize their Christ-receptive form potencies of character only if the gift of the Holy Spirit imprints onto it a likeness unto that of the Son. It is grace *and* the Christian character dispositions or virtues that unite us with God. The transformation of our character, therefore, is what I already pointed to in my formation science as the fruit of interformation between the formation mystery and human life. Our interformation with Christ implies the formation and the exercise of Christian character dispositions or virtues. These virtues imprint on our Christian character the features of God's character shining forth in Jesus of Nazareth.

Human nature, as described in my seven pretheological volumes, is thus from its very beginning fashioned by God in such a way that it can and should coform our Christian character. This clarifies some of the differences as well as some of the relationships between my pre-Christian formation science and the Christian formation theology I shall present in volume 8.

The shift from pretheological formation science is thus made possible by a deepening of the idea of a general formation mystery. I placed this idea at the center of the interformation paradigm of my formation science. It took the place of the "self" at the center of other contemporary sociological, psychological, and educational anthropologies. At the same time, this mystery of formation, as I define it in my pretheological formation science, is not incompatible with the Christian mystery of the most Holy Trinity. This trinitarian mystery can only be known by the Christian revelation. As such, it does not exclude that non-Christians may know something of the formation mystery too. On the contrary, such human knowledge may prepare people for the potential disclosure of its deepest revealed meaning by grace. For it is grace alone that makes us enter into its inner treasures. This awesome transformation is made possible by the epiphany of Christ. He opens our minds and hearts to the riches of the Divine Mystery without unveiling all of its ultimate concealments in the Godhead.

In brief, my formation paradigm as a whole points to the magnificent trinitarian formation mystery, the mystery that embraces all eons while transcending them all eternally. The heart of God's providential plan for universe and humanity is the Word of God himself. By his sweet condescendence, compassion, and compatibility the Word became one of us. He shared the sufferings and joys, the victories and defeats (except sin) occasioned in all spheres of our human formation field. As a loving sufferer in the pain-filled field of fallen humanity, he disclosed to us the eternal mercy and loving compassion of the Father. He let his own loving person and character shine forth epiphanically in his human form. He manifested in his own person the ultimate divine love-will embedded in the multispheric fields of his own human character and personality formation. I believe that Jesus Christ through the Spirit has inspired me over the years to point to this field of divine love as the guiding intuition behind my theology of Christian character and personality formation.

My paradigm of Christian interformation identifies the mystery of the Incarnation as the heart of the divine unfolding of creation and salvation. The universal role of the formation mystery, which I underlined so emphatically in my formation science, finds its true significance in my original form- theological paradigm that will undergird all of volume 8. The mystery of the divine love-will unfolding God's merciful plan of formation for universe and history is a source of profound meditation in my personal life and work.

My pre-Christian formation science by itself cannot disclose this restoration by Christ of our original nature and its inherent direction. This divine reformation and transformation will thus constitute the heart of the next volume on Christian formation. To prepare for its graced disclosure I used constantly in my pretheological formation science such expressions as epiphany, consonance, dissonance, appreciative abandonment, forming, reforming, and transforming. These terms and others like them will help me to describe in volume 8 how in Christ the human love-will is directed by the epiphany of the divine love-will.

Love is the epiphany of God. This insight nourishes my reflections on the epiphanic character formation of the Christian. Through his suffering for us, Christ received the form or imprint of love in his human character. He is the firstborn of many. The only purpose of this receptivity was to imprint this divine love into our Christian character as a gift of grace. That is why Christ's life and character are the original form of God's epiphanic love and image. We are God's image or form by creation and by Christ's redeeming call to reformation. In this life we can already participate in Christ's character, if our human character is rooted in that of Christ himself. This is the ineffable mystery of the *divinization* of human character. As Christ allowed his character to shine forth in his outward appearance, we, too, are called to let him do the same through the true apparent or appearing form of our character.

I will have much to say about the role of the outward appearance of our Christian character. I had to prepare my readers and audiences for the new theological formulations I had worked on from the very beginning before the additional development of my formation science in Holland. One of the preparatory concepts in this pretheological science was that of the apparent form. The reader will find it mentioned in all seven volumes that prepare for my formation theology, volumes which from the start have been designed to be conducive to and compatible with the Judeo-Christian revelation without pretending to be identical with it.

My formation theology considers the Christian character to be an indispensable element of the profession of the Christian faith. My theology of Christian character formation posits that each true Christian character is a *condensed* version of the Christ-story. Christ's representation in each Christian character is made possible by the Spirit's gift of contemplation and by the unique incorporation of the character of Jesus of Nazareth in the whole of human history, our own included.

Bibliography

Books

Adler, Alfred. *The Education of the Individual.* New York: Philosophical Library, 1958.

Argyris, C. *Personality and Organization: The Conflict between System and Individual.* New York: Harper Torchbooks, 1970.

Edelwich, J., and A. Brodsky. *Burn-Out: Stages of Disillusionment in the Helping Professions.* New York: Human Sciences Press, 1980.

Bogdan, R. C., and S. K. Biklen. *Qualitative Research for Education. An Introduction to Theory and Methods.* Boston: Alyn & Bacon, 1992.

Bolin, Frances S. *Growing Up Caring.* Lake Forest, IL: Glencoe, 1992.

Burrett, K., and T. Rusnak. *Integrated Character Education.* Bloomington, IN: Fastback Series, Phi Delta Kappa Educational Foundation, 1993.

Erikson, Erik H., ed. *Adulthood.* New York: W. W. Norton, 1978.

———. *Identity, Youth and Crisis.* New York: W. W. Norton and Company, 1968.

Freudenberger, H. J. *Burn-Out.* New York: Bantam Books, 1980.

Gilligan, C. *In a Different Voice.* Cambridge: Harvard University Press, 1982.

Katz, R. L. *Empathy, Its Nature and Uses.* New York: Free Press of Glencoe, 1963.

Keen, E. *A Primer in Phenomenological Psychology.* New York: University Press of America, 1975.

Keniston, K. *The Uncommitted: Alienated Youth in American Society.* New York: Brace and World, 1965.

Kline, H. F., and R. A. Feldmesser. *Program Evaluation in Moral Education.* Princeton, NJ: Educational Testing Service, 1983.

Knowles, Richard T. *Human Development and Human Possibility: Erikson in the Light of Heidegger.* New York: University Press of America, 1986.

Kohlberg L. *Essays in Moral Development: Philosophy of Moral Development.* San Francisco, CA: Harper and Row. 1981.

Leech, K. *Soul Friend.* London: Sheldon Press, 1977.

Levinson, D. J. *The Seasons of a Man's Life.* New York: Ballantine Books, 1978.

Macquarrie, John. *In Search of Humanity: A Theological and Philosophical Approach.* New York: Crossroad, 1985.

May, Gerald. *Will and Spirit.* New York: Harper and Row, 1982.

May, R. *Love and Will.* New York: W. W. Norton, 1969.

Mayeroff, M. *On Caring.* New York: Harper and Row, 1971.

McClelland, David. *The Achievement Motive.* New York: Appleton-Century Crofts, 1953.

McLean, G. F., and O. Pegoraro. *The Social Context and Values: Perspectives of the Americas.* New York: University Press of America, 1989.

———, and F. E. Ellrod, eds. *The Philosophical Foundations for Moral Education and Character Development: Act and Agent.* 2d ed. Washington: The Council for Research in Values and Philosophy, 1992.

Muto, Susan. *Caring for the Minister or Caregiver.* New Rochelle, NY: Don Bosco Multimedia, 1990.

———. *John of the Cross for Today: The Ascent.* Notre Dame, IN: Ave Maria Press, 1991.

——— . *John of the Cross for Today: The Dark Night.* Notre Dame, IN: Ave Maria Press, 1994.

———. *Late Have I Loved Thee: The Recovery of Intimacy.* New York: Crossroad, 1995.

———. *Pathways of Spiritual Living.* New York: Doubleday; Rpt., Petersham, MA: St. Bede's Publications, 1988.

———. *A Practical Guide to Spiritual Reading.* Revised edition. Petersham, MA: St. Bede's Publications, 1994.

———. *Meditation in Motion.* New York: Doubleday, 1986.

———. *Womanspirit: Reclaiming the Deep Feminine in Our Human Spirituality.* New York: Crossroad, 1991.

———, and Adrian van Kaam. *Commitment: Key to Christian Maturity.* Mahwah, NJ: Paulist Press, 1989.

———, and Adrian van Kaam. *Divine Guidance: Seeking to Find and Follow the Will of God.* Ann Arbor, MI: Servant, 1994.

Nouwen, H. J. M. *Reaching Out.* Garden City, NY: Doubleday, 1975.

Piaget, J. *The Moral Judgment of the Child.* New York: Free Press, 1989.

Rubin, T. *The Angry Book.* New York: Collier Books, 1969.

Ryan, K., and T. Lickona, T. *Character Development in Schools and Beyond.* 2d ed. Washington: The Council for Research in Values and Philosophy, 1992.

Scott, Nathan A., Jr. *The Poetics of Belief.* Chapel Hill, NC: The University of North Carolina Press, 1985.

Selman, R. L. *The Growth of Interpersonal Understanding: Developmental and Clinical Analyses.* New York: Academic Press, 1986.

Sorokin, P. *Social and Cultural Dynamics: A Study of Change in Major Systems of Art, Truth, Ethics, Law, and Social Relationship.* New Brunswick, NJ: Transaction Books, 1985.

van Kaam, Adrian. *The Art of Existential Counseling.* Wilkes-Barre, PA: Dimension Books, 1966.

———. *The Demon and the Dove: Personality Growth through Literature.* Pittsburgh: Duquesne University Press, 1967.

———. *Dynamics of Spiritual Self Direction.* Pittsburgh, PA: Epiphany Association, 1992.

———. *Existential Foundations of Psychology.* Garden City, NY: Doubleday, 1969.

———. *Foundations for Personality Study: An Adrian van Kaam Reader.* Denville, NJ: Dimension Books, 1983.

———. *Living Creatively.* Denville, NJ: Dimension Books, 1978.

———. *The Transcendent Self: The Formative Spirituality of the Middle, Early, and Later Years of Life.* Pittsburgh: Epiphany Association, 1991.

———. *The Roots of Christian Joy.* Denville, NJ: Dimension Books, 1985.

———. *Formative Spirituality. Volume I. Fundamental Formation.* New York: Crossroad, 1983.

———. *Formative Spirituality. Volume II. Human Formation.* New York: Crossroad/Continuum, 1985.

———. *Formative Spirituality. Volume III. Formation of the Human Heart.* New York: Crossroad/Continuum, 1986.

———. *Formative Spirituality. Volume IV. Scientific Formation.* New York: Crossroad, 1987.

———. *Formative Spirituality. Volume V. Traditional Formation.* New York: Crossroad, 1992.

———. *Formative Spirituality. Volume VI. Transcendent Formation.* New York: Crossroad, 1995.

———. *The Mystery of Transforming Love.* Denville, NJ: Dimension Books, 1982.

———. *The Music of Eternity.* Notre Dame, IN: Ave Maria Press, 1990.

————. *Religion and Personality.* New York: Prentice-Hall, 1964; rev. ed. Pittsburgh, PA: Epiphany Association, 1991.

————, and Susan Muto. *The Power of Appreciation: A New Approach to Personal and Relational Healing.* New York: Crossroad, 1993.

Wynn, Edward A., and Kevin Ryan. *Reclaiming our Schools: A Handbook on Teaching Character, Academics, and Discipline.* New York: MacMillan Publishing, 1993.

————, and Kevin Ryan. *Reclaiming our Schools: A Handbook on Teaching, Character, Academics, and Discipline.* New York: MacMillan Publishing Company, 1993.

Zukav, Gary. *The Seat of the Soul.* New York: Simon and Schuster, 1990.

Articles

Blasi, A. "Bridging Moral Cognition and Moral Action: A Critical Review of the Literature." *Psychological Bulletin* 88 (1980): 1-45.

Chandler, M. J. "Egocentric and Antisocial Behavior. The Assessment and Training of Social Perspective-taking Skill." *Developmental Psychology* 9 (1973): 326-32.

Ellrod, Frederick E. "Contemporary Philosophies of Moral Education." Ed. G. F. McLean and F. E. Ellrod. In *The Philosophical Foundations for Moral Education and Character Development: Act and Agent.* 2d ed. Washington, D.C. The Council for Research in Values and Philosophy, 1992.

Fabiano, E. A. "How Education can be Correctional and How Corrections can be Educational." *Journal of Correctional Education* 42/2 (1991): 100-106.

Freudenberger, H. J. "Staff Burn-Out." *Journal of Social Issues* 30 (1974): 159-685.

————. "The Staff Burn-Out Syndrome in Alternative Institutions." *Psychotherapy: Theory, Research and Practice* 12 (Spring 1975): 73-82.

Gorman, M. "Life-Long Moral Development." Ed. R. T. Knowles and G. F. McLean. In *The Psychological Foundations of Moral Education and Character Development: An Integrated Theory of Moral Development.* 2d ed. Washington, DC: The Council for Research in Values and Philosophy, 1992.

Grim, P. K., L. Kohlberg, and S. H. White. "Some Relationships Between Conscience and Attentional Processes." *Journal of Personality and Social Psychology* 8 (1968): 239-52.

Knowles, Richard T. "The Acting Person as Moral Agent: Erikson as the Starting Point for an Integrated Psychological Theory of Moral Development." Ed. R. T. Knowles and G. F. McLean. In *The Psychological Foundations of Moral Education and Character Development: An Integrated Theory of Moral Development.* 2d ed. Washington: The Council for Research in Values and Philosophy, 1992.

Kohlberg L. "Development of Moral Character and Moral Ideology." Ed. M. L. Hoffman and L. W. Hoffman. *Review of Child Development Research* New York: Russell Sage Foundation, 1964.

———. "Stage and Sequence: The Cognitive-Developmental Approach of Socialization." Ed. D. Goslin. Pp. 347-480 in *Handbook of Socialization Theory and Research.* Chicago, IL: Rand McNally, 1969.

Luna. G., and T. Price. "Qualitative Research: A New Approach for the Correctional Education Teachers as Researcher." *Journal of Correctional Education* 43/3 (1992): 118-21.

Muto, Susan. "Erosion and Depletion of Social Presence in the Helping Professions—A Formative Perspective." *Studies in Formative Spirituality* 9/3 (1988).

Piaget, J. "Moral Judgments by Normal and Conduct-Disordered Preadolescent and Adolescent Boys." *Merrill-Palmer Quarterly* 35 (1965): 463-78.

Selman, R. L. "Correction Counseling and Moral Education." *Journal of Correctional Education* 37 (1986): 48-53.

van Kaam, Adrian. "Transcendence Therapy" in *Handbook of Innovative Psychotherapies.* Ed. Raymond J. Corsini. New York: John Wiley and Sons, 1981: 855-72.

———. "The Goals of Psychotherapy from the Existential Point of View." In *The Goals of Psychotherapy.* Ed. Alvin R. Mahrer. New York: Appleton-Century-Crofts, 1966.

———. "The Psychology of Falling Away from the Faith." In *The Star and the Cross.* Ed. Catherine T. Hargrove, RSCJ, Milwaukee, 1966.

———. "Counseling from the Viewpoint of Existential Psychology." In *Counseling and Psychotherapy: An Overview.* Ed. D. S. Arbuckle. New York: McGraw-Hill, 1966.

———. "Formative Spirituality." In *Dictionary of Pastoral Care and Counseling.* Nashville, TN: Abingdon Press, 1990.

———. "Readings in Existential Psychology and Psychiatry" In *Readings of Existential Psychology and Psychiatry.* Ed. Keith Hoeller. Seattle, WA, 1990.

———. "Freud and Anthropological Psychology." *The Justice* (Brandeis University, May 1990).

———. "The Nurse in the Patient's World." *The American Journal of Nursing* 59 (1959).

————. "Clinical Implications of Heidegger's Concepts of Will, Decision, and Responsibility." *Review of Existential Psychology and Psychiatry* 1/3 (1961).

————. "Counseling and Existential Psychology." *Harvard Educational Review* (Fall 1962). (This article was later published in *Guidance—An Examination* [New York: Harcourt, Brace, and World, 1965]).

————. "Commentary on 'Freedom and Responsibility Examined.'" *Behavioral Science and Guidance*. Ed Lloyd-Jones and Westervelt. New York: Teachers College, Columbia University Press, 1963.

————. "Existential Theory and Therapy" (with Rollo May). *Current Psychiatric Therapies* 3 (1963).

————. "The Addictive Personality." *Insight* 4/ 2 (1965).

————. "Motivation and Contemporary Anxiety." *Humanitas* 1/1 (1965).

————. "The Addictive Personality." *Humanitas* 1/2 (1965).

————. "Religious Anthropology and Religious Counseling." *Insight* 4/3 (1966).

————. "Dynamics of Spiritual Self-Direction." *Spiritual Life* 21/4 (Winter 1975).

————. "Formation Counseling." *Studies in Formative Spirituality* 7/2 (1986).

————. "Correction Counseling and Moral Education." *Journal of Correctional Education* 37/2 (1986).

————. "Counseling from the Viewpoint of Formation Science." *Studies in Formative Spirituality* 12/3 (1991).

————. "Goals and Transcendence Therapy from the Viewpoint of Formation Science (Part One)." *Studies in Formative Spirituality* 13/1 (1992).

————. "Goals and Transcendence Therapy from the Viewpoint of Formation Science (Part Two)." *Studies in Formative Spirituality* 13/2 (1992).

————. "Principles and Practice of Spiritual Healing." *Advances* 9/4 (Fall 1993).

————. Guest Editor. *Journal of Correctional Education* 44/2 (June 1993).

————. "Phenomenal Analysis: Exemplified by a Study of the Experience of Really Feeling Understood." *Journal of Individual Psychology* 15 (1959).

————. "Counseling from the Viewpoint of Formation Science. Part One" *Studies in Formative Spirituality* 12/2 (May 1991).

Walker, L. J. and J. H. Taylor. "Family Interaction and the Development of Moral Reasoning." *Child Development* 62 (1991): 264-83.

Wiley, L. "The Correctional Educator as Moral Change Agent." *Journal of Correctional Education* 40 (1989): 12-15.

Index

socio-interphobia, 79
Socrates, 115
solitude, 229, 247
source of renewed presence, 237
sphere: interformational, 87
spirit: human, 3, 6; of transcendency, 183
spiritual: direction, 202, 203; director, 89;
  see also: counselor; transtherapists
spontaneity, 166
Stalin, Joseph, 224
structure: syncretic character, 168
subject-object criterion, 13
subjectivism, 13
subtraditions, 24
superego, 76: pretranscendent, 76
superiority: male, 51
symbiosis, 33
symbols: transcendent, 69
sympathy: dissonant, 187
symptoms: somatic, 53
syncretism, 168
syndrome: hostility, 132
system: of congruity, 59; neuroformational, 139

Taizé, 43
teaching: therapeutic, 128
temper form, 77
temperament, 42, 164
tendencies: pantheistic, 219; refusal, 231
Teresa of Avila, 20
testing: functional reality, 208; transcendent reality, 208
theologians: informational, 10, 12
theology: formation, 1, 57, 259, 262;
  information, 57, 132; informational,
  179
theory: counseling, 181; psychoanalytical, 32
therapists: pretranscendent, 51
therapy: pretranscendent, 19; private,
  131, 132; sessions, 131; transcendence,
  1, 4, 14, 16, 109, 118, 129, 183, 194
tradition: American theater, 73; capitalist,
  71; coforming power of, 30; communal

memory of, 61; culture reflecting, 84;
  deformed, 86; democratic, 71; dissonant, 9; Franciscan, 24; functionalistic,
  140; fusional we, 48; ideological, 136;
  Islamic, 53, 73; Judeo-Christian, 28;
  popular, 167; psychoanalytic, 32, 95;
  pyramid, 72; self-actualizing, 46, 140;
  transcendent, 152; transcendent-immanent, 46, 69; tyranny of unappraised,
  99; vital-fusional, 48; *see also:* faith
  tradition; formation tradition
tradition-modulation coformant, 81
transmission of form traditions, 71
trans-pression, 55
transcendence: anxiety, 164, 231; gnostic,
  51, 140
transcendent: dimension, 210; reading
  direction, 106
transference, 103
transformation, 47, 186, 249: unifying, 9,
  12
transpersonalism, 3
transtherapists, 22, 182
transtherapy, 7, 8, 10, 15, 19, 27, 29, 48,
  51, 59, 97, 102, 106, 142, 153, 181,
  198, 220: aim of, 148; dialogue of, 163;
  practice of, 11; spirit of, 173, 174, 175;
  sessions-in-common, 63, 119, 229
trust, 245

uniqueness: transcendent, 209

values: clarification, 37, 38
vital: we-form, 88
vitalism, 89

we: fusional, 78; -experience, 177; relationships, 77
willfulness, 224
wisdom: of continuous transcendence,
  109; transcendent-immanent, 61
women: control of, 93
women's movement, 50
World War II, 49